GCSE

English Language and English

for CCEA®

Series Editor: John Andrews
Authors:
Jenny Lendrum
Aidan Lennon
Pauline Wylie

HODDER
EDUCATION
AN HACHETTE UK COMPANY

The Publishers would like to thank the following for permission to reproduce copyright material:
Photo credits – see page 216.

Acknowledgements
Unit 2A p55 Baroness Susan Greenfield, "How Facebook addiction is damaging your child's brain" from *Daily Mail online*, 23/04/09; **p56** Tour Egypt, "Dive into the Mediterranean" from *http://www.touregypt.net*; **p58** NHS, "Smoking - The Facts" from *http://smokefree.nhs.uk*; **p59** "Smokefree United" from *http://smokefree.nhs.uk/united/kick-the-habit* ; **p60** Age UK, "Help the Aged letter" from *http://www.ageuk. org.uk* (Christmas 2002); **p64** Neil Tweedie, "Camping: Is it Nuts in May?" from *Telegraph online*, http://www.telegraph.co.uk/travel/ campingholidays/5323901/Eurocamp-camping-in-the-UK-Is-it-nuts-in-May.html (15 May 2009), © Telegraph Media Group, 2009; **p70** Tom Rawstorne, "Why Red Bull is Britain's real drink problem" from *Daily Mail online*, htpp://www.dailymail.co.uk/news/article-1024654/School-bans-Red-Bull-energy-drink-disrupts-classes.html (31 October 2009); **p71** Andrew Malone, "Have WE turned sharks into maneaters: Baiting leads to rise in Great White attacks" from *Daily Mail online*, http:www.dailymail.co.uk/news/article-1243355 (15 January 2010); **Unit 2B: p83** Sean Hamilton, "Katie flogs Pete's dog" from *The Sun*, http://www.thesun.co.uk/sol/homepage/showbiz/tv/2707582 (31 October 2009); **p84** Greig Box Turnbull, "Barack Obama in Hawaii holiday alert after family friend is injured" from *The Mirror*, http://www.mirror.co.uk/news/top-stories/12/29 (29 December 2009); **p97** Pete McCarthy, extract from *McCarthy's Bar: A Journey of Discovery in Ireland* (© St Martin's Press, 2003); **Unit 3: p108** Charles J. Sykes, extract from *Dumbing Down Our Kids; Why America's Children Feel Good About Themselves But Can't Read, Write, Or Add*, 2/e (© St Martin's Press, 1996); **Unit 4.1: p124** Robert Pattinson, transcript from MTV interview with Larry Carroll from *http://www.mtv. com/news/articles/1613220/20090603/story.jhtml* (3 June 2009); **p130** Charles Earl Spencer, transcript of eulogy to Princess Diana at Westminster Abbey (6 September 1997); **p131** Halle Berry, transcript of Acceptance Speech at the Oscars (Academy of Motion Picture Arts & Sciences, 2002); **Unit 4.2: p139** Arthur Miller, extract from *All My Sons* (© Penguin Modern Classics, 2009); **p146** John Steinbeck, extract from *Of Mice and Men* (Penguin Modern Classics, 2000); **Unit 4.3: p170** Alan Gibbons, extract from *The Defender* (Orion Children's Books, 2004), © Alan Gibbons 2004; **p173** Alan Gibbons, extract from *The Edge* (Orion Children's Books, 2002), © Alan Gibbons 2002; **p174** John Steinbeck, extract from *Of Mice and Men* (© Penguin Modern Classics, 2000); **p176** Louis Sachar, extract from *Holes* (© Bloomsbury, 2003); **p179** Priscilla Higham, "Angels of the Slums" from *London Daily Telegraph magazine* (18 November 2000), © Telegraph Media Group, 2000; **Exam Section: p195** Fubra Ltd, Recycling facts from *http://www.recycling-guide.org.uk*; **p197** Bill Bryson, extract from *Notes from a Small Island* (© Black Swan, 1996); **p198** Bill Bryson, extract from *Neither Here Nor There* (© Black Swan, 1998).

Crown copyright material is reproduced under Class Licence Number C02P0000060 with the permission of the Controller of HMSO.

Although every effort has been made to ensure that website addresses are correct at time of going to press, Hodder Education cannot be held responsible for the content of any website mentioned in this book. It is sometimes possible to find a relocated web page by typing in the address of the home page for a website in the URL window of your browser.

Hachette UK's policy is to use papers that are natural, renewable and recyclable products and made from wood grown in sustainable forests. The logging and manufacturing processes are expected to conform to the environmental regulations of the country of origin.

Orders: please contact Bookpoint Ltd, 130 Milton Park, Abingdon, Oxon OX14 4SB. Telephone: (44) 01235 827720. Fax: (44) 01235 400454. Lines are open 9.00–5.00, Monday to Saturday, with a 24-hour message answering service. Visit our website at www.hoddereducation.co.uk.

© 2010 John Andrews, Jenny Lendrum, Aidan Lennon and Pauline Wylie

First published in 2003 by
Hodder Education,
An Hachette UK Company
338 Euston Road
London NW1 3BH

This edition first published 2010

| Impression number | 2 |
| Year | 2011 |

Cover photo © Richard Cummins/Corbis
Illustrations by Barking Dog Art
Typeset in 12/13pt Bembo Regular by Servis Filmsetting Ltd, Stockport, Cheshire
Printed in Italy

A catalogue record for this title is available from the British Library

ISBN: 978 1444 110 944

Contents

Contents

Introduction
Welcome to GCSE English Language and English for CCEA

Welcome to the GCSE English Language and English Student's Book. This book focuses on helping you to understand the requirements of CCEA's two GCSE English specifications for English Language and English and shows you how to succeed in the examinations and Controlled Assessments. Although some students will naturally find this subject area easier than others, this book will show you that, whatever your skill level at the start of the course, you can improve and do well. It will develop your essential skills and allow you to become more confident in the key areas of reading, writing and speaking and listening.

This book has three main aims:

- to help you become familiar and comfortable with the four different units of the English Language or English course.
- to create an awareness of what exactly will be being tested within the four units.
- to offer a step-by-step approach to developing the combination of skills, knowledge and techniques that will allow you to maximise your potential in the examinations and Controlled Assessments.

On pages 2–5, there are detailed outlines of the two specifications and their Assessment Objectives. These provide a clear overview of what you will be learning and the skills you will need to develop in order to fulfil your potential in these courses.

Each section in this Student's Book provides guidance on how best to tackle each element of your GCSE course. There are activities throughout the book that help to build up essential skills and techniques. There are also model responses that show examples of student work so you can get a feel for how you should be answering. At the end of each section, there is advice on how to succeed in your exams/Controlled Assessments.

Make sure you keep:

- on top of your work and try to stick to deadlines
- all your notes and pieces of work filed and organised
- a positive attitude to your work
- focused and work hard on all parts of the course (even though there will inevitably be some parts that you enjoy more than others!).

Taking note of these simple points will go a long way to helping you to maximise your achievement at GCSE. Also, try to remember the **five Ps**:

Proper Preparation Prevents Poor Performance!

With all the support and advice provided in this book and your own efforts and preparations, your English Language and English courses should be both enjoyable and rewarding. The more positive your approach and the more thorough your preparation, the better you will do.

English Language: At a glance

The table below outlines what you will be working on for the next two years for GCSE English Language. Whilst the course will be demanding, it will hopefully also be engaging and rewarding. You can use this table for reference from time to time so that you can see what you have completed and what remains to be done.

While the various elements of the exam are displayed in the order of the two units that are tested by external examination followed by the two Controlled Assessment units, this is not necessarily the order in which you tackle these in school.

Unit description	Content of each unit	Assessment options
Unit 1 External examination 1 hour and 30 minutes 20% of your final GCSE grade	Section A: Personal Writing Section B: Reading Multi-Modal Texts	Every Summer from 2011 and every January from 2013
Unit 2 External examination 1 hour and 30 minutes 20% of your final GCSE grade	Section A: Functional Writing Section B: Reading Non-Fiction	Every Summer from 2012 and every January from 2013
Unit 3 Controlled Assessment 20% of your final GCSE grade	Speaking and Listening Task 1: Individual Contribution Task 2: Group Discussion Task 3: Role-Play	Every Summer from 2012 and every January from 2013
Unit 4 Controlled Assessment 40% of your final GCSE grade	Task 1: Study of Spoken Language Task 2: Study of Written Language (Literature) Task 3: Writing Creatively	Every Summer from 2012 and every January from 2013

The Assessment Objectives and their role in the examining process

The English Language specification sets out to test four Assessment Objectives (AOs). Your ability to use the four English Language AOs will be tested in the four units of the exam.

This section looks at:

- the four AOs for English Language
- where they are tested within the four units.

The four Assessment Objectives are:

AO 1 Speaking and Listening

i) Speak clearly and purposefully – this will require you to structure and sustain talk; match it with audience and situation; and use standard English and a series of techniques, depending upon the circumstances of your talk.

ii) Listen and respond to speakers' ideas and viewpoints.

iii) Engage with others – so that co-operatively you can make and create meaning as a result of suggestions, comments and questions and draw these points together in the form of a summary.

iv) Create and maintain different role-play scenarios.

AO 2 Study of Spoken Language

i) Understand variations in spoken language as well as how this type of language alters as a result of the situation in which it is used.

ii) Be aware of the effect that choices can have in your own and others' use of spoken language.

AO 3 Studying Written Language (Reading)

i) Read with insight and select appropriate material from different sources for the purposes of cross referencing and making comparisons.

ii) Develop an interpretation of a piece of writing.

iii) Understand and assess how writers use language to create their desired effects.

AO 4 Writing

i) Write clearly, effectively and imaginatively.

ii) Use a style that matches purpose and audience.

iii) Organise ideas/information logically into sentences and paragraphs.

iv) Make use of language and structural features for effect.

v) Use a range of sentence structures as well as punctuate and spell accurately.

Where the Assessment Objectives are assessed within the four units

The table below shows where the individual AOs are assessed and the overall weightings for each AO.

Assessment Objective	Component weighting						Overall weighting
	External examination		Controlled Assessment				
	Unit 1	Unit 2	Unit 3	Unit 4i	Unit 4ii	Unit 4iii	
AO1	–	–	20%	–	–	–	20%
AO2	–	–	–	10%	–	–	10%
AO3	10%	10%	–	–	15%	–	35%
AO4	10%	10%	–	–	–	15%	35%
Total weighting	20%	20%	20%	10%	15%	15%	100%

English: At a glance

The table below outlines what you will be working on for the next two years for GCSE English. Whilst the course will be demanding, it will hopefully also be engaging and rewarding. You can use this table for reference from time to time so that you can see what you have completed and what remains to be done.

While the various elements of the exam are displayed in the order of the two units that are tested by external examination followed by the two Controlled Assessment units, this is not necessarily the order in which you tackle these in school.

Unit description	Content of each unit	Assessment options
Unit 1 External examination 1 hour and 30 minutes 20% of your final GCSE grade	Section A: Personal Writing Section B: Reading Multi-Modal Texts	Every Summer from 2011 and every January from 2013
Unit 2 External examination 1 hour and 30 minutes 20% of your final GCSE grade	Section A: Functional Writing Section B: Reading Non-Fiction	Every Summer from 2012 and every January from 2013
Unit 3 Controlled Assessment 20% of your final GCSE grade	Speaking and Listening Task 1: Individual Contribution Task 2: Group Discussion Task 3: Role-Play	Every Summer from 2012 and every January from 2013
Unit 4 Controlled Assessment 40% of your final GCSE grade	The Study of Literature and Writing Creatively and Writing for Purpose Tasks 1, 2 and 3: Study of Literature – drama (Shakespeare), prose and poetry Tasks 4 and 5: Writing for Purpose (Creatively)	Every Summer from 2012 and every January from 2013

The Assessment Objectives and their role in the examining process

The English specification sets out to test three Assessment Objectives (AOs). Your ability to use the three English AOs will be tested in the four units of the exam.

This section looks at:

- the four AOs for English Language
- where they are tested within the four units.

The three Assessment Objectives are:

AO 1 Speaking and Listening

i) Speak clearly and purposefully – this will require you to structure and sustain talk; match it with audience and situation; and use standard English and a series of techniques, depending upon the circumstances of your talk.

ii) Listen and respond to speakers' ideas and viewpoints.

iii) Engage with others – so that co-operatively you can make and create meaning as a result of suggestions, comments and questions and draw these points together in the form of a summary.

iv) Create and maintain different role-play scenarios.

AO 2 Reading

i) Read with insight and select appropriate material from different sources for the purposes of cross referencing and making comparisons.

ii) Develop an interpretation of a piece of writing.

iii) Understand and assess how writers use language to create their desired effects.

iv) Understand texts in their social, cultural and historical contexts.

AO 3 Writing

i) Write clearly, effectively and imaginatively.

ii) Use a style that matches purpose and audience.

iii) Organise ideas/information logically into sentences and paragraphs.

iv) Make use of language and structural features for effect.

v) Use a range of sentence structures as well as punctuate and spell accurately.

Where the Assessment Objectives are assessed within the four units

The table below shows where the individual AOs are assessed and the overall weightings for each AO.

| Assessment Objective | Component weighting | | | | | Overall weighting |
| | External examination | | Controlled Assessment | | | |
	Unit 1	Unit 2	Unit 3	Unit 4 Tasks 1–3	Unit 4 Tasks 4–5	
AO1	–	–	20%	–	–	20%
AO2	10%	10%	–	20%	–	40%
AO3	10%	10%	–	–	20%	40%
Total weighting	20%	20%	20%	20%	20%	100%

Unit 1
English Language and English

Section A: Personal Writing

Introduction to Personal Writing

Unit 1 is externally examined and is made up of two sections. The first section is Section A and it assesses **Personal Writing**.

Target outcome: Structured writing that seeks to create a rapport with the reader by developing a clear engagement with the subject.

Target skills

The target skills you will learn about in this Personal Writing section will enable you to:

 write clearly and fluently

 organise ideas in order to support the purpose

 use an appropriate writing form

 select language to engage the reader

 use grammar, spelling and punctuation effectively.

Assessment Objective

Your Assessment Objective in this Personal Writing section is:

Writing

i) Write clearly, effectively and imaginatively to engage the reader.

ii) Use a style that matches vocabulary to purpose and audience.

iii) Organise ideas/information logically into sentences and paragraphs.

iv) Make use of language and structural features for effect.

v) Use a range of sentence structures as well as punctuate and spell accurately.

Exam question

 You will have 45 minutes in which to produce a single piece of writing on a given subject. The audience will be the examiner.

You can go to the Exam Practice section at the end of this book (page 183) for more practice.

1 Planning

Planning is central to success. It is the foundation of the writing process and it is even more important in the exam because you will have only 45 minutes to complete this section.

So, what happens to this key practice when it comes to the actual exam? You are anxious; there is an overwhelming desire to 'get stuck in'; you see others around you writing furiously so you panic and start before you have sorted out what you should actually be writing.

The 5–10 minutes you spend preparing **before** you begin to write is vital if you are to produce your best work.

The benefits of planning are:

- A piece of writing that has been planned nearly always achieves a higher mark in the exam.
- You will find it easier to write because you will not be trying to think about the direction of your piece at the same time as you are attempting to compose it in a fluent and interesting manner.
- You will have all your ideas written down before you begin – therefore you won't forget them as you are writing.
- You will be able to group your ideas together and organise them clearly and coherently.
- The ideas you decide to present will be more likely to be relevant and will directly link to the title of the writing task.
- You will be able to plan the writing techniques that you will use in particular paragraphs so that you demonstrate variety and maintain interest.

Use the following sample task in order to explore the planning processes that will help you to tackle the demands of personal writing in an organised and appropriate manner.

Sample task

You have been asked to make a presentation to next year's Year 8 students, telling them about your school and what they might expect next year. This talk will be given to groups of between 15 and 20 Year 7 students during an induction day for them in June.

How to plan the sample task

The first thing to do is to apply the 'Why?', 'What?' and 'Who?' questions.

Why?

*Why are you writing? What is the **purpose** of your writing?*

In this case you are preparing a speech in which you have to share your experience and advice about what your school is like.

Your task is to make next year's Year 8 students aware of what they might expect – so you need to be reassuring in what you say and make their arrival in school next term seem a relatively painless affair.

What?

*What is the **context** or situation?*

For the purpose of this task you are a mature Year 11 or 12 student who is giving younger children, who are liable to be quite nervous, the benefit of your experience.

Who?

*Who is your **audience**?*

This talk is aimed at children aged about 11 years old but it is likely that some of your teachers will be present and that will also have a bearing on what you say.

The fact that these children are quite young will have an impact on the range of language you are likely to use. Your language needs to be chosen so that they understand you.

Once you have answered these questions the next step is to consider the content of your speech by initially making a list of ideas or points that you might want to include.

Three planning options follow – the bullet-point list, the spider diagram and the flow chart; which one you use is a matter of personal choice.

Bullet-point list

You might create the following list when planning your speech.

 Subject: Settling into life in secondary school

- memories of your own first day – humorous story/stories
- the biggest differences in comparison to primary school
- asking for help if you get lost
- how to recognise the prefects
- how the school day is structured
- how to address your teachers
- how teachers will address students
- assembly – what happens
- your 'best bits'
- registration
- lockers and bags
- opportunity for them to ask questions or speak to you when the talk is over

This process is useful because it allows you to identify all of the points you want to cover. Group ideas together and place them in the order in which you want to include them.

ACTIVITY 1

In pairs:
1 Discuss how you might usefully combine some of the points in the bullet-point list.
2 Place them in the order that you would choose to use them in your speech – feel free to add further ideas of your own.
3 Note down your revised plan and be prepared to justify your decisions as you share them with the class.

Spider diagram

- Write the subject 'Settling into life in secondary school' in a bubble in the middle of a page. Then add outer bubbles, labelling each with a different aspect of your subject. List ideas under each heading – just one or two ideas for each heading.
- Number the bubbles in the order you want to write your ideas. When the planning is done, you would then go on to expand your ideas into sentences, which would then form paragraphs. You would probably write a separate paragraph for each bubble.

ACTIVITY 2

Create and fill out a spider diagram using the title provided.

Write about an occasion when you had a really good time.

Flow chart

If you prefer, you could use a flow chart to plan your writing:

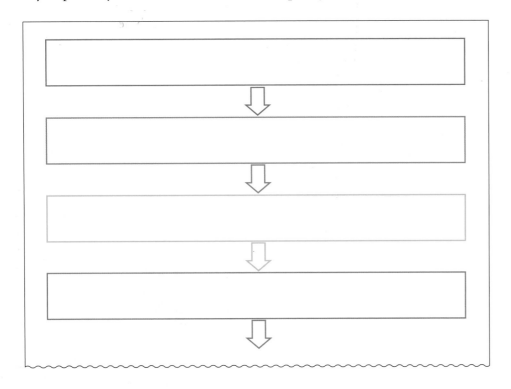

Regardless of the type of approach you take, the key to successful writing is to plan!

All plans should:

- include the points to be covered in the writing task – aim for six as a rough target
- have the points numbered to indicate the order in which they should be written up
- identify the writing techniques that you will use throughout the writing task, especially at the beginning and the end (see pages 14–17)
- identify the structure of the writing (see pages 14–17)
- be brief – write in note form and use key words – no lengthy sentences and no paragraphs!

2 Using an Appropriate Form of Writing

As well as planning, you will also need to consider what form is appropriate for your writing. To do this, think about the **purpose** of your writing.

- Are you being invited to inform the reader?
- Are you being asked to explain something?
- Does the task require you to describe a place or perhaps a situation?

When you have sorted out the purpose, decide what **form** your writing will take. Will it be:

- a letter
- a magazine article
- a speech
- a diary
- an essay – a story or account?

ACTIVITY 4

In pairs, discuss and note down the key characteristics or features of each of these forms of writing. Be prepared to share these with your class and note down any important features that you missed.

Who is the **audience** for your writing? This is very important because it will set the tone for the piece of writing and you will need to choose words and phrases that are appropriate for your audience. The audience could be:

- Year 8 or Year 12 students
- classmates/parents
- a specific person – for example, a friend
- the examiner.

ACTIVITY 5

As a class, briefly discuss what impact each of these audiences would have on your choice of language and tone.

ACTIVITY 6

Identify the **purpose**, **form** and **audience** for the writing questions below. Use this example to help you:

> The audience will be a mixture of students, parents, staff and interested local people like past students.

> The form

You have been selected to write an article for the school magazine on one of your personal highlights from the last school year.

> The purpose is to describe these experiences in an entertaining way.

1 You are making a presentation to your classmates. Select a particular interest or hobby that you have. Explain how your interest has developed and why it is important to you.

2 Write a review of a place you know and really like for a travel website. Describe why people should choose to go to this place on holiday.

Once you have identified the purpose, form and audience of the two writing questions above, write your response for each question. Remember to:

- ✓ demonstrate that you are aware of the specified audience
- ✓ use suitable opening and concluding paragraphs that show that you recognise their purpose in that particular type of writing
- ✓ use appropriate and convincing development to hold the audience's interest
- ✓ make sure the writing is lively and engaging
- ✓ use convincing, descriptive language – it adds interest
- ✓ include examples and anecdotes to add interest, realism and a personal voice
- ✓ possibly use humour – if it's appropriate
- ✓ use rhetorical devices (see page 90) to hold the audience's attention.

3 Structuring Your Writing

Openings

Openings set the tone for everything that follows. Always try to begin with a powerful opening line to grab the reader's attention. For example, you could use:

- an exclamation, e.g. 'Never, ever again!'
- a question, e.g. 'When was the last time you were really glad to see a teacher?'
- a rhetorical question, e.g. 'Does anyone like the dentist?'
- a quotation, e.g. '"Only dull people are bright in the morning" according to Oscar Wilde. He's right!'
- an intriguing statement, e.g. 'Marley was dead: to begin with.'
- a shocking fact, e.g. 'Over 50% of Londoners have never spoken to their neighbours.'
- an anecdote from your own experience, e.g. 'Only last week I was . . .'
- a general statement, e.g. 'It was the best of times, it was the worst of times . . .'
- a direct appeal to the audience, e.g. 'If you have a brother or sister then you will know how really annoying . . .'.

ACTIVITY 7

Below are a series of openings. In pairs discuss which you think are engaging and which are not. Be prepared to justify your decisions.

1 I am going to write about the worst day of my life . . .

2 I'm sure you have all heard the expression 'getting out on the wrong side of the bed in the morning' . . .

3 I am going to tell you about the day I went to see my granny. It was a Thursday and the sun was shining . . .

4 The piercing 6.30 a.m. alarm jarred me out of a restful sleep. It didn't get any better after that!

ACTIVITY 8

Write **three** interesting and lively opening statements that you could use to begin an piece of writing called 'A Really Good Time'. Be prepared to share these with the rest of the class.

As a class, decide which of the openings are most effective and why.

Chronological structure

This means organising your writing by relating events chronologically – in the order in which they happened.

You might use a chronological structure if you are writing about:

- an important aspect of your life or important events and people that have shaped you
- several events – you can trace how you were involved or how your interest developed by describing the events very briefly
- a single event or person – you could focus on that one event and recount it hour by hour, or focus on the life events of the person you are describing.

When writing chronologically, make sure you:

- keep the reader aware of the order of events and keep the story generally moving forward – gloss over the dull bits and don't tell more of the story than you need to make your point
- start and end with the action and have everything take place within the context of the story
- describe events, people and places in specific, colourful terms
- make sure that you use rhetorical techniques (see page 90).

Here is an example of chronological writing:

> A twinge of excitement pulsed through my body that night. I don't know how I slept but I did. When I awoke I was refreshed but it wasn't long before I found my mind swarming with jumbled exhilaration. After a quick breakfast . . .

Flashback structure

You can use flashback in different ways to structure your writing.

You could start with the present and cut to the past before ending with the present again. Jennifer Johnston uses this approach in her book *How Many Miles to Babylon?*

It opens: and finishes:

> Because I am an officer and a gentleman they have given me my notebooks, pen, ink and paper.

> Because I am an officer and a gentleman they have not taken away my bootlaces or my pen, so I sit and wait and write.

You could also begin and end your writing with two halves of the same event. The middle might give an interpretation of or background to the event. Suppose, for example, you are writing about a memorable occasion, such as your surprise sixteenth birthday party, and you decide to describe in detail the moment when you blew out your candles as everyone sang 'Happy Birthday'. You could:

- begin your piece with the first lines of 'Happy Birthday'
- cut to the beginning of the day, when you woke up completely unaware of the party to come
- describe what you did that day, including the puzzling things that happened because your family were keeping the party a secret
- describe arriving at the party and being completely surprised
- describe how everything then made sense
- describe the party itself
- end with the last lines of 'Happy Birthday' or the words 'Make a wish!'

Conclusions

Conclusions are an extremely important part of any writing. Often students find it difficult to write conclusions as they run out of ideas by the time they get to the end! However, conclusions should not be overlooked. They:

- complete the reading experience for the reader
- leave the reader with a lasting impression
- sum up the main point of a piece of writing
- help you to stay on task.

Your conclusion needs to show that you have purposefully brought your piece of work to an end, rather than leaving the reader with the feeling that you have run out of time. Equally, don't go over everything again; this is boring.

Remember that the conclusion is the last part of your writing that the examiner will read. It should therefore be engaging and interesting in order to leave a positive and lasting impression.

When you write your conclusion, avoid:

- beginning with the cliché 'In conclusion . . .'
- making your main point(s) in the conclusion – you should have made them during your writing
- including evidence to support your previous points – you should have done this as you made your points.

Strategies for writing an effective conclusion

Try using one or more of the following strategies to help you write an effective conclusion.

'Full circle' strategy

You could refer again to the theme or themes that you explored in your introduction. For example, if you began by describing a scenario, you could end with the same scenario. You might use the same key ideas or images that you used in the introduction. These first and last paragraphs of a piece of writing below are an example of this approach:

As I stepped out of the car I took time to look around and I have to admit that I felt apprehensive. The large, grey building towered over me and the windows seemed like eyes glaring at me as I made my way towards the door . . .

. . .

My first day at school had been much more enjoyable than I had thought it would be. It was time to go home. As I walked down the school drive I looked back and felt a warm feeling inside. I knew everything would be all right.

'Make the reader think' strategy

You could make a **statement** or ask a **rhetorical question** to encourage the reader to think about their own life or think in a different way. Here a **statement** is used:

Thus, my personal experience challenges us all to think about our past, present and future.

Here a **rhetorical question** delivers a challenging conclusion:

As a school it is our duty to progress so that those who follow will enjoy the best educational experience possible. They deserve it, don't they?

Predictions strategy

You may want to make predictions for the future based on the topic of the piece. In other words, you could raise further questions linked to the topic, like this:

Unless we change our ways dramatically and quickly it will be too late to reverse these global changes. If the situation continues in this way, the future for generations to come will be bleak.

'Pull it all together' strategy

You could include a brief summary of the main points that you have made. Be careful with this approach as you can end up repeating everything again in a longwinded fashion. Keep it brief! For example:

Evidently my Grandad is important to me because of his kind heart, sense of humour, sense of pride and his unwavering support of me over the years.

'Use a quotation' strategy

You could use a quotation linked to the subject, a well-known phrase that ties in or perhaps even a quote from someone related to the subject:

It is therefore clear that the old adage 'an eye for an eye' is not one which is applicable to the 21st century.

ACTIVITY 9

Write two engaging conclusions that use two of the strategies outlined on the left. The conclusions should be for a piece of writing called 'A Really Good Time'.

Be prepared to share your conclusions with the rest of the class. As a class decide which of the conclusions are the most effective and why.

4 Editing Tips

The last 5 minutes spent reviewing and editing your writing could make that all-important difference to your final grade. Reviewing and revising your writing is one of the best ways to maximise your performance.

Examiners are impressed by students who correct their work, so don't be afraid to cross things out and make changes: it shows you are a thoughtful writer.

Make sure you keep changes readable and make your corrections clear.

Check your writing to get the best possible mark:

✓ Does it make **sense**?

✓ Have you included **full stops**, **semicolons** and **commas**? Also check for speech marks, colons, question marks and apostrophes.

✓ Could you **vary** the sorts of **sentences** you've used? Could you reorder some sentences to make them more descriptive and detailed?

✓ Do any of the words you've written look as though they're not quite right? If so, try writing them again on rough paper, **spelling** them differently; keep trying until they look right and then correct them in your work.

✓ Have you divided your work into **paragraphs**? If not, read it carefully and decide where you think the breaks ought to go. Mark // where you want to end a paragraph and then **NP**. This will indicate that you want to begin a new paragraph.

✓ Have you **included all that you wanted** to say? If not, mark the place where you want to add something with an asterisk ★, make the same mark at the end of your piece, where you have some space, and then write the points or ideas you wish to add by the second mark. If you want to add extra points or ideas somewhere else use a different mark, such as ★★. Do not make than one or two additions, otherwise your work will begin to appear unplanned!

Matching grades to personal writing

In Section A the essential qualities the examiners will be looking for are highlighted at the important grade boundaries. Read these descriptions *carefully*; they tell you what your answer should be like.

Grade C writing displays:

 development that holds the reader's attention

 an appropriate sense of audience and purpose

 clearly structured and increasingly fluent expression

 a series of sentence structures, competently handled

 accurate use of basic punctuation that makes the meaning clear

generally accurate spelling and the use of a widening range of language.

Grade A/A* writing displays:

 development that is sophisticated and commands the reader's attention

 a sense of a positive relationship with the audience

 an assured use of structure and a confident style

 sentence structuring that enhances the overall effect

 a range of punctuation, confidently employed to enhance fluency

accurate spelling and use of an extended vocabulary – errors tend to be one-off mistakes.

ACTIVITY 10

Here is a sample writing task:

The answer on page 20 was written under exam conditions by a student of your age. The examiner's comments have been added to help you recognise the key strengths of the work.

Take 10 minutes to read it over and look closely at the examiner's comments.

1 Do the examiner's comments fairly represent the quality of the work?
2 Do any of these remarks surprise/puzzle you?

Exam-style question
Write a speech to be delivered to your classmates in which you tell them about the most worthwhile experience you have ever had.
Response time: 45 minutes

Fellow classmates, I am going to tell you about the most worthwhile experience I've had – hearing my little sister first say my name.

It all began on the sixth of October 2006. My brother and I were staying at our granny's when she recieved (sp) the call saying that Dad would come and pick us up, we were going to the hospital to see our new baby sister.

When we walked into the ward, as you can imagine, we were deafened by the sound of crying babies, exhausted mothers, and family members cooing over the 'little miracles'. As we walked cautiously up to my mother's bed, we could see our little sister was no different – in fact she was almost purple in the face she was screaming so loudly!

However, that all stopped the minute my mother scooped her up in her arms and cuddled her. I remember thinking that she looked so small and fragile that I was scared to hold her, but my Dad encouraged me to 'go on' and so I climbed carefully up beside my mum and waited as she was gently placed into my arms by my Dad. My first thought as I held her was 'She's not as light as she looks' – in fact she weighed a tonne!

Then my mum made the dreadful mistake of asking my brother and I what she should be called and seconds later we were shouting out the names of our favourite singers, childhood novels and even our favourite TV chefs, I'm sure she regretted the decision, wouldn't you??

It wasn't until we were hushed and told 'there are babies sleeping', although from the noise they were making I was sure my dad was going slightly deaf, that my aunt suggested the name 'Flora'. We all agreed on this, and one year later she was crawling on the kitchen floor, on the very same day that she uttered my name.

On a hot June day, I was sitting at the kitchen table drinking the most delicious lemonade you have ever tasted. My mother and I had just started discussing in depth why Tracy from CBBC got her own mobile phone yet I didn't, when Flora suddenly came over to me and pointed. Then she said 'Sue' in that child like way she had. I felt so amazed and shocked that I asked her to repeat what she said.

This was the most worthwhile experience because it showed me that even the best things can happen unexpectedly.

So while I remember that day like it was yesterday, now Flora is nine years old and she never stops talking and saying my name, so I'm sure you can imagine, the novelty has definately (sp) worn off!!

This answer demonstrates:

 confident awareness of purpose and audience

 a developing, confident style

 deliberate manipulation of a range of sentence structures

 some extended use of vocabulary.

Personal Writing: Key to success

Read these key pointers and then complete the exam-style question below.

 Your own experiences will provide you with the best sources for a piece of personal writing that has to be completed in a short period of time.

 The best writing results from the following process: **Think, Plan, Write**. Resist the temptation to start immediately; taking the time to think and plan is essential to produce your best work.

 Make your writing lively and engaging. Let your personality come through in the writing – the last thing the examiner wants is to read something dull!

 Remember you have only 45 minutes in which to complete the writing process.

 There are no prizes for finishing first so use all of the time wisely – the only reward for finishing early could be a low grade if you do not make the most of the time available.

 Review your finished work – you must review your work to get the most out of your answer because everyone makes mistakes when they are working quickly and under pressure. Remember too that there are no marks for extreme neatness – it is much better that your work is accurate even if it contains a few corrections. As you check your work, consider the following questions and correct any mistakes that you find:

i)   Have you paragraphed the essay?

ii) Did you use a range of sentence lengths?

iii) Did you vary the sentence openings?

iv) Have you used a varied vocabulary?

v)   Have you left out any words or are there any sentences where the meaning is less than clear?

> **Exam-style question**
> Write about an occasion when you were really pleased with yourself!
> *Response time: 45 minutes*

Checklist for success: working towards Grade C	✔
Have you shown understanding of the **purpose** and **structure** of the task?	
Have you shown and maintained awareness of the reader/ intended **audience**?	
Does the content fit the **purpose**?	
Is the piece **paragraphed** and does each paragraph have a **topic sentence**?	
Have you used some **stylistic devices** (rhetorical questions, emotive language, etc.) that are in keeping with the purpose and audience?	
Is there a range of appropriate **vocabulary** used to create effect?	
Is there appropriate **variety** in the **sentence structures**?	
Is there **clear punctuation** and is it used to vary pace and clarify meaning?	
Have you checked your **spelling**?	

Checklist for success: working towards Grade A/A★	✔
Does your writing show an understanding of the **purpose** and is your writing **structured** appropriately?	
Have you shown an ongoing awareness of the reader/intended **audience**?	
Is the content coverage **detailed**, and fitting for the **purpose**?	
Have you made sure the paragraphs have a **topic sentence**?	
Have you used a range of **stylistic devices** (rhetorical questions, emotive language, etc.) adapted to purpose and audience?	
Is there a wide range of appropriate, extended **vocabulary** and is it used to create effect or convey precise meaning?	
Is there confident and effective variation of **sentence structures**, use of **simple**, **compound and complex sentences** to achieve particular effects?	
Is there **accurate punctuation** used to vary pace, clarify meaning, avoid ambiguity and create deliberate effects?	
Is virtually all **spelling**, including that of complex irregular words, correct?	

Unit 1
English Language and English

Introduction to Reading Multi-Modal Texts

Unit 1 is externally examined and is made up of two sections. The second section is Section B and it assesses **Reading Multi-Modal Texts**.

Target outcome: A purposeful comparison demonstrating an understanding of the features that have been combined to generate the desired outcome of particular multi–modal texts.

Target skills

The target skills you will learn about in this Reading Multi–Modal Texts section will enable you to:

 read and understand texts

 select material appropriate to purpose

 make connections between ideas, texts, words and images

 analyse how the language used varies according to audience

 explain how writers use language in particular ways and employ presentational features to capture the reader's attention

 draw together material from different sources.

Assessment Objective

Your Assessment Objective in this Reading Multi–Modal Texts section is:

Reading/Studying written language

i) Read with insight and select appropriate material from different sources for the purposes of cross referencing and making comparisons.

ii) Develop an interpretation of a piece of writing.

iii) Understand and assess how writers use language to create their desired effects.

Exam question

You will have 45 minutes in which to answer two questions that will require you to compare and/ or contrast two pieces of stimulus material.

These will focus on the ways in which:

- presentational devices influence the reader
- words and phrases are used to achieve a purpose.

You can go to the Exam Practice section at the end of this book (page 185) for more practice.

1 Multi-Modal Texts

Multi-modal texts combine two forms of communication (written, spoken, visual or non-verbal). Texts include sound, print, film, electronic and multimedia presentations.

The term 'text' has a very broad meaning. Texts include not only:

- picture books
- novels
- newspapers
- letters

- conversations
- speeches
- plays
- feature films

- TV programmes
- computer graphics
- advertisements

but also:

- maps
- charts
- diagrams

- graphs
- timelines
- databases

- flow charts
- concept maps
- photographs.

When you are approaching a multi-modal text, the first two basic issues you need to sort out are:

- What is it for? (**purpose**)
- Who is it aimed at? (**audience**)

The text's **purpose** and **audience** should be reflected in almost every aspect of its appearance and language, from its layout and use of pictures to its words and phrases and its style.

For example, a children's story which has been written to entertain is likely to include colourful illustrations, short sentences and a relatively simple vocabulary. In contrast, a textbook, with the purpose of educating and informing, will probably be much more formal and serious. It will use a specialised vocabulary and complex sentences, and illustrations may be limited to photographs or diagrams which will convey information more effectively than words alone.

In order to help you identify a text's audience and purpose, look for clues as to the **type of text** you have been given and its **context**.

For example, an advert can usually be easily recognised because it uses the conventions of this **type of text**: features like slogans, logos, images and written text. A printed advert may be found in a magazine or newspaper or on a billboard. Its purpose may be to persuade its audience to buy a certain product or act in a particular way (e.g. give money to a charity), or it may be designed to raise awareness about a particular issue or brand.

An article in a women's magazine, for instance, will probably use conventions like columns and pictures with captions. It could be intended to advise women about a particular health issue or inform them of the latest fashions.

Key Terms in Analysing Media and Non-Fiction Texts

2

When you have sorted out the basics of purpose and audience, the next major task is to work out how **linguistic** and **presentational features** are used to engage the reader.

This table shows the terminology that you need to discuss multi-modal texts. You are probably familiar with most of these terms but some may be new to you.

Alliteration	Repeating sounds for effect
Article	Non-fiction writing in a newspaper or magazine
Bias	Use of words or phrases that deliberately present a one-sided view; language used deliberately to make you agree with the view the writer is putting forward
Bullet points	Way of highlighting key points
Caption	Information under a photograph or image
Content	What the text is about
Emotive language	Words or phrases that appeal to your feelings
Fact	Something that can be proved
Formal	Official style of writing
Headline	Large text introducing an article
Informal	Chatty or casual style of writing
Layout	How a text is laid out on the page
Logo	Easily recognisable company design, e.g. the Nike tick
Masthead	Name of the newspaper on the front page
Opinion	Personal point of view
Photographs	These may be long-distance shots or close-ups. They are used for effect: to show what a place looks like or to create drama, emotion, etc.
Presentational devices	Ways of presenting things on a page
Pun	A play on words for humorous effect
Repetition	When a word or phrase is repeated for effect
Representation	How a group, person or place is presented by the media
Rhetorical question	Question asked for effect rather than expecting an answer
Slogan	Catchword or phrase, e.g. 'Just do it!'
Statistics	Facts, figures and graphs
Target audience	Group of people 'targeted' by the media
Tone	Way in which the text is written, e.g. using flattery

3 Presentational Devices in Multi-Modal Texts

There is usually a lot to comment on when you are assessing **layout** and **presentation**, but remember you must *always explain the effect on the reader.*

It is not enough to say, for example, that bullet points are used to make the information more user friendly, because this is true in just about every text in which bullet points are used! Make sure your analysis of the bullets says something specific about the text and remember to write about the effect of their use on the audience.

ACTIVITY 1

Below is an advertisement for a Land Rover Defender. Analyse this advert and how it works. Write comments for each part arrowed. How many of the key terms on page 25 can you use in your analysis?

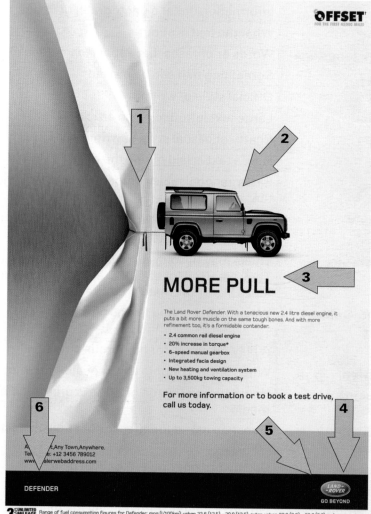

Here are some of the main techniques or **presentational devices** you need to look out for and the impact that each has.

Alliteration (in headings)	Makes the text catchy – quick to read – grabs attention
Bullet points	Eye-catching way to organise a text or make information more accessible
Captions	Help readers understand pictures
Colour	Lots of connections and links – colours reinforce messages, e.g. blue = crisp, cold, clean; red = dangerous, passionate
Columns	Way of organising text – help make text clearer to the reader
Fonts	Classic, formal, old-fashioned, modern fonts, etc., are chosen to impact on different audiences and to grab attention
Graphs and diagrams	Help make difficult information easy to grasp
Headings	Important as a way to inform, to organise the text or to sustain interest
Imagery	Similes (like/as) or metaphors (direct comparisons) create images in words – so you can 'see' the thing being described
Italics	Emphasise information
Logos	Symbols – often representing a company or organisation
Maps	Give information about places – where they are and how to find them
Paragraphs	Organise text – may be small, short and easy to read or longer and more detailed – this will affect the text and the reader in different ways
Pictures and images	Grab attention and bring the text to life – also useful for breaking up the text
Underlining	Emphasises points made

ACTIVITY 2

On the next page are three pages from a leaflet produced for Northern Ireland entitled 'Your Body, Your Life Your Choice'. Which of the presentational devices outlined above are used in these three pages?

Front cover

First Aid

**Watch out for your friends if they
have taken drugs or solvents and
they start feeling:**

- dizzy or faint
- sick (ie want to vomit)
- suddenly tired
- sudden headache or
  cramps (especially in
  the arms and legs)
- scared or confused
- short of breath

If they are drinking water
to cool down, don't let them
gulp down too much as this
can be very dangerous

If someone collapses
If the person is breathing, put them in the
recovery position by:

- turning them onto their side
- tilt their head back to make sure their
  airway remains open (see picture)
- clear their airway if blocked and
  loosen their clothing
- check breathing and pulse regularly
- stay with them until help arrives

If the person is not breathing and you
know how to do mouth to mouth
resuscitation, do so. **If not**, wait until
help arrives.

Inside page

acid Tabs microdots
Strawberries BLOTTERS Trips

If a trip is bad, this can be very frightening

Watch out for friends if they are having a bad
trip - reassure and comfort them

**Another inside
page**

**Flashbacks (reliving the trip) can occur
weeks or months after a trip - they can
be frightening and may be dangerous as
they come unexpectedly**

Magic Mushrooms - similar effects and risks as LSD
Additional risk of picking poisonous mushrooms by mistake

To assess how a multi-modal text creates its effects, you need to consider these **key questions**:

- What overall effect is created by the size and/or choice of images, colours and font styles?
- Is the title a question, statement or concept?
- Is the title based on description, information or opinion?
- Does the title take a particular stance or viewpoint on the topic?
- Do the headings help to construct a series of viewpoints on the topic?
- How do the headings relate to the reader or get them to engage with a particular stance on the topic?
- Is the choice of wording based on a concept, information or questioning?
- Does the content reveal depth or breadth of knowledge?
- Do the choices of colour, template design, image and font style 'match' the topic?
- Are the colours appropriate and visually pleasing?
- What relevance or effect do any graphics or symbols in headings have?
- Do the images add impact to the communication of meaning?
- Does the presentation of information engage the reader visually? Is it striking in its effect?
- What do the visual elements do that the words alone would not?
- Are the images as informative as the words – or even more informative?
- Is the meaning in the text communicated mainly through the images or the words?
- How do the words and pictures interact to communicate meaning?

To help you analyse aspects of multi-modal texts, you can also use these three groupings to organise your reflections and comments in response to the key questions:

Visual meaning

How the whole text appears to the reader: angles, framing (long, medium, close shot), colour, composition, layout or positioning, message and purpose, perception, perspective, expected prior knowledge, lighting, amount of text, text related to graphics, sequencing.

Spatial meaning

The relationship between the following items and their effects: size of text and graphics, position of text and graphics, shape, composition, amount of text on page, arrangement of elements on page.

Linguistic meaning

The overall impact of the words and phrases: effective use of words, effective choice of words, absence of any words or text, the way words and text are presented.

Visual meaning is the most important element here. This has probably struck you already and it will become even more apparent as you analyse more multi-modal texts.

When analysing colour you need to be aware of the subtle and not so subtle effect that different colours have on us. Here is a breakdown of their impact.

Colour	Influences
Grey	gloomy, depressing, bland, stability, wisdom, old age, boredom, decay, dullness, dust, pollution, urban sprawl, balance, neutrality, mourning
White	purity, neutrality, cleanliness, truth, snow, winter, coldness, peace, innocence, simplicity, surrender, cowardice, fearfulness, unimaginative, bland, empty, unfriendly
Black	death, funerals, the bad guy, evil, power, sophistication, formality, elegance, wealth, mystery, style, fear, seriousness, rebellion, slimming quality (fashion)
Red	passion, strength, energy, fire, love, excitement, speed, heat, arrogance, ambition, power, danger, blood, war, anger, revolution, aggression, summer, stop, communism, Mars (planet)
Blue	seas, men, peace, harmony, sadness, tranquility, calmness, trust, coolness, confidence, water, ice, dependability, cleanliness, depression, coldness, obscenity, Earth (planet), strength, steadfastness, light, friendliness, conservatism (UK and European politics)
Green	nature, eco-friendly, spring, fertility, youth, environment, wealth, money (US), good luck, vigour, generosity, go, grass, aggression, jealousy, illness, greed, envy, renewal, natural abundance, growth, health, calming
Yellow	sunlight, joy, happiness, wealth (gold), summer, hope, air, liberalism, cowardice, illness, hazards, weakness, summer, friendship, a sign of hope (yellow ribbon)
Purple	royalty, wisdom, nobility, spirituality, creativity, wealth, ceremony, arrogance, flamboyance, gaudiness, mourning, riches, romanticism (light purple), delicacy (light purple), penance, bravery (purple heart)
Orange	energy, enthusiasm, happiness, balance, heat, fire, flamboyance, playfulness, arrogance, warning, danger, autumn, royalty
Brown	boldness, depth, nature, richness, rustic, stability, tradition, fascism, dirt, dullness, filth, heaviness, poverty, roughness, down-to-earth, wholesomeness, steadfastness, dependability
Pink	femininity, sympathy, homosexuality, health, love, marriage, joy

On the next page is a commentary on the presentational devices used in a film poster. The poster is assessed in terms of the layout, the use of images and the use of colour.

ACTIVITY 3

Compare and contrast the presentational devices (the layout, colour and images) used in the logos of the following two popular soft drinks.

The title of the film is clearly presented and dominates the top of the poster.

WE WERE WARNED

2012

Dramatic tagline emphasises main theme of movie – a cautionary tale about the end of the world.

Muted colours match the seriousness and tragic nature of the film.

Dramatic picture dominates entire poster and confirms genre of film as blockbuster disaster movie.

Uses a world-famous landmark familiar to all audiences to reinforce the genre – a disaster movie.

Release date clearly displayed at bottom of the poster.

AT CINEMAS NOVEMBER 13

ACTIVITY 4

Use the commentary to help you analyse the presentational devices used in the film poster. Write about:

1 the layout
2 the use of images
3 the use of colour.

ACTIVITY 5
Study the presentational features of this poster. What do you learn about the play?

Language Devices in Multi-Modal Texts 4

So far you have focused on presentational features in multi-modal texts. Now you are going to assess the role played by words and phrases.

Fact and opinion

You need to able to tell the difference between fact and opinion; this is a very important basic skill.

- A **fact** is something that is accurate and can be supported by evidence.
- An **opinion** is a belief that is not supported by evidence. An opinion is normally a personal statement or viewpoint that can be the result of an emotion or an individual analysis of a situation or fact.

It is important to know the difference between what people think and what people know, between what people believe to be true and what has been proved to be true.

- Facts are *known* for certain to have happened or be true or exist.
- Opinions are *believed* to have happened or be true or exist.

For example:

> **Fact:** Monday is the day after Sunday.
> **Opinion:** Monday is the longest day of the week.
>
> **Fact:** The flower is yellow.
> **Opinion:** The flower is pretty.
>
> **Fact:** The legal age for drinking alcohol is 18.
> **Opinion:** The legal age for drinking alcohol should be 21.

ACTIVITY 6

Separate these into fact and opinion:
1 The best way to choose a partner is based on brains, not beauty.
2 Paris is the capital city of France.
3 The car probably stopped running because it ran out of petrol.
4 The river Amazon is 3900 miles long.
5 The boiling point of water is 100 degrees Celsius.
6 Students should get less homework.

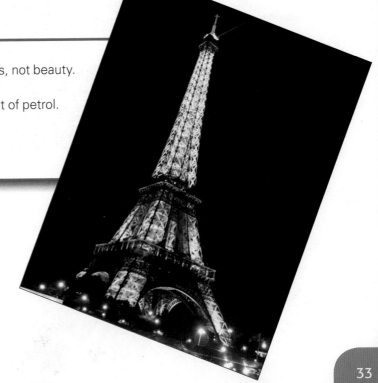

5 Persuasive Language Techniques

Persuasive use of fact and opinion

Fact and opinion can be combined to 'colour' the information being conveyed. Here's an example:

> A worrying 17% of children are overweight.

The fact in this sentence is '17% of children are overweight'. The element of persuasive opinion comes from use of the word 'worrying'. This is the writer's view on this statistic and they are trying to colour the reader's point of view by implying that we too should be concerned by this percentage.

More persuasive techniques

Combining fact and opinion is just one way in which multi–modal texts such as advertisements, leaflets and websites use persuasive language techniques. Writers may also use one or more of the following persuasive techniques.

ACTIVITY 7

Use the internet to gather facts on obesity. (Use a search engine – obesity/uk/facts will provide what you need.)

Then write a 150-word piece on 'Obesity and young people'. Treat the issue of obesity as very serious and deliberately try to alarm your readers with your presentation of the information and the language you use.

Directly addressing the reader

This engages the reader and therefore retains their interest and concentration because the material seems directly relevant to them. For example:

- I ask you.
- Don't you agree that . . .?

Indirect involvement with the reader

Here are two examples:

- Imagine a time when . . .
- Consider the following advice . . .

Emotive language

Words and phrases are selected to create a certain type of reaction. Here are some examples of emotive language used in newspapers:

- Money deficits result in havoc in schools.
- Political gathering results in riot.
- Hundreds of peasants slaughtered by troops.

Graphic language

This paints a picture for the reader and may be used to generate anger, fear, pity or whatever emotion supports the mood the writer is trying to create. Metaphors can be very useful because they paint pictures and also say a lot through their connotations. For example:

- Tony Blair talked of his aspiration for Britain to be a 'beacon' to the world.

This has a lot of positive associations, suggesting light in the midst of darkness or lighting the way to safety for others or leading the way.

Creating a rapport with readers

Using words to create a bond with the reader creates the illusion that the writer is on the same side as the reader. So, psychologically, this makes it more difficult for the reader to disagree with the writer. For example:

- Friends . . .
- Fellow students . . .

Repetition

The conscious repeated use of a word or words creates drama and impact. Many politicians and effective public speakers employ repetition. President Lyndon B Johnson used repetition in his 'We Shall Overcome' speech in 1965:

- There is no Negro problem. There is no Southern problem. There is no Northern problem. There is only an American problem.

Rhetorical questions

These are questions used simply to emphasise a point. For example:

- Isn't it true that . . .?
- Isn't it a bit frightening that doctors call what they do 'practice'?

Assertive language

Using forceful or self-confident language makes your point seem indisputable. It also makes your opinion sound as if it is a widespread belief. For example:

- Everyone knows . . .
- It is abundantly clear that . . .

Hyperbole

This is the use of exaggeration to create an effect. For example:

- I could eat a horse.
- He has a brain the size of a pea.

Groups of three (or triads)

These can be the same three words or different words. For example:

- Life, liberty and the pursuit of happiness.

This technique is very effective if used rhetorically. Three sentences which are very similar in structure also work well.

Triads also sound better to the ear than a list of two or four. For example, most people quote Winston Churchill this way:

- 'I have nothing to offer but blood, sweat and tears.'

What Churchill actually said was:

- 'I have nothing to offer but blood, toil, tears and sweat.'

Alliteration

Repetition of consonant sounds at the beginnings of words which are in close succession makes the point more memorable. For example:

- Nerds can naturally make nukes from nickels.

Assonance

This is repetition of vowel sounds for effect. For example:

- The moon is a balloon.
- It beats as it sweeps as it cleans. (Slogan for Hoover vacuum cleaners.)

Appeal to greater authority

Using experts or research to support a viewpoint adds credibility to what the writer is saying and can make opinion sound like fact. For example:

- Scientists believe that . . .
- A recent survey indicated that . . .

Quotations

These add credibility to an argument and can be used to show that research has been carried out. For example:

- As Winston Churchill said: 'We make a living by what we get, we make a life by what we give.'

Statistics

Statistics provide a factual basis for an argument. For example:

- 7% of the light bulbs tested were defective.

Humour

In the right context, humour lightens the tone, establishes a closer rapport between writer and reader and adds variety, which in turn helps maintain interest.

Superlatives

These words describe something as of the highest degree or extreme, such as 'best', 'most', 'greatest', 'highest', 'prettiest'.

Personal anecdote

This may convince the reader of the authenticity of the writer's views but, like humour, it is best used wisely and sparingly. For example:

- I was in the shop the other day and you wouldn't believe who came in to buy milk.

Tone

The tone can be indignant, angry, shocked, disgusted, sad, happy, calm or reflective. It can be adapted according to the point being made and the reaction the writer wants to generate in the reader. Here are examples of comments that are sincere, sarcastic, envious and insulting in tone:

- She rose from her chair when I came in and exclaimed with a smile, 'Wow! Nice outfit!'
- She gave me one look and said, with a short laugh, 'Yeah, right! Nice outfit!'
- She glanced at me quickly and muttered reluctantly, 'Um, yeah . . . nice outfit.'
- She looked at me incredulously and said, 'Eww! Nice outfit!'

Contrast

The difference or dissimilarity of things or situations can be contrasted. For example:

- 'It was the best of times, it was the worst of times'.

ACTIVITY 8

The text below is taken from a leaflet written by a GCSE student as part of her coursework. Its aim is to persuade people to visit Belfast.

Some persuasive language techniques have been used to support its purpose.

Read the text carefully. Note down, with examples, which of the following techniques have been used:

1 Repetition
2 Hyperbole
3 Groups of three
4 Rhetorical questions
5 Alliteration (repetition of consonants)
6 Assonance (repetition of vowels)
7 Addressing the reader directly
8 Statistics or examples
9 Contrast
10 Superlatives (e.g. best, most, greatest)

You Can Bank On Belfast

If you're looking for something to do over the summer holidays why not visit Belfast? Belfast is steeped in history and rich in cultural diversity. Whether you prefer shopping and nightlife or walking and exploring, culture or nature, life in the town or the country you'll find it all in Belfast.

Belfast is proud of its pools, parks and pitches if it's sport you're into. If you've got troublesome teenagers on your hands you could take them to Castle Court Shopping Centre and if you've got younger ones why not try out Cheeky Monkeys play centre? And if you're looking for a night out Belfast's many restaurants boast some of the best cuisine to be found in the world. You could also catch the latest show at the Odyssey Arena or the Waterfront Hall.

Belfast has a state-of-the-art transport system so it couldn't be easier to get about and it's surrounded by beautiful countryside. That's why over a million tourists visited Belfast last year and that's why you should too.

ACTIVITY 9

Could you do better? In approximately 200 words, use a range of the persuasive techniques or features you have been studying to write a promotional piece for your local city, town or area.

6 Analysing a Multi-Modal Text

The two sample answers that follow were written under exam conditions by students of your age. The students were answering this question:

> Analyse the presentational devices used in this promotional leaflet for a folk park.

ACTIVITY 10

Take 10 minutes to read over the sample answer below and look closely at the examiner's comments. The examiner's comments will help you recognise the key qualities of the answer.

1 Do the examiner's comments fairly represent the quality of the work?
2 Do any of the examiner's remarks surprise/puzzle you?

⬤ First student response

A key feature of the advertisement is the use of photographs. The main body of the first page is made up of photos, each depicting bright images. The images show the best features of the park and of an idealised trip to the area – sheep and donkeys mingle among smiling employees upon the pleasant backdrop of a cottage with a 'cosy' fire. Families are pictured enjoying themselves taking part in various activities around the park. This presents a clear image of the park's intention, which is to promote an idyllic day out for the whole family.

The second page shows yet more photos, spaced attractively so as to provide an enjoyable visual experience. A border constructed of colourful images runs across the top and bottom of the page. Beautiful images of buildings entice us in and lure us to come and experience the park for ourselves. The pictures also come with a visual description of the activities available at the site.

The layout is very visually pleasing. The title is the first thing that draws your attention and is written in black bold writing. This makes it stands out. The title is further emphasised by the warm block of colour which it sits on. The whole first page is edged with a green broken border. This border reminds you of a country landscape which emphasises the rural nature of the site.

Bright, bold colours encourage a family audience. It is easy to imagine a young child becoming attracted to these and the pretty pictures and thus begging his parents to visit the park.

The numerous sub-headings are outlined in bold and help break up the text and they emphasise the context of each section.

The logos and official badges of various companies that sponsor and support the park further promote the park as a reputable place to visit.

Details such as phone numbers and the park's official website are displayed clearly at the end of the leaflet, and make it easy to get in contact with the park and receive more information.

Examiner comments
This answer demonstrates:

 a range of relevant evidence

 a clear appreciation of presentational details

 some perceptive assessment.

ACTIVITY 11

Read the second student's response below. Assess its strengths and weaknesses and write your comments in a table like the one below.

The strengths of this answer	The areas that need to be improved

Second student response

When we first open the leaflet we see two large pictures to grab our attention. The first picture shows a bright, happy photograph which makes the park look pleasant, the second photograph shows a woman from the 19th Century who is smiling at two visitors who seem to be enjoying themselves. From the first two photographs we are lead to believe that the park's setting and people are pleasant and that we will enjoy a day here.

On the second page there is the five pictures which are in order down the page in the same order they are reffered to in the text, this allows us to become more involved with the park and that we agree on what the writer has said about the park.

When we first see the leaflet we notice that there is very bright colours to create a pleasant atmosphere and to make the reader feel as if they would want to read it, after the bright colours have caught their eye.

7 Analysing a Pair of Multi-Modal Texts

ACTIVITY 12

The DVD cover on page 41 helps to advertise and sell the film.

1 How do **presentational devices** help to sell this DVD? In your answer consider:
- the layout
- the use of images
- the use of colour.   (9 marks)

2 How do the **words and phrases** used support the presentational devices and help to sell this DVD?   (15 marks)

Use a planner like this to help you organise your reactions to and analysis of this multi-modal text:

Basic information for both questions	Purpose	
	Audience	
	Form – type of text	
Question 1	Use of presentational devices	
	Structural devices	
Question 2	Use of persuasive language devices	
	How these language devices support the effect created by presentational devices	

BOUNCE

BOUNCE

Bounce is the latest film from the studios that brought you Caterpillars! It's the uplifting story of a young boy and his favourite pet who travel the world, getting into exciting scrapes with pirates and bandits, and also making friends with the most unlikely characters. It will make you laugh and cry, and it might make you wish you were off on an adventure too!

Bonus special features

- Audio commentary by the director
- Music video performed by the artists
- Never-before-seen extended scenes
- Never-before-seen deleted scenes
- Interviews from the star cast
- Interviews from the special effects team

Simply brilliant!

'Bounce is the best children's film this year!'

★★★★★ 5 stars

DVD VIDEO

U

This widescreen presentation preserves the film's original aspect ratio

Widescreen TV   Standard TV

ENTERTAINMENT PRESENTS BOUNCE
A PRODUCTION PRODUCT BY ASSOCIATES MIDDISH EXECUTIVE PRODUCER NAME & NAME MUSIC BY SOUNDS GOOD TO ME MUSIC SUPERVISION BY COULD SOUND BETTER COSTUME DESIGN BY LOOKS GREAT FEELS NASTY DIRECTOR OF PHOTOGRAPHY MOVIE THE LIGHT 'TIL I SAY IT LOOKS RIGHT SCREENPLAY BY AUTA WORDS

LANGUAGE OPTIONS   ENGLISH   5.1
SUB-TITLE OPTIONS   ENGLISH
Colour
Feature running time: 100 minutes

ISBN 78-1-44 1-1082-1

8144 10821

The two publicity posters below and opposite are advertising the same film.

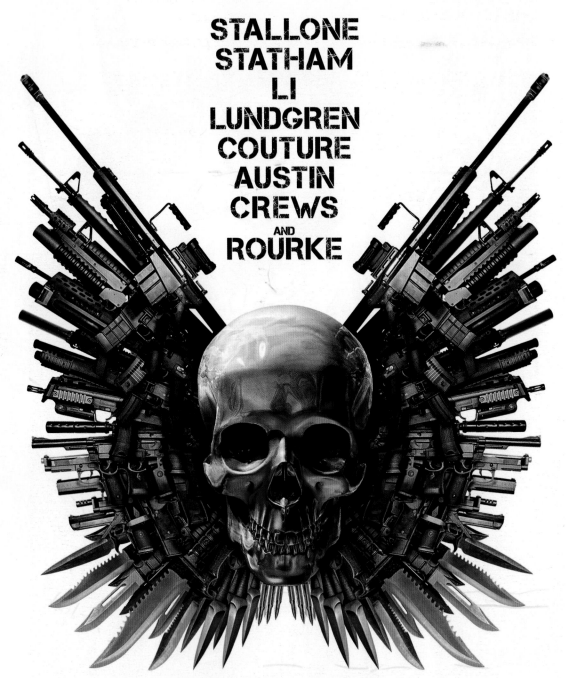

ACTIVITY 13

Which of these two posters would you use to advertise this film? Be prepared to justify your choice by presenting a series of supporting arguments.

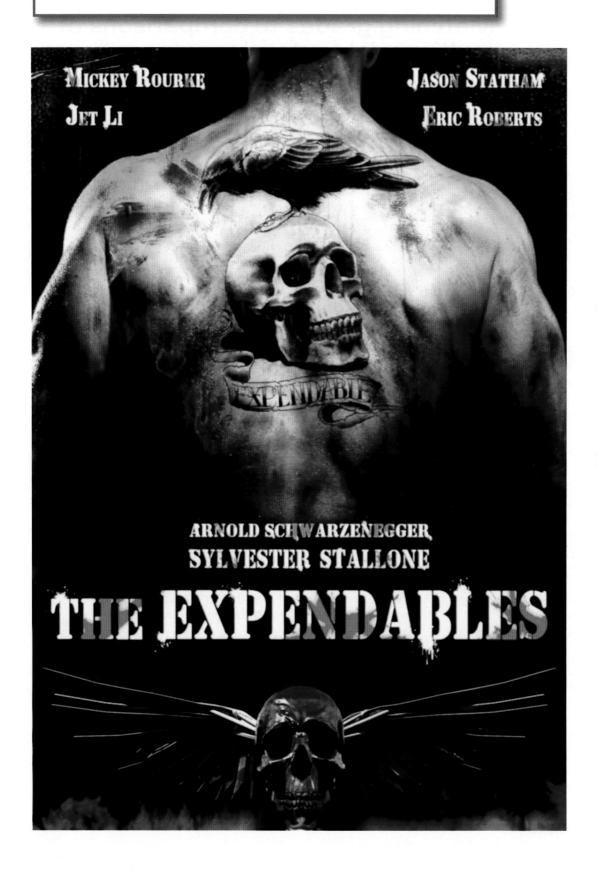

8 Reading Multi-Modal Texts: Exam Success

Matching grades to comparisons of multi-modal texts

In Section B the essential qualities the examiners will be looking for are highlighted at the important grade boundaries. Read these descriptions *carefully*; they tell you what your answer should be like.

Grade C work displays:

(a)   in comparing **presentational devices**:

✓   evidence of an overall evaluation of *how* these devices have been used to achieve particular effects

✓   a straightforward explanation and comparison of *how* these devices have been used to engage the intended audience

✓   some valid interpretations that draw supporting evidence together from both sources

(b)   in comparing use of **language**:

✓   evidence of some evaluation of *how* language and structural devices have been used to reinforce and support the visual message

✓   an explanation and comparison of *how* these devices have been used to positively engage the target audience

✓   a development of an appropriate interpretation that draws relevant supporting evidence from both texts.

Grade A/A* work displays:

(a)   in comparing **presentational devices**:

✓   an assured evaluation of *how* these devices achieve their particular effects

✓   a confident explanation of *how* these devices positively influence and aim to engage the target audience

✓   a perceptive interpretation based on an insightful selection of consistently relevant supporting material from both sources

(b)   in comparing use of **language**:

✓   an assured evaluation of *how* linguistic, grammatical and structural devices achieve their particular effects

✓   a confident explanation and comparison of *how* these devices positively influence and generate positive engagement with the target audience

✓   a perceptive interpretation based on a purposeful comparison of precisely selected evidence.

ACTIVITY 14

On page 45 are extracts taken from the responses to multi-modal texts made by two students. The examiner comments have been added to help you recognise the key strengths and weaknesses of the work.

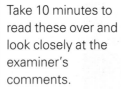

Take 10 minutes to read these over and look closely at the examiner's comments.

1 Do the examiner's comments fairly represent the quality of the work?

2 Do any of the remarks surprise/puzzle you?

First student response

The front pages of these two leaflets are laid out very neatly and both are very eye-catching. The 'environmental' leaflet appropriately makes use of a green background that reinforces the whole notion of driving 'more greenly' whereas the leaflet for the latest MM car is only concerned with using colour on the front cover in a dramatic way to make their car seem more attractive.

Examiner comments

This student is working comfortably at grade C level. This extract demonstrates:

 an overall consideration, explanation and comparison of how these devices attempt to engage the reader

 appropriate interpretation – draws together relevant evidence from both sources.

Second student response

In the 'green leaflet', the use of the colour coded table makes the information accessible at a glance as well as playing on the reader's conscience; it is intended that they will want to move down into the green band and reduce their carbon emissions and road tax. There is no such consideration from the MM motor company whose major consideration seems to be to appeal to the 'boy-racer' fraternity – their latest offering 'bursts' from the front on their leaflet, plunging through a flaming orange and red background!

Examiner comments

This student is working comfortably at grade A/A★ level. This extract demonstrates:

 an assured evaluation of the presentational devices and their intended effects

 a confident comparison and explanation of how these devices are intended to work

 perceptive interpretation and purposeful comparison.

ACTIVITY 15

As a class take 5 minutes to discuss how the first student might have improved this segment of his/her answer.
Consider it sentence by sentence assessing:

- what is good about the answer
- what the examiner might view as general and of therefore of no merit
- what could usefully be sharpened up to improve the point being made.

Comparison of multi-modal texts: Key to success

In the exam, time is limited and so focused comparison is vital. Read the pointers and then complete the exam-style question opposite.

 The best answers will result from the following process: **Think, Plan, Write**. Resist the temptation to start immediately; taking the time to think and plan is central to producing work that offers an organised and thoughtful comparison.

 Begin by considering the two key issues:

i)   What is the *purpose* of each of the texts? (What is being presented or promoted?)

ii) Who is the intended *audience* in each case?

Addressing these two questions about the texts will set you off on the correct path.

  You have strict time limits to adhere to if you are to maximise you performance so make sure you stick to them:

- Spend the first 15 minutes carefully reading and analysing the texts.

- Spend 10 minutes answering the first question on presentation.

- Take 20 minutes to answer the question on language.

 Reviewing your finished work isn't quite as significant in this section which is testing reading – spelling, grammar and punctuation is therefore not being assessed. If, however, you have a few spare moments when you have finished both questions, check over what you've written, making sure it all makes sense and that you have expressed your points clearly.

 Respond to the question on presentational devices offering a comparison that:

i)   evaluates the presentational devices and their effects

ii) explains how these devices combine to create the desired impact on the target audience

iii) offers an interpretation that is supported by drawing together a purposefully selected range of evidence.

 Respond to the question on the use of language and structure offering a comparison that:

i)   evaluates the role of language and structural devices in creating the desired outcome

ii) explains how these devices create a connection with the target audience and positively support the desired outcome

iii) offers an insightful interpretation of the stimulus material bringing together a range of precisely chosen pieces of evidence.

Exam-style question

Look at the multi-modal texts on pages 48–49 and then answer the questions below.

1. How have the presentational devices been used in both DVD covers to persuade you that these are exciting films?
   Compare the use of images, colour and layout in each of the covers.
2. How has language been used in both DVD covers to support the idea that these are exciting films?
   Compare how language has been used to reinforce this sense of excitement in titles, headings and captions.

Response time: 45 minutes

Below is a version of the table you will have already used to analyse a single multi-modal text. This latest table is designed to help you to focus on producing the required comparison of the two multi-modal texts that conclude this unit.

Copy and complete a table like the one below to assist with the initial planning of your answer. Note down the main features from each text and then use these notes as the basis for your comparisons.

Features	Text 1	Text 2
Purpose		
Audience		
Form – type of text		
Presentational devices		
Structural devices		
Main language strategies		
How are they developed?		
Language devices		

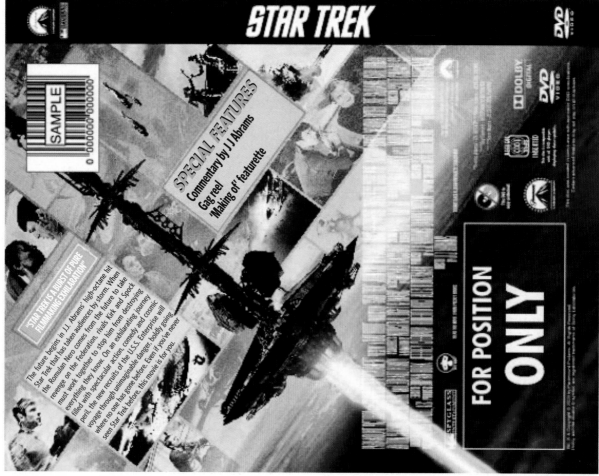

Checklist for success: working towards Grade C	✔
Have you developed your two answers in a style that **cross-references relevant material from the two multi-modal texts?**	
Has your answer on presentational devices offered **a sound overall assessment that compares/contrasts how the presentational devices in both multi-model texts set about achieving their effects?**	
Has your answer on the use of language been presented to offer **a straightforward explanation and comparison of how words and phases and structural devices have been used** in order to engage and influence the reader?	
Have both answers developed **appropriate conclusions** about the stimulus materials that are **supported by relevant examples/ evidence from both sources?**	

Checklist for success: working towards Grade A/A★	✔
Have you developed your two answers in a style that **confidently cross-references precisely selected material from the two multi-modal texts?**	
Has your answer on presentational devices offered **an assured evaluation that purposefully compares/contrasts how the presentational devices in both multi-modal texts set about positively achieving their effects?**	
Has your answer on use of language presented a **confident explanation and comparison of how linguistic, grammatical and structural devices generate engagement and positively influence the reader?**	
Have both answers developed **perceptive interpretations** of the stimulus material that are **supported by precisely selected evidence from both sources?**	

Unit 2
English Language and English

Introduction to Functional Writing

Unit 2 is externally examined and is made up of two sections. The first section is Section A and it assesses **Functional Writing**.

Target outcome: Clearly ordered writing offering an engaging treatment that displays an appropriate sense of audience and purpose.

Target skills

The target skills you will learn about in this Functional Writing section will enable you to:

 write accurately and effectively

 use an appropriate writing form

 express ideas and information precisely and accurately

 form independent views

 select vocabulary to persuade and inform the reader

 use accurate grammar, spelling and punctuation.

Assessment Objective

Your Assessment Objective in this Functional Writing section is:

Writing

i)   Write clearly and effectively in a way that engages the reader.

ii) Use a style that matches vocabulary to purpose and audience.

iii) Organise information/ideas logically into sentences and paragraphs.

iv) Make use of language and structural features for effect.

v)   Use a range of sentence structures as well as punctuate and spell accurately.

Exam question

You will have 45 minutes in which to write on a given topic. Different stimulus material will be provided for the two tiers.

You can go to the Exam Practice section at the end of this book (page 191) for more practice.

No one, not even a famous writer such as J.K. Rowling, can create an effective piece of writing without putting time and effort into the process involved.

In Unit 2, Section A, you have only 45 minutes to create an interesting piece of functional writing which informs or persuades your audience. It needs to be time well spent!

You will be required to express your views and opinions on a given topic to a specified audience. The task will also tell you what form your writing should take. The form may be one of the following:

- a speech or talk
- a letter
- a magazine article
- a discursive essay.

You will be provided with some facts and opinions related to the topic which you may use to stimulate your own ideas and to help support your discussion and arguments.

In order to produce an effective piece of writing in the time allowed there are three essential elements you must consider:

- **What** you are going to write – the need to plan
- **Why** you are writing – the need to be clear about purpose
- **Who** you are writing for – the need to connect to your audience.

The three Ws

What are you going to write?

Effective planning is the foundation for successful written work.

Advice on planning in terms of timing is given in the examination papers themselves and also later in Exam Practice (page 91).

Start by carefully reading not only the functional-writing task but also the stimulus materials provided and then think through the ideas and arguments you are going to present on the given topic.

Your plan could take the form of:

- a bullet-point list (see page 9)
- a spider diagram (see page 10)
- a flow chart (see page 11)
- a thought tree.

It does not matter which of these you use. We all think in different ways and so may prefer different ways of planning. What is important is that you take 5–10 minutes to organise your thoughts and ideas before you start your writing.

ACTIVITY 1

Planning for success

Work in pairs. Imagine you are going to write an article with the title 'Give Teenagers a Break!' for the magazine *Over Sixty*. In your piece you are to defend young people against many of the criticisms directed against them by the older generation.

1 Consider your audience – what is the best approach to use to get through to them?

2 Spend 10 minutes planning ideas and arguments you could present to your audience.

3 Display your planning sheets and share your ideas with the rest of your class.

Below are some negative comments to get you started. Think carefully about how you might challenge such views:

> Young people just don't want to learn. Behaviour in schools today is appalling.

> Under-age drinking is a real problem.

> They roam the streets in gangs, intent on causing as much trouble as possible.

> This generation is all about 'Me, Me, Me!'

> Teenagers are such a waste of space. All they're good at is watching TV and playing computer games.

It is always advisable to plan a strong **introduction** to your written piece as you need to bring your audience over to your viewpoint from the start.

It is particularly important to write an arresting **opening sentence** which commands attention. There are many different techniques you could use to achieve this effect. For example:

- humour
- a quotation
- immediately making your view clear
- a shocking statistic
- emotive language
- a list
- direct appeal to the audience
- an emphatic or provocative statement
- a question
- an anecdote.

There is nothing but rubbish on television!

With your partner, identify the techniques used in the following openings for the issue: 'There is nothing but rubbish on television!' Discuss their effectiveness in attempting to capture interest about this issue.

- Wildlife programmes, documentaries, round-the-clock news, costume dramas, live sport . . . Does this sound like rubbish to you?
- What's important in life – world peace or who's going to win *X Factor*?
- Maybe Orson Welles spoke for all of us when he said, 'I hate television. I hate it as much as peanuts. But I can't stop eating peanuts.'
- Our obsession with television means we're in danger of becoming a nation of couch potatoes. The fact is that for most of us the only exercise we get is making a cup of tea when the adverts are on.
- By the time we are fourteen, on average we will have seen around 11,000 murders on television. Surely this can't be acceptable?
- Television has been described as 'chewing gum for the eyes'. And we all know what happens to chewing gum when it loses its flavour!
- More young people vote in reality television shows than take part in general elections. This is the sad reality of reality television!
- 19.2 million people tuned in to watch the final of *Britain's Got Talent*. That's 19.2 million people who need to get out more.
- Let me take you back to when we were children. I treasure the magical memories of television programmes I watched back then. I'm sure it is the same for you. Who could forget . . .?

Writing an effective opening

With your partner, write an interesting opening paragraph for the magazine article 'Give Teenagers a Break!' that you planned in Activity 1 (page 53). You need to come up with a punchy paragraph which is sure to grab the attention of your audience.

Share your opening with your classmates. Identify the range of techniques used by the class and discuss their effectiveness.

Why are you writing?

Every piece of writing has a **purpose**; in other words, a **reason why** it was written. This is also referred to as the writer's **intention**.

A piece of writing may have **more than one** purpose. The writer's intention may be to:

- persuade
- stimulate
- inform
- advertise or sell
- entertain
- explain
- motivate
- argue a point of view
- express feelings
- provoke emotions
- challenge or confront
- warn
- inspire
- deliberately shock.

Writers often deliberately manipulate words and phrases in order to achieve their intended purposes. You need to do this in your written work too.

The newspaper article opposite was written by Susan Greenfield, a leading neuroscientist (a specialist in the human brain and nervous systems). In it she sets out to express strong opinions and to persuade the reader to agree with her viewpoint about the dangers of using Facebook. The comments show how this writer uses language intentionally to achieve her purposes.

The reference to 'your child's brain' is meant to reinforce the sense of anxiety.

Note how the writer opens by speaking directly to the reader in the form of a question. This has the effect of drawing the reader into the issue.

HOW FACEBOOK ADDICTION IS DAMAGING YOUR CHILD'S BRAIN

Can you imagine a world without long-term relationships, where people are unable to understand the consequences of their actions or empathise with one another?

Such conditions would not only destroy our happiness and achievements – they could threaten our very survival.

Yet this imagined existence isn't as far away as it seems. It is likely to be our future. For we are developing an ever deeper dependence on online websites such as Facebook, Twitter and Second Life – and these technologies can alter the way our minds work.

But while adult brains *can* change, it is children who are most at risk, for their brains are still growing and developing. Yet 99% of children and young people use the internet, according to an Ofcom study. In 2005, the average time children spent online was 7.1 hours per week. By 2007, it had almost doubled to 13.8 hours. As an expert on the human brain, I am speaking out as I feel we need to protect the young.

Half of young people aged 8 to 17 have their own profile on a social networking site. What features of the young mind are being threatened by these sites?

With Facebook, real conversation has been replaced by screen dialogue. This will damage children's ability to communicate properly – and build relationships with others. In fact, it could completely change how conversation happens. Another aspect of brain development is empathy. This cannot develop through social networking because we are not aware of how other people are really feeling – we cannot pick up on body language when we are communicating through a screen.

We must take this issue seriously because what could be more important than the brains of the next generation?

Words in the title such as 'addiction' and 'damaging' are intended to shock the reader from the outset.

The first two paragraphs paint a bleak scenario for the future. Negative language such as 'a world without' and 'threaten our very survival' is clearly intended to frighten the reader.

The language changes to focus on children's brains. Statistics such as '99% of children' and references to time spent online support the writer's point about the risk to children's brains. She then plays her ace card as 'an expert' so the reader will trust her judgement.

Again, there is a direct appeal to the reader reinforcing the possible threat. This question leads the reader into the next paragraph.

The writer goes into detail about how young minds will be damaged. The intention is to worry the reader about the dire consequences of using Facebook.

The piece concludes with a warning to 'take this issue seriously'. The plea 'what could be more important' plays on the reader's fears.

ACTIVITY 4

Language to achieve purpose

Advertisers set out to sell their products. You can learn much from how they use language for this purpose.

Read the piece of writing below and identify the writer's intentions, using the list on page 54 as a guide.

Assess the techniques the writer has employed in order to achieve their intentions.

Dive into the Mediterranean; Drive onto the Eighth; Delve into History – It Could Only Be Egypt

A warm, friendly welcome is par for the course in the land of the Pharaohs, whatever your holiday interests may be.

From Cleopatra's city of Alexandria on the shores of the Mediterranean to the Red Sea's ultra-modern resorts like Sal Hasheesh, Marsa Alam, Ras Sudur and the Sinai's hallowed biblical sites, there's something for everyone in this country of sun-drenched sands and breathtaking treasures.

The Red Sea, for instance, boasts exhilarating water sports, pristine white beaches lapped by crystal-clear waters; scuba diving on tropical coral reefs and spectacular five-star holiday accommodation.

And yes, there are even lush, championship-quality golf courses should you fancy a round or two.

Just a day trip away from Egypt's holiday coastlines you'll find the unforgettable civilisation of the Pharaohs, whose reign inspired some of the most beautiful and spectacular structures ever built.

Why not crown your Egyptian holiday with a soulful, romantic cruise along the magical Nile, stopping off to explore the fabulous temple of Karnak or the magnificent Valley of the Kings?

Don't forget to save a day for Cairo's colourful bazaars though. There are bargains galore for those who like to haggle, and relaxing tea houses for those who prefer to watch the world go by.

Your travel agent has some very attractive deals on Egypt right now. Call in today or contact the Egyptian Tourist Authority on 09001 600299 or visit www.touregypt.net

Who are you writing for?

As well as identifying clear reasons why you are writing, you need to consider the **intended audience** for whom you are writing.

For example, your intended audience might be:

- newspaper readers
- your classmates
- a specific audience, e.g. parents of teenagers
- a particular age group, e.g. adults or young children
- people with a specific interest, e.g. in sport.

Purpose and audience are closely linked. You must keep both in mind when you plan what to write and how you are going to write it.

The following activity will help you focus on this important aspect of creating an effective piece of writing.

ACTIVITY 5

Considering audience and purpose

The two pieces of writing on pages 58 and 59 target different audiences but both have the same purpose – to caution people about the dangers of smoking and to encourage them to stop.

Read both texts. Working in groups:
1 Identify the target audience for each text.
2 Compare how language is manipulated differently in the two texts to target the different audiences.

Smoking – The Facts

Cigarette smoking is the greatest single cause of illness and premature death in the UK. This leaflet gives reasons why smoking is so harmful. It also lists the benefits of stopping, and where to go for help.

Some shocking figures

About 106,000 people in the UK die each year due to smoking. Smoking-related deaths are mainly due to cancers, COPD (chronic obstructive pulmonary disease) and heart disease.

Cigarette smoke contains over 4000 chemicals, including over 50 known carcinogens (causes of cancer).

About 30,000 people in the UK die from lung cancer each year. More than 80% of these deaths are directly related to smoking.

About half of all smokers die from smoking-related diseases. If you are a long-term smoker, on average your life expectancy is about ten years less than for a non-smoker. The younger you are when you start smoking, the more likely you are to smoke for longer and to die early from smoking.

Smoking increases the risk of developing a number of other diseases. Many of these may not be fatal, but they can cause years of nasty symptoms.

Other problems with smoking

- Your breath, clothes, hair, skin and home smell of stale tobacco. You do not notice the smell if you smoke, but to non-smokers the smell is obvious and unpleasant.
- Your sense of taste and smell are dulled. Enjoyment of food will be reduced.
- Smoking is expensive.
- Life insurance is more expensive.
- Finding a job may be more difficult as employers know that smokers are more likely to have sick leave than non-smokers. Around 34 million working days are lost each year because of smoking-related sick leave.
- Potential friendships and romances may be at risk – smoking is not the attractive thing that cigarette advertisers portray.

The good news

The benefits of stopping smoking begin straight away. You reduce your risk of getting serious disease no matter what age you give up. The sooner you stop, however, the greater the reduction in your risk.

If you have smoked since being a teenager or young adult:

- If you stop smoking before the age of 35, your life expectancy is only slightly less than people who have never smoked.
- If you stop smoking before the age of 50, you decrease the risk of dying from smoking-related diseases by 50%.

Many people have given up smoking. In 1972 just under half of adults in the UK were smokers. By 1990 this had fallen to just under a third. At present, just over a quarter of UK adults are smokers.

Help is available if you want to stop smoking but are finding it difficult:

- **Quit** – charity that helps people to stop smoking
  Quitline: 0800 00 22 00
  Web: www.quit.org.uk
- **Smokefree** – information from the NHS
  Helpline: 0800 022 4 332
  Web: www.smokefree.nhs.uk

http//www.

Smokefree United

A club of footie fans who want to quit smoking. Get all the coaching and support you need to stamp out the ciggies.

Kick the habit

There are plenty of great reasons for giving smoking the boot – like the difference you'll make to your wallet and body.

We know quitting can be tough, but with NHS support you're four times more likely to quit. That's Champion's League form. Sign up for Smokefree United and see what we can offer you.

Life's better Smokefree

Your body is more likely to develop health problems if you are smoking.

For footballers, that means your performance will suffer. Smoking lowers oxygen in the body and reduces your speed and power. You'll struggle to catch your breath and your muscles will tire sooner – allowing nippy non-smokers to run rings around you. And because smokers are more likely to get injured, you'll end up spending more time on the subs' bench.

Quitting smoking means you'll get more out of your game. Within 24 hours your blood pressure, pulse rate and oxygen rates will return to normal. Within a week your breathing will be noticeably better and you'll be able to exercise for longer.

Free support to help you quit

OK, so you may not be able to improve your team's chances of FA cup glory, but you can improve your chances of quitting by using local support from the NHS. You're onto a winner!

NHS support is completely free, and there are loads of services to choose from – so you can find the support that works best for you. Trust us; we're a team worth joining. Inspired and designed by smokers who have successfully quit, you'll get the best advice from people who are on your side.

Show smoking the red card. Get in touch with your local NHS adviser today – it's the signing of the season.

Meet Paul Scott

'I found the NHS Stop Smoking Service easy to use and helpful. I feel that I have now quit for good.'

Paul had been a regular smoker since being caught up in the wrong crowd at the age of 11.

Paul's main motivation for quitting was his passion for football and his desire to be fitter and faster.

Since quitting, Paul has already seen a marked improvement on the pitch and feels healthier and more energetic.

Effective writing makes an **impact with the audience**. This can be achieved only by developing a **rapport** with your reader or listener. This is a tall order in 45 minutes but practice really helps so take every opportunity to hone your skills during your GCSE course.

The following piece is an excellent example of how a writer sets out to establish a **connection** with the intended audience. This is vital to achieve the intended purpose: this writer wants to persuade the reader to give money to the charity Help the Aged.

Dear Friend,

What *does* Christmas mean to you? For most of us, it means decorations, laughter, presents, carols and, above all, family and friends.

But for 78-year-old Maud, who wrote to Help the Aged, it suggests very different images. For her, Christmas means loneliness, desolation, silence and despair.

Since her husband died 7 years ago, Maud has spent every Christmas Day completely alone.

There is no one for Maud. No one to buy her presents or send her a card. No one to share a traditional turkey dinner. No one to hug her and wish her a Happy Christmas.

She doesn't have much money, and so she decorates her flat with a few sprigs of holly and strands of tinsel. But with only the television for company, she is lonely to the point of despair.

As the world around her celebrates Christmas amongst family and friends, Maud, and many others like her, will sit in tortured silence, staring at four walls, wishing the day away. I simply can't imagine what that must be like. Can you?

If you are as moved by Maud's situation as I am, please help today with a gift of £14. Without help, an estimated 400,000 older people like Maud will struggle through Christmas alone. Your £14 could help stop this tragedy.

Help the Aged needs to act right now if we are to reach as many lonely, isolated men and women as possible this Christmas and throughout the year. But we can't do it without the help of people like you. That's why I'm counting on you to give whatever you can to our Alone at Christmas Appeal.

Let me tell you about the joy that your gift of £14 could bring. It would mean that someone like Maud could be amongst people who really care. It would mean a day of smiles, laughter, conversation and presents.

Without help, Maud and thousands like her will have to spend not just another Christmas alone, but the days and weeks that follow. Please don't let that happen.

Thank you.

ACTIVITY 6

Establishing a positive rapport

This exercise will help you to focus on how important it is to connect with the audience in order to write effectively.

Read the letter and answer these questions:

1 This charity appeal takes the form of a letter. How does this help to establish a connection with the reader?
2 Pick out examples of when the reader is being spoken to directly. What does the writer intend to achieve by doing this?
3 What is the effect of using a real-life example?
4 The reader feels a strong sense of pity for Maud. How does the writer achieve this?
5 What words are intended to shock the reader? Why does the writer want to do this?
6 The writer uses repetition in the fourth paragraph. What effect do they wish to achieve?
7 What other persuasive techniques does the writer use to convince the reader to give money to the Christmas appeal?

2 Using Appropriate Forms and Techniques

The form your writing needs to take will be specified in the examination paper. You may be required to write a speech, a letter, a discursive essay or an article for a magazine or newspaper.

Whichever form you are instructed to employ, you must use and adapt it in a way that will engage and influence your audience. So, in the examination, remember to apply what you have learnt about **writing effectively**.

An easy way to remember this formula for success is to use the mnemonic PPA:

P	**Plan**	Have you spent time thinking about **what** you are going to write?
P	**Purpose**	**Why** are you writing and how will you achieve your intentions?
A	**Audience**	How are you going to connect to **who** is going to read your work?

Writing to inform and persuade has a number of key features. These are **techniques** which you can use to influence your audience. (You will have already met some of them in the previous section, on 'writing effectively'.)

You can make a convincing impression when writing to inform and persuade by:

- grabbing the audience's attention with a memorable opening
- addressing the audience directly through rhetorical questions and using 'you' and 'your'
- using a suitably flexible and lively style of writing – there is no need to be boring
- using humour (where appropriate) to engage or entertain the audience
- revealing something of yourself in personal anecdotes so that the audience will empathise with you
- being aware of tone and varying this for effect
- using words to stir up emotions in the audience such as pity, guilt or shock
- using words to challenge the audience's thoughts and opinions
- expressing feelings – showing concern or outrage or pleasure
- using direct speech – e.g. for humorous effect
- using devices such as alliteration, repetition and lists of three to sustain interest
- presenting a series of convincing arguments, demonstrating an ability to sustain a viewpoint
- supporting views and opinions with facts, examples and anecdotes.

The next two activities will help you to reinforce these important writing skills.

Key features in writing a speech

Churchill was well aware of the power of the spoken word to influence, persuade and inspire. It is said that he sometimes spent weeks perfecting his speeches.

The extract below is part of a speech he delivered at the start of the Second World War.

> I say to the House as I said to ministers who have joined this government, I have nothing to offer but blood, toil, tears and sweat. We have before us an ordeal of the most grievous kind. We have before us many, many months of struggle and suffering.
>
> You ask, what is our policy? I say it is to wage war by land, sea and air. War with all our might and with all the strength God has given us, and to wage war against a monstrous tyranny never surpassed in the dark and lamentable catalogue of human crime. That is our policy.
>
> You ask, what is our aim? I can answer in one word. It is victory. Victory at all costs – victory in spite of all terrors – victory, however long and hard the road may be, for without victory there is no survival . . .
>
> I take up my task in buoyancy and hope. I feel sure that our cause will not be suffered to fail among men. I feel entitled at this juncture, at this time, to claim the aid of all and to say, 'Come then, let us go forward together with our united strength.'

ACTIVITY 7

Read the Churchill speech again and then consider the analysis below. The speech uses the following key features to inform the audience about the serious situation and to uplift them at a difficult and worrying time:

- negative language in the opening paragraph to reinforce the hardship ahead: 'blood, toil, tears and sweat', 'ordeal', 'grievous', 'struggle and suffering'
- emotive language to highlight the harsh reality of the enemy being faced: 'monstrous tyranny', 'dark and lamentable'
- reference to God to offer some reassurance: 'with all the strength God has given us'
- use of question and answer: 'what is our aim? I can answer in one word.'
- deliberate use of repetition, e.g. to reinforce the important message to defeat the enemy: 'Victory at all costs – victory in spite of . . . victory, however long . . .'
- change of tone (tonal shift) to one of hope conveyed in language such as: 'buoyancy and hope', 'I feel sure that our cause will not . . . fail'
- final direct appeal to the audience to unite to pursue a common goal: 'Come then, let us go forward together'
- use of inclusive language (here and in other parts of the speech) creates a bond which connects the speaker with his audience: 'We have before us', 'with all our might', 'our united strength'.

ACTIVITY 8

Using the list on page 62 and what you have learnt in Activity 7, analyse the key features which make the article on page 64 an effective piece of writing.

Key features of a magazine article

In this magazine article, the writer expresses his views on camping in a persuasive and entertaining manner.

Camping: Is It Nuts in May?

Now I understand the mind of Robert Falcon Scott when, nearly a hundred years ago, he wrote with shivering, half-frozen hand the despairing words, 'Great God! This is an awful place.'

Forget the Antarctic; Scott was quite obviously referring to his tent! Camping is one of those things: you either hate it or you hate it. There is no other rational approach.

Why would a sane human being in possession of a solid, brick-built house exchange hot water and central heating for the shelter afforded by a big nylon bag? And pay for it!

I asked myself this a fortnight ago, as, stirred yet again by the cold, I awoke to find myself staring up at a patch of orange nylon illuminated by the grey light of a new day.

Outside, the dawn chorus was clearing its throat. I was bang awake at six on a Sunday. I wanted to cry.

My wife, Penny, has been camping many times and claims to have enjoyed the experience. Friends have been camping too – mostly in France during the summer – but never have I been even remotely tempted by the call of the canvas.

When on holiday, I prefer buildings – buildings with Four Seasons written on the outside; and inside a barman called Raul, who has a talent for mixing cocktails and works next to the infinity pool, which is next to the hot tub, which is next to the Caribbean.

'Are we well today, Mr Tweedie?'

'We certainly are, Raul. We certainly are.'

'The usual?'

'Silly not to.'

'And Mrs Tweedie?'

'She's in the spa having a volcanic rock rub.'

Not that we actually go on holidays like this – but one can dream.

Bracelands campsite in the Forest of Dean is a big, sloping, field – short on charm. The reason for my visit, prompted by the Telegraph travel desk, was Eurocamp which, this year, has decided to dip its toe in the British camping market.

Eurocamp's reputation for good facilities produced high expectations in the Tweedie family. Our daughters will happily spend half a day in the swimming pool and here was the chance to tire them out, get them to bed early and enjoy a glass of wine by the dying light of the barbecue under a star-sprinkled sky. I almost forgot my camping phobia. Disillusionment came swiftly.

On arrival at the tents our hearts sank: no swimming pool, no games hall, no nothing – except for an uninviting loo-and-shower block.

We fired up the small barbecue, tossed on some burgers and made up the beds. The sky was cloudless and the first stars were winking in the darkening sky. We opened a bottle of wine and enjoyed, ooooh, a good 12 minutes of relaxed conversation before the girls began to moan about being cold and tired. That was when the reality of camping in Britain kicked in.

In Antarctic conditions, Penny spent the night huddled with the girls in the double bed under layers of blankets, sleeping bags and coats. I shivered under a duvet brought from home, observing my breath.

Eurocamp may work as a gentle introduction to camping in the Mediterranean, when the days are hot and the night air is balmy; but not in Britain in May. It's just too cold!!

As the great Bill Deedes, no stranger to physical hardship, once remarked, only the stupid endure discomfort when they don't have to!

Expressing ideas – confident communication

In order to **communicate** your ideas successfully you need to develop your point of view in a series of persuasive arguments and express these in a **confident** manner.

Developing your flow of ideas in this way is all about effective structuring – in other words **how** you present your thoughts to your audience. Structure is the skeleton of a piece of writing – it literally gives shape to the 'body'!

To make your written work coherent, your ideas and arguments need to be organised into paragraphs. The following examples show you how to do this.

The introduction

Writing an opening paragraph which captures the interest of the audience is the first step in persuading an audience to your viewpoint. The importance of this is highlighted on pages 53–54. Here is an example of an opening paragraph:

 Student response

> Bright yellow slices of plastic pretending to be cheese; chicken nuggets and burgers pretending to be meat; fluorescent fizzy drinks; chips, with chips on top of more chips and – horror of horrors – WHITE bread! Despite all the warnings, this is just some of the rubbish parents today are still feeding their young children with. Do they not care? Can they just not be bothered to cook proper meals? Whatever the answer, this country's obsession with junk food is storing up untold health problems for future generations.

The PEE (Point, Evidence, Explain) technique

This is a useful strategy for developing individual paragraphs. Keep to one key point per paragraph, support the point to add weight to your opinion and offer comment to further reinforce your viewpoint. For example:

 Student response

> Obesity in children has reached epidemic proportions. Sir Liam Donaldson, the Chief Medical Officer, recently described obesity as 'a time bomb' waiting to explode. Today, one in twelve 6-year-olds is obese. Among older children the proportion is even higher: here the figure is one in seven 15-year-olds. These are figures which should shock us all but, more important, shock irresponsible parents into changing disastrous diets into healthier options for their children. After all, it is only what they deserve!

Using links

These are sentences which act like links in a chain to join paragraphs together so that your ideas flow more fluently. Consider these examples of how the writer might lead the audience to the next key point and introduce the audience to the next idea:

- Obesity is not the only problem linked to pigging-out on junk foods.
- We also need to consider the link between junk foods and the increasingly poor behaviour in schools.
- Do these overweight children get bullied? Of course they do!

Sentences like these will add variety and interest to your writing as well as conveying that all-important sense of confidence in expressing your views and opinions.

The conclusion

The final paragraph is as important as the first. You should be aiming not only to capture the audience's attention, but to sustain it right to the end. Here are some possible concluding sentences:

- It has been said that this is the first generation of kids who will die before their parents. Surely we cannot allow this to happen?
- How did we allow this to happen? It is a question I have no answer to.
- Let's all do something about this – before it really is too late!

Look out for interesting openings and conclusions. Good places to find them are the school library, newspaper and magazine articles, travel writing, biography and autobiography.

ACTIVITY 9

Choose one of the three link sentences above and write a paragraph to follow it.

Which of the three conclusions seems to you to be the most powerful? Be prepared to give reasons for your choice.

Appreciate and enjoy them – you never know, you may even be inspired to read more as well as improve your writing skills!

Other persuasive structural devices

When writing to inform and persuade, don't forget about other structural devices which you could use for added impact as well as to convey strength of feelings. For example:

- sentences that use devices such as repetition, lists of three or question and answer
- a variety of sentence lengths: short sentences, long sentences, juxtaposition of short and long sentences
- a variety of sentence forms: questions, direct speech, emphatic statements.

ACTIVITY 10

Which of these persuasive structural devices can you spot in this paragraph?

 Student response

'Mum, please buy me sweets.' The word 'sweets' could be substituted by 'crisps', 'chocolate' or 'cola'. How often do parents hear such words? I suspect over and over and over and over again. Should parents give in to such unrelenting pressure? The answer is no, never! Not if they consider themselves to be responsible parents. I can hear the protests: 'Surely kids deserve a treat now and again' or 'That's cruel'. Well, I simply don't agree. Stuffing junk food into our children has resulted in a dramatic rise in obesity, hyperactivity and downright bad behaviour in our little darlings! Can giving junk food to children ever be justified? I don't think so!!

If you can recognise such strategies being put to effective use in other people's work, this will help to build up your own skills in writing to inform and persuade. Practising these strategies will then give you the confidence you need to take into the examination.

Expressing information

Prove your point!

In the examination, you will be given some stimulus material containing images, facts or opinions related to the topic you are to respond to. This is intended to stimulate your thinking about the issue but you may use some of the information in your written response.

- **Don't** regurgitate this information or simply copy it out.
- **Do** put thought into how to include **selected** facts within your response.
- **Don't** limit yourself to the stimulus material – it is there only as a starting point.

Supporting your arguments with information and/or opinion reinforces your viewpoint and is very persuasive for the audience. This is because you are giving evidence to support your claims.

If you follow this with **further explanation** and/or use **rhetorical devices** to emphasise your key points then you will be well on your way to creating effective persuasive writing. For example:

- 80% of people who smoke 20 cigarettes a day for 20 years will have a smoking-related disease. Fact! Half of them will die of cancer. Fact! Want to hear more? Probably not – if you're a smoker – but I make no apology for what I am about to say next.
- Couch potatoes, hoodies, druggies, layabouts, vandals, hoodlums – just some of the labels teenagers today have been branded with. Is this fair, I ask you?

Expressing **opinions that appear to be facts** is an effective way to provoke a reaction from an audience and can be most persuasive:

- The truth is that most football fans are thugs!
- Everybody knows that women are better drivers than men.

Facts and opinions integrated into and combined with a **variety of sentence constructions** can have powerfully persuasive results:

- Smoking kills. It's as simple as that!
- No less shocking is the fact that . . .

Speaking **directly to the audience** can be very effective:

- Does the fact that . . .? Well, it should.
- I'm sure you'll all agree with me when I say . . .

Embed quotes and opinions into constructions such as:

- It could be said . . .
- While I agree to a certain extent with those who think that . . .
- There's no other way to say this . . .

Another technique is to **state an opinion** and **then dismiss it** in an emphatic way:

- Some people think that . . . What nonsense!
- It has been said . . . How could this possibly be the case when . . .?

The next activity gives you an opportunity to manipulate factual information and opinions into constructions that will impact on an audience.

ACTIVITY 11

Write a 250-word article for your school magazine entitled 'Stay Safe in the Sun' which gives advice and warns about the dangers of exposing our skin to the sun.

Read the 'facts and figures' and opinions on the opposite page. How might you combine these in the body of your article?

> **Facts and figures**
>
> - Unprotected skin can be damaged by the sun's UV rays in as little as 15 minutes.
> - 80% of skin cancers are preventable through simple and cheap sun protection such as covering up and applying sun screen.
> - Children's skin is especially vulnerable. Sunburn in childhood can increase the risk of developing skin cancer in later life by 50%.
> - Skin damage can occur during normal activities – not just on the beach or on holiday.
> - Cloudy days are dangerous as a lot of UV rays still get through.
> - The intensity of UV rays in some sunbeds can be more than ten times stronger than the midday sun.

Spending too much time on sunbeds is just as dangerous as staying out too long in the sun.

Moderate exposure to UV produces vitamin D which some studies say protects against cancer.

Tanned skin is damaged skin!

Form independent views

Practise expressing factual information in an original way so that it conveys some of your personality. This will make your writing more effective.

ACTIVITY 12

Don't be a drag!

Write a speech in which you:
- inform your classmates about the dangers of smoking
- persuade them not to smoke.

A speech like this is frequently written in a dull, earnest fashion. See if you can bring some of your personality into your writing to give it a 'lift'.

You could use selected information from the texts on pages 58 and 59 to help support your own ideas and strengthen your arguments.

ACTIVITY 13

Put your point of view!

This activity allows you to 'have your say' on a subject which you are sure to have some views about.

Read the newspaper article on the following page and then write a letter to the newspaper responding to the opinions expressed in the article.

Make sure you put into practice what you have learnt so far about how to create a successful piece of writing which will influence and engage your audience. Remember: the audience for a letter to a newspaper is the people who read the paper!

School bans Red Bull after pupils run wild. But the true effects of this cynically marketed 'energy drink' are far more toxic and disturbing.

As Principal of Chatsmore Catholic High School, Anne Ward is no doubt all too familiar with the day-to-day challenges of running a school – sloppy dress, over-enthusiastic use of make-up, even the occasional unacceptable haircut.

Never, however, can she have imagined that she would find herself in a war of words over a fizzy drink. But this is exactly what happened when Miss Ward hit the headlines by banning her pupils from drinking the caffeine-based Red Bull.

Her reasoning was simple: children consuming the energy drink (with the advertising slogan 'Red Bull gives you wings') had been mis-behaving.

'We noticed a change in the behaviour of some of our students, and when we investigated we found they had been buying this drink on the way to school,' says the head of the school in Worthing, West Sussex.

'They were drinking more caffeine, which made them hyperactive in some lessons because they hadn't had the time to run off all that energy. They were noisier and didn't always respond to instructions. Some were coming in later than they should do.'

Strong words – and ones that the drink's manufacturer does not want to hear.

Red Bull sells more than three-and-a-half billion cans and bottles a year in 143 countries worldwide. In Britain alone, it sells £271 million worth of the stuff each year.

But this product is coming in for growing criticism.

Red Bull has been banned from sale in Norway, Denmark, Uruguay and Iceland, while health departments in France, Ireland, Turkey, Sweden and the U.S. have expressed grave concerns. A succession of medical studies have also highlighted serious health issues.

What is also a problem is the role of Red Bull in our binge-drinking culture.

In a devastating analysis of the 21st-century binge-drinking epidemic, Chief Constable Stephen Otter, head of the Devon and Cornwall police, found that the typical consumption for a young woman on a night out was eight vodka and Red Bull cocktails.

What he did not point out is that, in terms of caffeine intake, this is equivalent to drinking 16 cups of coffee!

And the real trouble, say experts, is that mixing caffeine, a stimulant, with alcohol, a depressant, is like getting into a car and applying the accelerator and brake pedals at the same time.

'They can't tell if they're drunk. They can't tell if someone else is drunk. So they get hurt – or they hurt someone else,' says Professor Mary Claire O'Brien who has researched the subject.

Could this really be true? Could a drink that is ruthlessly targeted at young thrill-seekers, and which increasing numbers of children consume in school playgrounds along with their packed lunches, also be a contributory factor to the violent, anti-social and dangerous binge-drinking mayhem on many of our streets each weekend?

Consider the following posting by a young man on Facebook:

'I was designated driver for the night when me and my mates went out. I had seven cans of Red Bull in a really short space of time. I was buzzin'. . .That night I crashed my two-week old car which wasn't so good. But you gotta still love the wings, eh?'

Not everyone would agree!

Selecting Vocabulary

4

Words are very powerful – they can destroy and demotivate or convey encouragement and enjoyment. In the examination you are required to write to inform and persuade so you must select language that is going to achieve this.

Emotive language

Your choice of words can trigger an emotional response in your audience. Particular adjectives and adverbs can make your audience feel a sense of guilt, worry, pity or shame.

ACTIVITY 14

Consider how the writer's choice of emotive vocabulary in this piece provokes a strong sense of fear.

Fiddling with his swimming goggles as he strolled across one of Cape Town's most popular beaches, the 37-year-old man did not notice anything amiss. With temperatures in the 90s, the sand was packed with families enjoying the delights of the South African summer.

The sea appeared calm – perfect to escape the heat. But as he waded out, something terrible started to happen. A strange ripple effect circled him in the water. On the beach, people started waving their towels and shouting at him desperately. It was too late. A great white shark struck the man with devastating force. The world's deadliest cold-blooded predator then turned and, amid thrashing water, pulled its human prey under the waves.

Astonishingly, he somehow managed to struggle to the surface as the sea turned red around him. He disappeared again moments later. The shark simply circled and struck again, knocking the man into the air before pulling him under once more. He has not been seen since.

This was no ordinary shark attack. The beast was enormous – indeed one eyewitness described it as being the size of a 'dinosaur or bus'.

Using its unique ability to detect the tiny electrical pulse emitted by a human heart, this fearsome creature – estimated to weigh more than 5 tonnes – had attacked the tourist, striking from beneath at up to 25mph. Only his goggles have been recovered.

Shark spotters are desperate to locate the Great White responsible. Because sharks are territorial creatures, experts say a beast this size is likely to return again and again to the same spot where prey is known to live.

Ever since the Steven Spielberg film *Jaws*, this lethal predator has been reviled and feared. But many believe humans, not the Great White, should be blamed for this horrific death.

Humans are now being hunted by Great Whites. Many believe this is due to the greedy, irresponsible actions of dozens of tour operators which have sprung up along a place known locally as 'shark alley'. They charge tourists £100 a time to be taken out in a boat, placed in a cage and lowered into the water, hoping for the Great White shark of *Jaws* legend to circle.

Environmentalists, swimmers and surfers blame these tourist boats for 'chumming': dropping bloody bait, such as meat and rotting fish, into the sea to lure sharks towards the tourists. They say chumming is behind the upsurge in lethal attacks as this pungent bait drifts all over the sea, luring sharks dangerously close to the shore.

Humans and Great White sharks are regarded by scientists as the number one and number two predators on the planet. In the water, however, the shark always wins.

Persuasive language

Advertisers are experts at selecting and manipulating words to persuade their target audiences. You too can use these techniques in your written work.

Emotive language is often used in adverts but other types of vocabulary are also selected:

- flattering adjectives – to increase interest in what the writer has to sell
- imperatives – special words which guide or instruct the audience: 'Look at this!'
- descriptive details – to entice the audience
- verbs in the present tense – to convey immediacy or excitement: 'It's thrilling to be telling you about . . .'
- informal language – to communicate friendliness: 'Hey, what are you waiting for?' or 'So, don't hang about . . .'
- the personal pronoun 'you' – for direct appeal
- modal verbs – to make suggestions and offer advice: 'Giving up smoking *would* be a good idea as this habit will affect your health.'
- puns and other forms of wordplay – often for humorous effect
- figures of speech such as similes, hyperbole/exaggeration and alliteration.

Tone

Consider the differences in tone in these sentences:

'Please be quiet.'
'Shut your mouth!'
'Would you ever shut that gob of yours?'

Each speaker wants someone to stop talking but the words used make all the difference to whether the effect is intended to be respectful, rude or insulting.

The tone you use can vary. In fact, tonal shifts in a piece of writing can add interest – humorous touches are often appropriate and always appreciated by any audience, even if the subject matter is serious.

Your tone should always be appropriate to the task. A sense of outrage is fine but there is no need to be inappropriate or abusive, even when expressing strong views. This would never persuade an audience to agree with your viewpoint – quite the reverse. It is important to be aware of your tone as this has an effect on the audience.

Choose words that convey a sense of liveliness and inject an enthusiastic tone into your writing. The audience is more likely to empathise with your views if you do.

Informal language is more conversational in tone and can sometimes be put to good use in written work:

- 'So, come on, let's think about this.'
- 'But, hang on a moment. What exactly are we talking about here?'

You have learnt how important it is to think about:

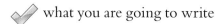 what you are going to write

who you are writing for

why you are writing

the form your writing is to take

how you are going to express your views

what vocabulary you are going to use.

This list is about the planning and writing process, but reviewing and checking your work for accuracy is also essential if you are to communicate your ideas as effectively as possible.

 Be sure to leave yourself at least 5 minutes in which to review and check what you have put down on paper. This is something you must always do if you want to maximise your performance!

Check your functional writing to get the best possible mark:

Have you structured the piece adequately?

Is there sufficient variety in sentence construction?

Does it all make sense – do any sections require reorganising so that the meaning is clear?

Has your word choice been precise enough?

6 Functional Writing: Exam Success

Matching grades to functional writing

In Section A the essential qualities the examiners will be looking for are highlighted at the important grade boundaries. Read these descriptions *carefully*; they tell you what your answer should be like.

Grade C writing displays:

- ✓ development that holds the reader's interest in the subject
- ✓ an appropriate sense of audience and purpose
- ✓ clearly structured and increasingly fluent writing
- ✓ a series of sentence structures, competently handled
- ✓ accurate use of basic punctuation that makes the meaning clear
- ✓ generally accurate spelling and the use of a widening range of vocabulary.

Grade A/A* writing displays:

- ✓ development that is sophisticated and commands the reader's attention
- ✓ a positive rapport with the audience
- ✓ an assured use of structure and a confident style
- ✓ sentence structuring that enhances the overall effect
- ✓ a range of punctuation, confidently employed to enhance fluency
- ✓ accurate spelling and use of an extended vocabulary – errors tend to be one-off mistakes.

ACTIVITY 15

Here is a sample writing task:

Consider the following issue and the questions it raises:

'Young people just don't respect those who are older and wiser.'

This statement presents one view on the topic of respect between the generations. The examiner wants students to to put forward their own thoughts and feelings on the issue.

The answer on page 75 was written under exam conditions by a student of your age. The examiner comments have been added to help you recognise the key strengths of the work.

Take 10 minutes to read it over and look closely at the examiner's comments.
- Do the examiner's comments fairly represent the quality of the work?
- Do any of these remarks surprise/puzzle you?

Student response

When hearing the word 'teenager' most people stereotypically think of somebody with a hood up over their face who is drunk and shouting abuse to somebody else, but is that always the case? Are all teenagers like that?

Actually the majority of teenagers are not like that. Most young people would still see the need to help an elderly lady across a road. There is still many young people who would give up their seat on the bus or train just so an elderly lady or gentleman can sit down. However there is still some young people who would not do this. Some would feel the need to steal off an elderly person as they are more vulnerable and to 'impress' their 'friends'.

Nobody deserves to live in fear because they are vulnerable. People should feel comfortable in their homes and not have to worry about going to the shop to get something like a newspaper or milk.

It is not the young people who should be blamed. It's the parents. They should teach their children to respect adults so it would become a habit. They should not let them be on the streets at night with nothing to do as they will find unhealthy ways of passing the time such as smoking and drinking alcohol. Parents should encourage their children to attend youth clubs, etc.

Why is knife crime and gun crime rates so high? Is it really an accident most likely yes but not for the reasons they claim. Most likely the youths have been bored and decided to drink alcohol or take drugs. This may have resulted in a small disagreement spiriling out of control and eventually resulting in someone being seriously injured or killed.

This is not always the case, most young people refrain from being involved in incidents like these, yet the small minority who do get involved create such vast disrupting it results in all the young people being 'labelled' as being rude, rowdy and rough.

Elderly people should be living in harmony with young people. Youths should look to adults for guidance and support. They should not have a clash of character. If young people do not respect adults now, who will respect the young people of today in the future? However most young people fail to see a future, they only see their today.

Clearly paragraphed throughout. The second paragraph begins by taking up the questions raised at the end of the first paragraph.

Again clear progression in the third paragraph, although it is all rather general.

A competent piece of development, appropriately expressed.

The thread of the argument is maintained. An engaging, alliterative, finishing paragraph.

Attempts a strong conclusion. The penultimate sentence doesn't quite work.

A strong, opening paragraph. Good use of language and questions to engage the reader.

Some effective initial development here, but by the end of the paragraph there is a theoretical quality – 'Some' which is less effective.

A paragraph that begins strongly, but is not quite sustained. Attempts to use a widening vocabulary – 'spiralling'.

This answer demonstrates:
- some development that maintains the reader's attention
- an appropriate sense of audience
- an increasingly fluent style
- a series of sentence structures
- generally accurate use of punctuation.

Functional writing: Key to success

Here are the key pointers in what is normally considered the most demanding written task in these exams. Read these pointers and then complete the exam-style question opposite.

 The best writing results from the following process: **Think, Plan, Write.** Resist the temptation to start immediately; taking the time to think and plan is essential to producing work that has a strong opening, demonstrates a clear train of thought and presents an effective conclusion.

 Begin with the three key questions: **Why, What and Who**? This will set you off on the correct pathway.

 Where appropriate, make your writing lively and engaging. Let your personality come through in the writing – the last thing the examiner wants is to read something dull! Your tone and vocabulary choice needs to match the audience and purpose.

 Remember you have only 45 minutes in which to complete the writing process.

 There are no prizes for finishing first so use all of the time wisely – the only reward for finishing early could be a low grade if you do not make the most of the time available.

 Review your finished work – you *must* review your work to get the most out of your answer because *everyone* makes mistakes when they are working quickly and under pressure. Remember too that there are no marks for extreme neatness – it is much better that your work is accurate even if it contains a few corrections. As you check your work, consider the following questions and correct any mistakes you find:

i) Have you paragraphed your writing?

ii) Did you use a range of sentence lengths?

iii) Did you vary the sentence openings?

iv) Have you used a varied vocabulary?

v) Have you left out any words or are there any sentences where the meaning is less than clear?

vi) Finally, does it all make sense – do any sections require re-organising so that the meaning is clear? Has your word choice been precise enough?

Here is an acrostic to help you remember the key messages:

P planning/purpose

E emotive language

R rhetorical devices

S structure/selecting vocabulary/supporting your points

U using factual information

A audience/anecdotes/arguments

D direct appeal

E empathy/expressing opinions and feelings

Exam-style question

Plan and write an essay in which you discuss your reactions to this opinion:

'Raise the school leaving age to eighteen years – we need all the qualifications we can get if we're ever to get a job!'

Response time: 45 minutes

Re-read your answer and then check it against the checklists for success on the next page.

Take 5 minutes to make amendments in the light of these reminders and then, without writing anything down, decide where you believe your answer sits when viewed against the standard of work described for grades C and A/A★ on page 78.

There is also an opportunity to swap and compare work here with a partner. You need to adopt the role of a 'sensitive friend' for this exercise (the idea is not to savage your partner but to treat him/her in the way you would like to be treated!).

1 Swap essays and carefully read/assess the piece of work you been given.
2 Constructively complete the table below.
3 Return the assessment to your partner.

The strengths of this essay	The areas that need to be improved
1.	1.
2.	2.
3.	3.
4.	4.
5.	5.
6.	6.

Checklist for success: working towards Grade C	✔
Have you **developed** your response in a manner that **will hold the reader's interest?**	
Have you clearly **planned, organised** and **structured** the writing so that you've presented your ideas in a **fluent** manner?	
Have you tried to maintain an appropriate sense of **audience** and kept your focus on the **purpose** (it could be a speech or an article)?	
Is the piece **paragraphed** and does each paragraph have a **topic sentence**?	
Have you used some **stylistic devices** (rhetorical questions, emotive language, etc.) that are in keeping with the purpose and audience and which help to hold your audience's attention?	
Is there a range of appropriate **vocabulary**, some of which is used to create effect?	
Is there **clear punctuation** and does it create variety and clarify meaning?	
Is there appropriate **variety** in the **sentence structuring**?	
Have you checked your **spelling** and tried to use some **ambitious vocabulary**?	

Checklist for success: working towards Grade A/A★	✔
Does your writing develop the topic in a **sophisticated manner**?	
Does your writing **positively engage and confidently hold the reader's attention**?	
Has your writing created a **positive rapport** with your reader?	
Does your writing demonstrate an assured use of **structure** and a **confident style?**	
Have you used a range of **stylistic devices** (rhetorical questions, emotive language, etc.) that are adapted to purpose and audience?	
Is there a wide range of appropriate, **extended vocabulary** and is it used to create an effect or to convey precise meaning?	
Is there confident and effective variation of **sentence structures**, making use of **simple, compound** and **complex sentences** to achieve particular effects?	
Is there **accurate punctuation** used to vary pace, clarify meaning, avoid ambiguity and is it used to create deliberate effects?	
Is virtually all **spelling**, including that of complex irregular words, correct?	

Unit 2
English Language and English

Section B:
Reading Non-Fiction

Introduction to Reading Non-Fiction

Unit 2 is externally examined and is made up of two sections. The second section is Section B and it assesses **Reading Non-Fiction**.

Target outcome: An understanding of how writers have employed the various strategies and skills at their disposal to create effective non-fiction writing.

Target skills

The target skills you will learn about in this Reading Non-Fiction section will enable you to:

 read and understand how meaning is constructed

 recognise the effects of language choices

 develop interpretations of writers' ideas

 draw together material from different sources

 explain how writers use linguistic, grammatical and structural features to influence the reader.

Assessment Objective

Your Assessment Objective in this Reading Non-Fiction section is:

Reading/Studying written language

i) Read with insight and select appropriate material.

ii) Develop an interpretation of a piece of writing.

iii) Understand and assess how writers use language to create their desired effects.

Exam question

You will have 45 minutes to answer one question that will require you to study a previously unseen non-fiction text.

This task will focus on the ways in which the views of the writer have been presented to hold the reader's attention.

You can go to the Exam Practice section at the end of this book (page 96) for more practice.

1   Non-Fiction Texts

Mark Twain

> The difference between fiction and non-fiction is that fiction must be absolutely believable.
>
> Mark Twain, author of *The Adventures of Huckleberry Finn*

Fiction and **non-fiction** are two types of writing that you will be familiar with. This section of Unit 2 is on reading non-fiction but there are overlaps between fiction and non-fiction so we shall look at some aspects of fiction as well as non-fiction. You will have the opportunity to study a fiction text for Controlled Assessment in Unit 4 (page 135).

The key thing to remember about fiction texts is that they are made up. They are imaginary. They are based on an imagined world and contain imaginary characters. What makes fiction successful is that whilst reading, you believe it to be real.

ACTIVITY 1

In pairs or groups:
1 Think about a piece of fictional writing that you have read which was completely believable and realistic to you. (It could be a book that you have studied at school or one that you read in your own time.) What made it so realistic?
2 Think about a piece of fictional writing that you did not find believable or realistic. Try to work out why it was unsuccessful as a work of fiction.

Fiction texts create imaginary worlds, situations and characters. **Non-fiction** texts are about reality and facts; the material can be authenticated. They are based on the real world – on real people, real things and real events. Non-fiction texts are all around us and are an important part of everyone's lives.

It is important to bear in mind that although non-fiction is based on the real world, it is not always factual or true. Non-fiction is an account or representation of a subject which is presented as fact. This presentation may be accurate or it may not be; that is, it can give either a true or a false account. However, it is generally assumed that authors believe their account to be truthful when they write them.

Often non-fiction writers are aiming to engage, entertain and persuade you so they choose language that has the desired impact on you as a reader.

Non-fiction texts include:

- textbooks
- essays
- newspaper articles
- websites
- blogs
- biographical writing
- travel writing
- letters
- diary entries.

ACTIVITY 2

The extracts below are different types of non-fiction texts. Sort them into the categories listed above.

1 In winter Hammerfest is a 34-hour ride by bus from Oslo, though why anyone would want to go there in winter is a question worth considering.

2 Knackered again. This camp has been really tough. It was the first foreign training camp of the Olympic run-up, a chance for the group to blow away the cobwebs that three weeks of holiday had gathered.

3 Cassius Clay entered the ring in Miami Beach wearing a short white robe, 'The Lip' stitched on the back. He was beautiful again. He was fast, sleek and 22. But, for the first and last time in his life, he was afraid.

4 ON LOCATION – VENICE
TV chef Gary Rhodes stops off while filming his new show to share the culinary delights of the famous floating city . . . 'I've had my eyes opened on this trip,' says Gary Rhodes as he enthusiastically pokes around the lively fish market at the world-famous Rialto Bridge in Venice.

5 Dear Mr X,
Thank you for taking the time recently on the phone to hear about our work . . . Not a lot of people realise that Praxis Care is Northern Ireland's largest charity . . .

6 The solid crust of the earth consists of rocks in great variety . . . The study of rocks is primarily the province of the geologist, but the geographer must also be interested . . .

7 Radio 5Live's bi-weekly Moron-a-thon, is a constant source of thought-provoking debate. Many of Britain's great contemporary philosophers are regular contributors to the show, commendably guided to previously unimagined heights of perception by intellectual titans of our era, sophists like Spoony, Tim Lovejoy and Alan Green.

Fiction and non-fiction texts differ but some elements overlap. Fiction texts borrow from non-fiction to help create a sense of reality and credibility. For example, sometimes authors use real place names or settings in their stories, real people may be mentioned or the story may be based on real events.

Strategies used by fiction writers	Examples
Using real place names or settings	He had come to Edinburgh from London at the age of nineteen; an assistant surveyor in Scotland's Board of Works. From *Arthur & George* by Julian Barnes
Making use of real events	We passed big houses with apple trees in the gardens, fountains, passed bungalows knocked together out of tin for victims of the Blitz. From *Number 5* by Glenn Patterson
Referring to real people	Over the next half hour, Langdon showed them slides of artwork by Michelangelo, Da Vinci and many others. From *The Da Vinci Code* by Dan Brown

Non-fiction writers likewise borrow elements from fiction to aid them with their writing. For example, to engage the reader they may present real people as 'fictional' character types, turning them into heroes, villains or victims to make them interesting.

Furthermore, the way in which non-fiction stories are structured can create suspense and tension which makes the reader continue to read. The newspaper extracts on the next two pages demonstrate how non-fiction stories can be given 'a slant'.

KATIE FLOGS PETE'S DOGS!!!

'Dog gone . . .'

Dogs of war . . . Jordan sold Pete's pets after split

PETER Andre was furious last night after he discovered ex Jordan had secretly sold his beloved dogs.

The singer, 36, is livid that he may never see British bulldogs Hugo and Pepsi again. Jordan, 31 – real name Katie Price – found new owners for the pair without letting him know. When they split in May, Peter said all he wanted from the divorce settlement was the dogs and his cars. A source said: 'Pete can't believe she has sold his dogs without telling him. He adored those dogs. He is worried about how the kids are coping because Princess Tiaamii and Junior especially were obsessed with them. Pete would have taken the dogs, but he didn't think it was fair to take them from the kids. Now they have gone for good.' The couple bought male Hugo 2½ years ago – while female Pepsi was Jordan's surprise Christmas present for Pete in 2007. But friends have been concerned that the dogs did not receive enough attention from the model, whose divorce from Peter was confirmed last Thursday.

In this newspaper article Katie Price is presented as the villain because:

- She sold Peter's dogs without discussing it with him.
- She denied Peter one of the two things that he wanted from the divorce, 'the dogs and his cars'.
- She has caused unhappiness for Peter and their children Princess Tiaamii and Junior, who all loved the dogs.
- She was not paying enough attention to the dogs.

In contrast, Peter is presented as the victim because:

- His dogs were disposed of without him knowing about it.
- He is concerned about the emotional wellbeing of his children.
- He has been denied one of his only two divorce demands.

ACTIVITY 3

Take the 'facts' of this story and see if you can spin them so that Katie Price appears to be the victim whilst Peter is presented as the villain. Create a new headline and caption to help you develop a different angle on these events.

Newspaper articles often present facts in an exciting and sensational way. They do this to increase readership and it often makes minor, simple stories fascinating. Look at how the following article creates something out of nothing.

Barack Obama in Hawaii holiday alert after family friend is injured

President Barack Obama was caught up in an emergency drama last night when a family friend was injured.

Obama ended a round of golf abruptly and sped back to his family's holiday home. He described the incident as a 'personal matter' as an ambulance headed to the compound in Kailua, Hawaii. It sparked fears the President had fallen ill. However, The White House quickly announced Obama was safe and the incident was not a matter of national security.

The son of Obama's friend Eric Whitaker suffered minor injuries which needed stitches. It was reported the victim suffered his injuries in an accident with a surfboard.

ACTIVITY 4

The reporter has cleverly based this story around the President of the United States. Phrases have been deliberately used to make it exciting and engaging. For example:

• 'Barack Obama was caught up in an emergency drama last night'.

List three more phrases of this type and then in your own words state what actually did happen.

ACTIVITY 5

Now that you are aware that fiction and non-fiction can overlap, choose **one** of these tasks:

1 Find an extract from a novel that uses one or more of the non-fiction ingredients discussed on page 82: real place names or setting, real people, or real events.
2 Find a newspaper or magazine article that either uses non-fiction ingredients spiced up with 'fictional' aspects such as heroes, villains and victims or presents a story structured to create excitement, suspense and tension.

In the exam you will be given an unseen piece of non-fiction writing. Because this piece of writing will be new to you, it is important to read the extract carefully and answer the **What? Who? Why?** and **How?** questions:

- **What** is the subject of the writing? What is it about?
- **Who** is the audience? Who has the text been written for?
- **Why** was the text written? What is the purpose of the writing?
- **How** has the text been constructed so that it works for its particular audience and purpose?

Answering these questions will help you plan your written response so let's explore each of them in more detail.

What?

Following your first reading of a non-fiction text you should have a good idea of its subject. For example, you can see at once that the subject of this extract from a letter is unsatisfactory service in a restaurant:

> Dear Sir/Madam,
>
> Following my recent visit to your restaurant, I am writing to express my anger in relation to the service that I received. . . .

ACTIVITY 6

Identify the subject of this extract from a diary entry:

> I can't tell you how oppressive it is never to be able to go outdoors, also I'm scared to death that we shall be discovered and shot. That is not exactly a pleasant prospect. We have to whisper and tread lightly during the day; otherwise the people in the warehouse might hear us.
>
> From *The Diary of Anne Frank* (entry for 11 July 1942)

ACTIVITY 7

Identify the subject of this extract from a piece of travel writing:

> It was a hot morning, and I had been at the temples since 5.30am to capture the magical moment when the sun rose over one of the ancient world's most amazing complexes – Angkor Wat.

Who?

It is vital that you identify who the text has been written for – its **audience**. Writers adapt their style of writing depending on their audience. For example, the intended audience for this website extract is adults who are interested in booking a family holiday:

Thompson Family Club

Your perfect family holiday
We've used our years of experience creating fantastic family-focussed holidays to bring you this, The Family Collection - so now it's even easier to find your perfect family holiday with Thomson. <u>Download a brochure here</u>.

ACTIVITY 8

Identify the intended audience for this extract from a recipe:

You will need

- 500g chocolate loaf cake, approximately 5cm thick and 20cm long
- 8 tablespoons double cream
- 8 tablespoons strawberry conserve
- 100g fresh strawberries
- 30g piece plain chocolate

Method

Cut the cake in half through the middle, and using a heart-shaped cutter, stamp out an even number of hearts . . .

ACTIVITY 9

Identify the intended audience for this magazine extract about smoking:

It's a common problem: You are trying your best to quit smoking but everyone around you still smokes. If you have a spouse or other family member who smokes, you are exposed to smoking every day. If your co-workers smoke, you probably have smokers around you at least five days per week. If your friends smoke, you'll be exposed to smoking whenever you get together to have some fun.

So how do you maintain your resolve to quit when everywhere you look you see someone lighting up? How do you deal with the personal conflicts that can develop when you quit but your family, friends and co-workers don't? Read on to find out how to beat the smoking battle for a healthier lifestyle.

Why?

Everything is written for a reason. It is important that you can recognise why the text has been written.

Non-fiction texts have various purposes, including:

- to entertain
- to explain
- to advise
- to persuade
- to inform
- to instruct.

Different types of non-fiction writing have different purposes. For example, instructions and procedures are written to describe or instruct how something is done through a sequence of steps, while biography allows someone other than the subject to tell a life story.

ACTIVITY 10

Match each of these non-fiction types with one of the purposes below:

1 autobiography
2 recount
3 explanation
4 discussion and argument
5 journalistic writing
6 diaries
7 interviews
8 public information leaflets.

a to present arguments and information from differing viewpoints
b to educate or inform
c to retell events
d to tell the writer's life story
e to reveal a person's thoughts and experiences
f to provide a personal account of an event or incident
g to retell events of public interest
h to explain processes involved in nature or how something works.

How?

In the exam, you will be expected to demonstrate that you understand:

- how meaning is created in non-fiction texts
- the effects of language choices
- how writers use linguistic, grammatical and structural features to influence the reader.

In order to do this, it is vital that you know the methods that non-fiction writers use to help them achieve their purpose. Non-fiction writers consciously adapt their style, language and structure to impact on the reader. The next section looks at each of these areas in turn.

Style

In any text the writer's aim is to create a style that will suit a particular kind of reader or audience to achieve a specific purpose.

Style describes how the writer uses **words**, **sentence structure** and **sentence arrangement** to establish **mood**, **images** and **meaning** in the text. Style also describes how the writer describes **events**, **objects** and **ideas**.

One easy way to understand literary style is to think about fashion styles. Literary style is like the clothes that a text puts on. The information underneath is like the wearer's body, while the specific words, structures and arrangements that the writer uses are like the clothes. Clothes can be formal and dressy, informal and casual, athletic, and so forth. Just as one person can be dressed in several different fashions, writers can dress a single message in several different literary styles. For example:

- **Informal:** 'Nothing like that ever happened,' Tony replied.
- **Formal:** 'That happenstance did not become a reality,' Tony stated.
- **Journalistic:** 'It did not happen,' Tony said.
- **Archaic:** 'Verily, it was a circumstance, to be noted, that appeared not so much to have been a reality as to have evolved as a thing that had not yet come to be,' Tony impelled.

The style that a writer uses influences how we interpret the facts that are presented. The version of a sentence that a writer chooses tells us a lot about the situation, the speaker and the person being spoken to (the audience).

ACTIVITY 11

Compare these sentences. What does each sentence tell you about the situation, the speaker and the person being spoken to?

1 He's passed away.
2 He's sleeping with the fishes.
3 He died.
4 He's gone to meet his Maker.
5 He kicked the bucket.
6 He's pushing up daisies.

Language

A writer who has information to present to an audience must choose very carefully how to present this information in order to achieve the intended effect. As with style, it's like choosing which clothes to wear. Different choices will create different effects. The same applies to language, so a writer needs to select words and phrases carefully.

These are of some of the techniques or features that a writer might choose to include in a piece of non-fiction:

- **Personal pronoun:** 'You' is called the direct-address pronoun: it can be used to add a personal touch and engage the reader, as the writer seems to be talking directly to you. It brings a friendly and inviting tone to the writing, e.g. 'Have faith in us; you just know it makes sense.'

- **Inclusive pronoun:** 'We' can make the reader feel part of a special group, which can be very persuasive, e.g. 'We're all in this together, aren't we?'

- **Personal viewpoint:** The use of 'I' can create a friendly tone and involve the reader, e.g. 'I couldn't believe it!'

- **Emotive language:** Language can be chosen to affect the reader's emotions. For example, to make you feel sympathy for someone or something, an author might write: 'Today, our fellow citizens, our way of life, our very freedom came under attack in a series of deliberate and deadly terrorist acts.'

- **Anecdotes:** Short anecdotes add interest and engage the reader's attention, e.g. 'One day as I was walking along the main street in my town I noticed . . .'.

- **Hyperbole** is when the writer uses words and phrases to exaggerate. Hyperbole can be persuasive and make normal events extraordinary, e.g. 'This earth-shattering event will blow your mind away!'

- **Description** creates imagery that can be very engaging and involving, even persuasive. Look out for similes and metaphors as these can be very vivid and effectively create mood and emotion, e.g. 'The boy was a cheeky monkey with a grin as wide as a Cheshire cat.'

- **Facts** and **opinions** can support a writer's point of view or argument but you must be able to recognise bias and opinions stated as fact when assessing how reasonable and effective the evidence really is.

- **Rhetorical questions** imply their own answer and certainly engage the reader. They help make a point in a more powerful and emotional way, e.g. 'Should this be allowed to continue?'

- **Repetition** and **lists of three** can emphasise the writer's purpose and often prove memorable as well as persuasive.

- **Different tones:** A **formal** tone can add authority and sound authentic or sincere; an **informal** or even **conversational** tone can add warmth and fun – it can be very persuasive, too.

- **Humour:** A writer may use humour (including jokes and puns) to engage the reader as it evokes a response and makes the writing enjoyable to read.

- **Quotations** and **evidence from expert sources** provide support and create added authority, e.g. 'Every three minutes a child in Africa will die because they do not have access to clean water.'

This is not an exhaustive list so don't be afraid to comment on other non-fiction writing techniques you have learnt about.

ACTIVITY 12

The letter below to the editor of the local newspaper uses a range of non-fiction writing techniques. Some have been identified for you. Identify as many more as you can.

Dear Editor,

Belfast City is facing a sticky problem – chewing gum. I hate the stuff, never more than on a bus when somebody sits behind you chewing noisily all through your journey. The sound of someone chewing gum incessantly, like some mindless cow chewing the cud, is enough to drive anyone insane!

> **Personal pronoun and personal viewpoint**

> **Personal anecdote and simile**

> **Emotive language**

This chewing of gum is one thing, but not disposing of it properly is another. It costs 3p a stick to buy, but 10p to prise it off the pavement. Dropping used gum irresponsibly is an unpleasant nuisance, an eyesore for the public and a major headache for those who have to clean it up. It's about time we tackled the blight of gum on our streets.

> **Statistics**

> **List of three**

> **Inclusive pronoun**

Chewing gum is a growing menace in the UK that is costing taxpayers millions each year to clean up. We need to think before we spit! Currently, the clean-up bill for local authorities across the UK is as high as £150m a year. Belfast Council spends £60,000 a year on gum removal, but could spend ten times that and not crack the problem. At any given time, on Belfast's main shopping street, Royal Avenue, there are more than 300,000 pieces of discarded chewing gum. It's a disgrace!

> **Facts**

Yours faithfully
A. Wrigley

> **Conversational tone**

Whilst it is essential that you can identify these techniques it is equally, if not more, important to explain the impact that these choices have on the reader. You must do this to demonstrate to the examiner that you understand why the writer has made these choices.

ACTIVITY 13

Re-read the letter above and think about why the writer has used each of the techniques identified and the others you have found. What impact does each of these have on you as a reader?

Structure

You also need to analyse the structure of non-fiction writing because this is another important feature used by writers. In other words, you should analyse how the writing has been put together. Think about:

- how the piece is introduced
- how the ideas are developed – study the piece paragraph by paragraph and look at how this is done, e.g. using examples, statistics, advice, expert opinion, details, anecdotes, interview, questions
- how the piece concludes.

Summarising style, language and structure

The style, language and structure adopted by a writer are intentional therefore it is vital to ask yourself:

- **What** is the writer trying to do? They could be trying to entertain, amuse, alarm, persuade, argue, inform, challenge, and so on.

- **How** does the writer achieve their goals? The answer to this question lies in the use of style, language and structure:

Techniques of style, language or structure	Examples
Choice of vocabulary	rich description used to engage reader, complex words used to seem more serious
Formal or informal style	dialect, colloquialisms, slang used to create familiarity with reader
Imagery	creates an image, picture in reader's mind – use of language, e.g. metaphors and similes
Technical devices	repetition, alliteration, onomatopoeia used to engage/entice reader
Sentence variety	length, simple, compound, complex, exclamations, questions
Variety in paragraph construction	short sentences for dramatic effect, longer sentences to provide detail

Remember: non-fiction texts are all around you, so look out for them and get into the habit of reading them to practise your close-reading skills.

Reading Non-Fiction: Exam Success

4

Matching grades to reading non-fiction texts

In Section B the essential qualities the examiners will be looking for are highlighted at the important grade boundaries. Read these descriptions *carefully*; they tell you what your answer should be like.

Grade C work displays:

 a straightforward consideration/some analysis of the features bullet-pointed in the question

 some examination of these bullet-pointed features that is supported by appropriate explanations

 a valid interpretation of the stimulus material that is supported by appropriate evidence.

Grade A/A* work displays:

 an assured evaluation of the linguistic and structural features as indicated by the bullet points. These are likely to include: style/use made of fact and opinion/the selection of words and phrases/the use made of sentence structuring and paragraphing

 a perceptive explanation/discussion of these features

 an insightful and focused interpretation that is supported by a range of precisely selected, appropriate evidence.

Sample reading task

Read the piece of travel writing on page 94 and consider this question:
The writer has created an entertaining and informative piece about the visit. How has this been achieved?
Comment on:

- the personal nature of the writing
- the lively nature of the descriptions
- the variety in sentence structure and the use of paragraphing.

This piece is describing the writer's visit to Our Dynamic Earth, a centre that 'combines the latest interpretative technology and special effects with cutting edge scientific thinking'.

ACTIVITY 15

Below is a sample reading task. There is an answer to this task on page 95 which was written under exam conditions by a student of your age. The examiner's comments have been added to help you recognise the key strengths of the work. Take 10 minutes to read it and look closely at the examiner's comments.

- Do the examiner's comments fairly represent the quality of the work?
- Do any of the remarks surprise/puzzle you?

Number One on my MUST visit list: the 'Our Dynamic Earth' centre, opposite the new Scottish Parliament building in Edinburgh. I liked the white tent roof effect − it looked very striking against the hills behind it. You need at least 90 minutes to do this one justice! It is an 'interactive' exhibition with sound effects, temperature changes and surround sound to go along with the video/film.

Our first stop was one of the eleven scenes they call 'earthscapes'. It was supposed to be an environmental monitoring station. Anyway, this is where you get into the Time Machine. It's a sort of souped-up lift that takes you back 15,000 million years. They had rigged it so it seemed like you were moving through starfields. The lift doors opened and we staggered out into the darkness; well, there was a neon light in the far corner but it was very dark and there was a lot of bumping and 'Sorry, was that your toe?' This was the deck of a spaceship. Through viewing windows we witnessed the awesome Big Bang, which started it all off − the birth of the Solar System. Did I mention the whole thing moved? We 'flew' forward in time, which was fine until we came to an earthquake. Rather good but I nearly lost my balance and the man beside me lost his wife who kind of slid gently away to bounce off the far wall.

Of course this earthquake threw up mountains and lava − spewing volcanoes, complete with blasts of air hotter than a furnace, to be dodged by our spaceship. They did it really well because when we came to the glaciers you got another blast, this time freezing cold.

Some people in my group looked quite queasy as we left the spaceship and walked across a nasty-looking mixture with the first life forms crawling out of it . . . they were almost the same shade as the heaving sludge! I'd hate to have fallen into those gooey, greenish bubbles! From here we followed a timeline through the age of dinosaurs to the appearance of Early Man before climbing into a yellow submarine and exploring the ocean.

There were loads of other areas, in fact it was a lot to take in. But we all loved the tropical rain forest, which was full of animated animals and snakes. One big snake appeared suddenly and threateningly from

the undergrowth. They even laid on a thunderstorm and real rain! No, you don't get wet but it's very convincing.

It's all terribly exciting but noisy from start to finish so you might end up with a headache. At least you get a sit down for the final bit, a film about how we are destroying the Earth, of course. Having watched this film about logging and pollution you leave, by way of a gift shop so, as you plan how to save the planet, you can buy a pencil or a mug at the same time!

Student response

Refers to personal style and its impact.

The writer uses their own personal style to engage the reader and to make the piece more 'user friendly' ensuring the language is everyday and easy to understand. The reader is addressed as, 'You need at least. . .' and this contributes towards the personal feel of the writing. We are introduced to the writer through personal feelings and through thoughts we can all sympathise with, 'I nearly lost my balance, I'd hate to have fallen. Did I mention.' This prevents the piece from becoming a lecture on 'Dynamic Earth' and serves to put the reader directly in the writer's shoes, giving a real sense of the experience and making it personal for the reader. The laid back style of writing engages, 'gooey, greenish' and the reader can read and enjoy this extract without having to try too hard to grasp the writer's meaning or visualize events.

Quote to support point.

Style referred to and quotes support.

Descriptions discussed.

The most entertaining parts of the piece are most definitely the descriptions. They are honest, reassuring and taken directly from real life events, 'Sorry was that your toe?' 'Kind of slid gently away', 'the whole thing moved', 'noisy from start to finish' and thus very funny as the reader can visualise the scene clearly as a result of the writer's distinctive use of informal language. The writer also makes witty observations, 'as you plan how to save the planet, you can buy a pencil or a mug'. The reader sees clearly the irony of this as, previously the group had watched 'this film about pollution'. All in all, these descriptions and observations serve to entertain the reader.

Irony picked up by reader.

Evidence to support throughout.

Impact of style explored.

The descriptions are not only entertaining but informative. They give a realistic view of what the 'Dynamic Earth' experience is really like. The writer describes all of these wonderful gadgets portrayed in the leaflet with a dry sarcasm and clarity, 'souped-up lift', 'staggered out into the darkness', 'we 'flew' forward in time.' These descriptions are very informative, giving actual impressions and experience which is useful to the reader as a gauge of the real value of Dynamic Earth.

Further points made and supported with quotes.

Focus on sentence structure and impact explored.

The writer varies sentence structure, making some short, to create more impact on the reader, 'This is where you get into the time machine' and others are longer, containing descriptions or lists, so as to provide a contrast and variety in style, preventing the piece from becoming monotone or too staccato, 'spewing volcanoes . . . . complete with. . .hotter than a furnace . . . .dodged by our spaceship.' Each paragraph has a self contained message and each takes us on a stage further in the journey, giving us the same feeling as the writer – being taken along history in steps. The writer adds all these devices to keep the writing entertaining and engage the reader. Overall the piece contains humour, wit and is useful as an informative piece of personal insight.

Quotes support points.

Overall impact of the piece summed up.

Non-fiction reading: Key to success

Read these key pointers and then complete the exam-style question below:

 Use the following **W, W, W, H** questions to help you with your analysis:

1 **What?** Subject matter – what is the piece all about?
2 **Who?** Audience – exactly who is being targeted?
3 **Why?** Purpose – what is the ultimate aim? To sell something/persuade/amuse/be provocative?
4 **How?** Style, structure and language – the 'nuts and bolts' that are employed to successfully achieve the desired outcome.

 Don't fall into the trap of judging a piece of writing aimed at a different kind of reader from yourself by seeing it only through teenage eyes; instead, try to 'become the text's reader' when you judge its style and appropriateness.

Now use all the strategies you have learnt in this section to respond to this question on non-fiction writing. Afterwards use the checklists for success on page 98 to assess your answer and/or the answer of a classmate.

Exam-style question

Read the piece of travel writing opposite and answer this question:

Analyse how the writer holds the reader's attention.

In your answer discuss how the writer has:

- used a style and tone that is personal and lively
- made use of humour
- selected words and phrases for effect
- used sentence structuring and paragraphing to sustain the reader's interest.

Response time: 45 minutes

It's almost four o'clock, the deadline for admission. I have an irrational hatred of guided tours, historical re-enactments and anything themed. Still, I have time to kill till around five o'clock so I park among the coaches and family cars and join the nearest queue.

I push my way through a coach load of amorous teenagers from France and make my way into an impressive hall. A guided tour is just beginning. The guide, a flame-haired young Irish woman, is extremely lively but it's hard to make out what she is saying. She's been talking for the best part of two minutes before it dawns on me that she is speaking French.

Outside the Folk Park there's a collection of traditional thatched cottages, showing the way of life of the small farmer, the blacksmith and so on. They're kitted out with old beds and cupboards, and a collection of holy pictures that range in tone from fairly gloomy to the deeply scary. In spite of myself, I find these cottages quite atmospheric; they're supposed to be nineteenth century but they're not far removed from my memories of my Auntie Annie's house. The smell of the turf adds to the effect – at any moment a wizened little lady dressed in black could leap out and start force-feeding me ham and potatoes.

Beyond the cottages sits a reconstruction of an Irish main street, which seems a bit pointless seeing the country's stuffed with the real thing. There are a few shops, a schoolroom and just one pub. All around me people are taking photos of each other outside the kind of shop fronts you'll find in any small town in Ireland. I stroll up the street and head for the school.

There are separate entrances for boys and girls. Inside the classroom, rows of traditional desks are packed with tourists pretending to be school kids. In front of them, a severe-looking sixty-year-old teacher is pointing at Irish words, chalked on a board. As I walk in I realise too late that there's nowhere for me to sit. He spots me and is on me.

'You boy. Where have you been?'

There's a ripple of laughter, then all eyes are on me, glad it's not them! I know it's silly, but I'm embarrassed. This is exactly how teachers made me feel on more occasions than I care to remember.

'Er. . . nowhere, sir.'

'Take your hands out of your pockets in class.'

The rest of the class is cracking up now.

'What's your name, boy?'

'McCarthy, sir.'

'McCarthy? A Cork man, is it? Well, stand up straight. That's better. Now, look at the board if you please.'

He reads out some Irish words and I do my best to copy him.

'Not bad. Now, the whole class.'

Sixty voices join in.

'Well done. Now, McCarthy, do you know what that means?'

All eyes are on me. Should I say something funny? Perhaps not. Too risky.

'No, sir.'

'It means "Where is the pub?" Well, it's just up there at the top of the street. You've been an excellent class. Good afternoon to you now and God bless.'

I head for the door as quick as I can, keen to avoid eye contract with smirking classmates – just like I used to at fourteen. As I head for the car, the schoolmaster is in the street heckling passers-by.

'You there, wake up! No holding hands! No eating sweets! Stop that smiling. . .'

Checklist for success: working towards Grade C	✔
Have you kept the **over-arching statement** in mind?	
Have you kept the focus on **how** the writer has achieved their **effects**?	
Have you developed an answer that considers all the **bulleted features** mentioned in the question?	
Have you clearly constructed your answer so that points are **supported by evidence** from the text?	
Have you tried to keep your focus on the writer's **purpose** and the **techniques** which they have used to accomplish their goals?	

Checklist for success: working towards grade A/A★	✔
Does your analysis sustain its focus on the writer's **purpose** – the main statement in the question?	
Have you presented a range of relevant evidence that supports perceptive conclusions on **how** the writer has achieved their **effects**?	
Does your answer present a **perceptive analysis of all the bulleted features** mentioned in the question?	
Have you focused your analysis throughout on the writer's **purpose** and the **techniques** which they have deployed to accomplish their goals?	

Unit 3
English Language and English

Speaking and Listening

Introduction to Speaking and Listening

Unit 3 is tested under Controlled Assessment conditions and is built around three different **Speaking and Listening** contexts.

Target outcome: Conscious use of the various skills of oral communication in order to deal effectively with individual scenarios as well as engaging appropriately in a range of group interactions.

Target skills

The target skills you will learn about in this Speaking and Listening unit are divided into three contexts:

- Individual Contribution
- Group Discussion
- Role Play.

In the **Individual Contribution** context, the target skills you will learn about will enable you to:

 communicate clearly and effectively

 present information and ideas

 use Standard English as appropriate

 structure and sustain talk

 choose and adapt language appropriate to audience

 respond appropriately to questions and the views of others.

In **Group Discussion**, the target skills you will learn about will enable you to:

 interact with others

 make a range of effective contributions

 express ideas clearly, accurately and appropriately

 listen and respond to others' ideas and perspectives

 challenge what is heard where appropriate

 shape meaning through asking questions and making comments and suggestions

 use a variety of techniques as appropriate.

In **Role Play**, the target skills you will learn about will enable you to:

 create and sustain different roles

 participate in a range of real-life contexts

 experiment with language to engage the audience.

Assessment Objective

Your Assessment Objective in this Speaking and Listening unit is:

Speaking and Listening

i) Speak to communicate clearly and purposefully; structure and sustain talk, adapting it to different situations and audiences; use standard English and a variety of techniques as appropriate.

ii) Listen and respond to speakers' ideas and perspectives, and how they construct and express meanings.

iii) Interact with others, shaping meanings through suggestions, comments and questions and drawing.

Controlled Assessment Tasks

You will be assessed under Controlled Assessment conditions in the context of an Individual Contribution, a Group Discussion and a Role-Play activity.

The range of Speaking and Listening tasks you undertake will give you the opportunity to respond in a variety of formal and informal situations. Your final mark will be based on your three best assessments.

The types of activity you might be expected to undertake:

- **Individual Contribution** – Deliver a presentation on a topic that interests you, followed by a question-and-answer session.

- **Group Discussion** – In a group of two or more, discuss the difficulties facing homeless people.
- **Individual Role Play** – You are a youth worker. At the monthly local council meeting, present your case for funding for your youth club.
- **Group Role Play** – You are members of the local council. Taking individual roles as Councillors, discuss whether you should provide funding for a local youth club.

'I can speak and I can listen: this will be easy, right?'

Wrong! This is what most people think, but a quick read through the target skills on page 99 should have started to ring a few alarm bells. We all secretly believe we have mastered speaking and listening but these are subtle and sophisticated skills.

Two-thirds of all communication is non-verbal. So words can have different meanings when non-verbal cues are added.

ACTIVITY 1

In pairs, see how many different meanings you can create by saying each of these seemingly simple words and phrases using different facial expressions, tone, use of eyes, posture, volume and pace:

- Yes
- I do
- Are you serious?
- No
- Never
- I know

Here's a scenario you have probably witnessed at your school. The teacher is moving around a Year 11 classroom, occasionally stopping to see how individual students are getting on:

STUDENT:	*(to teacher)* Excuse me, you are in my way. I can't see the Smart board.
TEACHER:	Don't you be cheeky with me. I'll report you to your Year Tutor.
STUDENT:	What do you mean? I only asked you to move so that I could get on with my work. I assume you do want me to get on with my work?
TEACHER:	Right that's enough lip from you – off you go to your Tutor; get out of my room!

In Speaking it is important that you:

- choose language that the audience will understand
- choose words and phrases that suit the situation
- use an appropriate tone
- control the speed and volume at which you talk
- are aware of the degree of formality you need to adopt
- control your body language
- make effective use of eye contact.

Like many students, you may find the Individual Contribution the most daunting of the three Speaking and Listening contexts. Take comfort from the fact that people often feel uncomfortable, even terrified, if they have to stand up and speak to an audience. How then do some speakers look as if they are naturals and make it seem easy to address and entertain a roomful of people?

ACTIVITY 2

The student may or may not have been trying to 'wind up' the teacher. It depends entirely on how they delivered the words they used.

In pairs, create two different versions of this dialogue where:

1 The student is an innocent victim of a tetchy teacher.
2 The teacher is justifiably angry at an ill-mannered student.

Mark Twain, the famous American writer of *The Adventures of Huckleberry Finn*, once said:

'It takes more than three weeks to prepare a good impromptu speech.'

'Impromptu' means not prepared – made up on the spur of the moment. Twain was saying clearly that the only way to give a good speech is to prepare thoroughly – good speeches do not happen spontaneously, they are the product of careful groundwork.

Always plan what you are going to say. Thorough preparation is the key to success not only in your Individual Contribution but in Group Discussion and Role Play as well. (For more on planning your work, look back at pages 8–12.)

These contexts are all interactive so listening to what others say is also very important. For example, have you ever been introduced to someone only to realise, moments later, that you have forgotten their name? If a stranger who has been introduced to you addresses you using your name, do you feel pleased that they have taken note of who you are? Listening skills are at the core of this – just simple, effective listening!

You can use rhetorical devices in order to sway, persuade, manipulate, entertain or engage your audience. How you do this will depend on the purpose and intention of your speaking and listening. (For more about rhetorical devices, see Units 2 and 4, pages 35 and 117.)

The next three sections suggest a range of practical tasks you can use to help you learn and practise skills you will need for your Speaking and Listening Controlled Assessment.

Here are some tips for how to prepare for making a presentation.

✔ Do	✘ Don't
Prepare thoroughly, bearing in mind **purpose** and **audience** – these will dictate the type of language you choose.	Don't write down all the words then read them out – your presentation must sound like talk being delivered to an audience.
Familiarise yourself with what you are actually going to say – where you intend to pause, where your tone and pace will alter.	Don't think that because you've read your speech twice you're ready; you won't be! Do at least six to ten slow readings or you will stumble.
Write your speech using fluent spoken English that takes account of your audience.	Don't write anything that is complex and hard to say aloud – change it.
Practise aloud in front of your bedroom mirror – you may feel uncomfortable to begin with but that's better than being a quivering jelly of awkwardness in front of the class!	Don't rush through your speech tripping over words. The larger the audience, the slower and louder your delivery needs to be.
Analyse your body language – plan your stance and remember that you can move your hands to help you present your speech in a measured way.	Don't fidget from foot to foot like someone who desperately needs the loo! Don't wave your arms around like a windmill – and don't scratch!
Keep your head up – pick a point or two at the back of the room and address them – your audience will think that you are maintaining eye contact with them when you're not.	Don't mumble. Most people feel shy and embarrassed so pretend that you feel comfortable making your presentation – that's what everyone else is doing!
If you are making a PowerPoint presentation, ensure that you are familiar with the technology and remember that you are addressing your audience *not* the screen.	Don't read out what is on PowerPoint slides! The audience will focus on the on-screen content, so your talk should enlarge upon these points.

ACTIVITY 3

Here are some possible topics for a presentation that you could use to practise your skills:

- An individual interest or achievement or sporting occasion or special occasion
- A current issue about which you feel strongly or could focus on to raise the audience's consciousness, e.g. global warming or cancer awareness

- The history of . . . (much more interesting if something personal or somewhere local)
- My local youth organisation or sports team or specialist-interest club and its impact on me
- The greatest day of my life
- My hero
- Five things I would change if I ruled the world!
- My family
- Five things I would like to do before I'm 30 (and past it!)
- The craziest thing that ever happened to me.

Choose one of these topics and prepare a presentation to give to your class.

ACTIVITY 4

While each member of the class delivers their presentation in turn, the audience should take notes under the following headings:

- What were the strengths of the presentations – which were the most enjoyable and why?
- What were the flaws that tended to spoil or detract from the presentations and how could these be overcome?

Feed back your constructive criticism in a whole-class discussion on making an effective presentation. On pages 112–113, you will find a chart and pointers that will help you assess your classmates' speeches.

Here are some tips for how to get the best out of group discussions.

✔ Do	✘ Don't
Prepare a range of points on the topic under discussion.	Don't think you just have to turn up and your natural brilliance will carry you through.
Present and respond to points in a measured way, e.g. 'That's interesting, Francis, but how would you see . . .?'	Don't be abusive or dismiss points put forward by others, e.g. don't say: 'Don't talk rubbish!' or 'What would you know about it?'
Listen to what others are saying and be prepared to give your opinion.	Don't monopolise the discussion even if it is on a topic about which you feel strongly.
Make sure you get involved – try to make meaningful contributions.	Don't leave the discussion to others – make sure you take an active role.
Move the discussion on to another issue within the topic if it seems to be flagging.	Don't talk over other group members.
Try to draw others who haven't made much of a contribution into the discussion, e.g. 'Another very real concern must be for the feelings of young people caught in this situation. What do you think, Peter?'	Don't get involved in one-to-one conversations at the expense of the group discussion.

ACTIVITY 5

Have a 2-minute debate on each of these points:

1 It is better to be a teacher than a student.
2 A bike is better than a car.
3 It is better to be a boy than a girl.
4 It is better to watch a soap opera than watch the news.

ACTIVITY 6

Student-based approach to bullying in school

Discuss how students can best tackle bullying in school. Consider:

- how bullying can be recognised
- what steps can be taken to stop or prevent it
- what help should be given to 're-educate' bullies and to support those being bullied.

ACTIVITY 7

Analysing performance in a discussion

A group of students is observed by the remainder of the class as they take part in a discussion.

Discussion group

Select some typical objects of our time to bury in a time capsule. Bring your own ideas to the discussion and, as a group, decide on the six most suitable objects that would best represent today's society.

Observers

Adopt the role of 'critical friend' and make notes about how each member of the group performs in the discussion. Summarise:

- what each member did well
- what each member could do to improve their effectiveness in group discussions.

Feed back your comments in a whole-class discussion. On pages 112–113 you will find a chart and pointers to help you assess your classmates' performance.

ACTIVITY 8

Here are some more discussions you could use to practise your skills:

1 The Board of Governors has asked your year group to put forward four to six potential changes that would improve the whole school experience from a student's viewpoint. Discuss a range of these possibilities and agree the proposals you would make.

2 'Educating boys and girls together is logical; it mirrors the world we live in!' Discuss the strengths and weaknesses of a co-educational approach to the education of young people.

3 Discuss which three ideas, methods or strategies you find least effective as a means of learning and agree three ideas, methods or strategies that make your learning more interesting. Remember, not everyone learns in the same way!

4 Does anyone have the right to tell you what to wear? Discuss the benefits and drawbacks of uniforms in school and the workplace.

5 Discuss whether or not 'rich countries' have a responsibility to assist 'poor countries'.

6 'Equality of the sexes – there's no such thing!' Discuss how far you agree or disagree with this statement.

7 'We still live in a class-based society where the rich get richer and the poor pay their bills!' Discuss how far you agree or disagree with this statement.

8 You are a steering group set up to plan a five-day Summer Scheme for children aged between six and ten in your area. Decide on a programme for these young people. Consider issues such as:

- the programme of events
- how each event will be organised
- staffing issues
- safety issues
- publicity.

ACTIVITY 9

The internet wrongly attributes the following rules on page 108 to Bill Gates. They actually come from Charles J Sykes' book *Dumbing Down Our Kids: Why America's Children Feel Good About Themselves But Can't Read, Write, Or Add.*

Read over the 'rules' and think about your own reactions to them.

In groups, discuss your reactions and decide:

- Which of the rules are fair and which are unfair?
- Is the author being harsh in his outlook?
- What does he think of young people? How far do you agree with these views?

11 maxims (truths) not taught in school

Rule 1: Life is not fair – get used to it!

Rule 2: The world won't care about your self-esteem. The world will expect you to accomplish something BEFORE you feel good about yourself.

Rule 3: You will NOT make $40,000 a year right out of high school (or college).

Rule 4: If you think your teacher is tough, wait till you get a boss.

Rule 5: Flipping burgers is not beneath your dignity. Your Grandparents had a different word for burger flipping: they called it opportunity.

Rule 6: If you mess up, it's not your parents' fault, so don't whine about your mistakes, learn from them.

Rule 7: Before you were born, your parents weren't as boring as they are now. They got that way from paying your bills, cleaning your clothes and listening to you talk about how cool you thought you were. So before you save the rainforest from the parasites of your parents' generation, try delousing the closet in your own room.

Rule 8: Your school may have done away with winners and losers, but life HAS NOT. In some schools, they have abolished failing grades and they'll give you as many times as you want to get the right answer. This doesn't bear the slightest resemblance to ANYTHING in real life.

Rule 9: Life is not divided into semesters [terms]. You don't get summers off and very few employers are interested in helping you find yourself. Do that on your own time.

Rule 10: Television is NOT real life. In real life people actually have to leave the coffee shop and go to jobs.

Rule 11: Be nice to nerds. Chances are you'll end up working for one.

Here are some tips for how to get the best out of role play.

✔ Do	✘ Don't
Prepare a range of points on the topic from the point of view of your character. Think about how would they respond: **get in role**.	Don't think getting in role will be easy – sustaining a character is difficult to carry off convincingly.
Be prepared to move the scenario forward if it is becoming bogged down.	Don't keep repeating the same point.
Use the language patterns that you would expect from your character.	Don't 'entertain' the audience with colourful words and phrases.
In your preparation, it is sometimes useful to have a broadly agreed course for your role play to follow.	Don't allow the scenario to descend into an abusive slanging match – none of you will have the opportunity to show your full potential.

ACTIVITY 10

Here are some role plays you could use to practise your skills:

1 Work in pairs. One of you is Worker A. It is 5 p.m. on Friday, but the boss has just asked you to work overtime to finish a project. That's terrible, because you have a date tonight! Beg Worker B to do the project instead of you. Start: 'Have you got any plans for tonight?'

2 Work in pairs. One of you is an experienced worker. You see a new worker. Ask them what their job is, and what they think of this company. Invite them to go to lunch with you. Start: 'Are you new here?'

3 Work in groups. You live in a small community and your local hospital is to be closed down and all its services moved to a town 25 miles away. Role play a public meeting called to discuss the issue. Each member of the group should adopt one of the following roles:

- the health-board official proposing the change
- a local councillor
- a patient needing regular hospital treatment
- a representative of the hospital workers who oppose the closure
- a local pensioner.

4 Work in groups. A large supermarket chain wants to open a new retail outlet, complete with car parking and a petrol station, on the outskirts of your town. Adopt one of the following roles and discuss whether or not this will benefit your town:

- the owner of a shop in the town centre
- a local shopper
- a local pensioner
- a local councillor
- the owner of the local petrol station
- a young unemployed person.

Choose one of these role plays and prepare a presentation to your class.

ACTIVITY 11

While each pair or group performs their role play, the audience should take notes under the following headings:

- What were the strengths of the role plays – which were the most enjoyable and why?
- What were the flaws that tended to spoil or detract from the role plays and how could these be overcome?

Feed back your constructive criticism in a whole-class discussion on making an effective role play. On pages 112–113, you will find a chart and pointers that will help you assess your classmates' performances.

ACTIVITY 12

Rent my house

This is a simple interview-style activity. Work in pairs, with one of you asking questions about a house for rent and the other answering as if they were renting out their family's home. Note details of the house and lease in a table like the one below to help give some structure to the interview.

Location – distance to city, school, shops, buses, type of neighbourhood	
Description – size, rooms, carpet, etc.	
Facilities – central heating, air conditioning, hot water	
Special features	
Lease – rent, deposit, time	

Speaking and Listening: Controlled Assessment Success

Matching grades to speaking and listening performances

In this unit the essential qualities the examiners will be looking for are highlighted at the important grade boundaries. Read these descriptions *carefully*; they tell you what your performances should be like.

Grade C speaking and listening displays the ability to:

- ✓ adapt talk to the demands of different situations and contexts

- ✓ recognise when Standard English is required and use it confidently

- ✓ use different sentence structures and select vocabulary so that information, ideas and feelings are communicated clearly and the listener's interest is engaged

- ✓ listen carefully and by developing their own and others' ideas, make significant contributions to discussion and take part effectively in creative activities.

Grade A/A* speaking and listening displays the ability to:

- ✓ select suitable styles and registers of spoken English for a range of situations and contexts

- ✓ use Standard English in an assured manner

- ✓ confidently vary sentence structure and select from an extended vocabulary so as to express information, ideas and feelings in an engaging manner

- ✓ initiate conversations and demonstrate sensitive listening through contributions that sustain and develop discussion

- ✓ recognise and meet the demands of different roles whether in formal settings or creative activities.

On page 112 is an assessment grid that can be used when assessing the various contributions/presentations of other classmates.

Filling in this chart will ensure that you analyse the performances of others and, as a result, grow to understand the ingredients that make for successful speaking and listening performances.

Remember your role is that of a 'sympathetic friend' – don't forget your own 'performance' will be open to assessment by others!

The strengths of _____'s Individual Contribution/Group Discussion/Role Play	The areas that could be improved
1.	1.
2.	2.
3.	3.
4.	4.
5.	5.
Level of performance:	

Here are separate lists of comments that you might want to include or adapt when making your assessments.

Individual Presentations

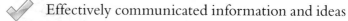

Effectively communicated information and ideas

Adapted talk to situation and audience

Range of appropriate vocabulary

Suitable use of Standard English

Briefly expressed points of view, ideas and feelings

Occasionally detail was used to aid development

Not always focused on target audience

Straightforward use of vocabulary

Some awareness of Standard English and when to use it

Can communicate complex and demanding subject matter, prioritising essential material

Used a sophisticated range of linguistic strategies

Assured choice and flexible use of Standard English

Grammar and extended vocabulary used where appropriate to situation

Group Discussion

Listened closely and attentively, engaging and responding with understanding

Made significant contributions, moving the discussion forward

Analytically engaged with others' ideas and feelings

Responded to what was heard

Showed some interest

Occasionally made brief contributions

Followed the main ideas

 Raised straightforward questions

 Sustained focused listening, demonstrating an understanding of complex ideas by asking penetrating questions

 Shaped and directed the content of the discussion showing flexibility and challenging assumptions

 Could initiate, develop and sustain the discussion by encouraging, participating and interacting with other group members

Role Play

 Developed and sustained role through appropriate use of language, gesture and movement

 Made contributions to the development of situations and ideas

 Showed insight into relationships and significant situations

 Drew on obvious ideas to create a basic character

 Related to situations in predictable if appropriate ways that showed some understanding

 Created a complex character to fulfil the demands of a challenging role using insightful and dramatic approaches

 Explored and responded to complex ideas, issues and relationships

The final row of the grid on page 112 is entitled Level of performance; in order to complete this row, read the checklists for success on page 111 before deciding which of the statements in the table below best describes the level of performance.

Levels of performance
Working towards Grade C level
Working at Grade C level
Working between Grades A/A★ and Grade C
Working at Grade A/A★ level

Checklist for success: working towards Grade C	✔
Communicating and adapting language in individual presentations:	
Have you ensured that you **communicated effectively** to promote ideas and issues?	
Have you **adapted talk** so that it matches the demands of different situations and audiences?	
Have you presented your ideas, using a **range of vocabulary** including **Standard English** where it is appropriate?	
Interacting and responding in discussion:	
Have you **listened closely** in order to engage with what you have heard?	
Have you tried to make **significant contributions** to move the talk forward?	
Have you made it possible for others to contribute even if their **views differ from your own**?	
Creating and sustaining roles in role play:	
Have you **developed a character** and **sustained** it through use of **appropriate language and stance**?	
Have you made **contributions** that **develop situations and ideas**?	

Checklist for success: working towards Grade A/A★	✔
Communicating and adapting language in individual presentations:	
Have you communicated **complex and demanding subject matter competently** and **with clarity**?	
Have you made use of a range of **strategies** to meet **challenging contexts and purposes**?	
Have you presented your ideas, using an assured and flexible choice of **vocabulary** and **grammar,** including **Standard English**, appropriately?	
Interacting and responding in discussion:	
Have you **listened with concentration** in order to critically question and manage complex ideas?	
Have you been flexible in order to **challenge assumptions** and **shape the direction** and the **content** of talk?	
Have you **initiated, developed and sustained discussion**, encouraging participation and positive outcomes?	
Creating and sustaining roles in role play:	
Have you created **complex characters** that fulfil **challenging roles** by the use of **insightful contributions?**	
Have you explored and responded to **complex ideas, issues and relationships** in varied scenarios?	

Unit 4
English Language

Task 1: The Study of Spoken Language (English Language)

Introduction to The Study of Spoken Language

Unit 4 is tested under Controlled Assessment conditions and is made up of three tasks. Task 1 assesses **The Study of Spoken Language**.

Target outcome: Making analytical comparisons of what is heard in relation to context, purpose, technique, delivery and register.

Target skills

The target skills you will learn about in this **Study of Spoken Language** task will enable you to:

 analyse the characteristics of spoken language

 understand the influences on spoken language

 understand the reason for and effect of language choices

 explore the impact of spoken language and how it is achieved

 explore how language is adapted in different contexts.

Assessment Objective

Your Assessment Objective in this Study of Spoken Language task is:

Spoken Language

i) Understand variations in spoken language, explaining why language changes in relation to contexts.

ii) Evaluate the impact of spoken language choices in your own and others' use.

Controlled Assessment Task

 In 1 hour and 30 minutes under Controlled Assessment conditions you will be expected to read and listen to examples (more than one) of motivational talk and then analyse:

- how language is used for a range of purposes
- influences on language choices

- regional variations
- variations due to time, place and context.

You will be expected to focus your answer on what you **hear** – including the structure of the talk, choice of language, rhetorical devices, tone and pace. You should not consider body language or appearance – **only what you hear**!

1   The Skills of Spoken Language

If you want to improve your skills in spoken language, listen to some of the best speakers to hear how they do it. Listen to storytellers, poets, politicians, film stars, comedians, TV soap stars, radio and TV reporters, newsreaders and weather forecasters.

Here are some practical tips related to Speaking and Listening:

- ✓ Think before speaking.
- ✓ Speak clearly.
- ✓ Speak loudly enough to be heard.
- ✓ Do not speak too quickly.
- ✓ Look at the person you are speaking to.
- ✓ Vary your expression.
- ✓ Take turns.
- ✓ Adjust what you say according to who you are talking to and why.
- ✓ Change the way you speak to suit the audience and situation.
- ✓ Let others contribute.
- ✓ Be prepared to change your ideas.
- ✓ Avoid repeating yourself.
- ✓ Remember people's feelings.

This task gives you the opportunity to explore **the way spoken language works** by looking at examples from:

- your own language
- the language of your own age group
- the language heard around you
- the language you hear through TV, radio, the internet and other electronic sources, etc.

We use spoken language for different **purposes**:

- to express our ideas, opinions and feelings
- to make sense of and confirm our understandings
- to question and test our assumptions
- to explore meaning.

Children develop their speaking and listening skills through contact with trusted adults and peers and learn to use language to develop their understanding of the world. They learn to interact with others for a variety of purposes and begin to develop understanding of registers, the types or groupings of words and phrases that are used depending upon the audience, tones and the use of expressive language.

In the Study of Spoken Language you will look at many different kinds of spoken communication, from everyday conversation to formal public speeches. Along the way you will explore and discuss language issues such as why and how language changes, and attitudes to regional accents.

Techniques Used in Spoken Language

2

Read through the following examples of techniques that can be used in spoken language.

Theme	Idea that recurs, e.g. 'A theme of healthy eating ran through the advertisement.'
Simile	Creating an image by describing one thing as **like** another, e.g. 'His eyes were **like** flames.'
Metaphor	Creating an image by describing one thing as if it **is** another, e.g. 'His eyes **were** flames.'
Personification	Creating an image by giving human qualities to a non-human, e.g. 'The flowers were dancing in the wind.'
Syntax	The way words are arranged in a sentence to change the emphasis or create a formal or informal tone.
Vocabulary	The words and phrases chosen. These could include colloquial words or phrases, e.g. 'He had butterflies in his tummy', or more formal, academic words, e.g. 'He experienced a release of adrenaline in his abdomen', single-syllable or multiple-syllable words, e.g. 'buy' or 'purchase'.
Tone	Attitude or mood of the writer communicated in the language they use and the way they speak.
Alliteration	Repetition of the same consonants at the start of several words in the same sentence, or near to each other, e.g. 'Harry hurried home with his heavy homework books.'
Assonance	Repetition of the same vowel sounds in several words in the same sentence, or nearby, e.g. 'The sheep bleat as they seek the jeep.'
Sibilance	Using words with repeated 's', 'sh' or 'z' sounds to create a hiss, e.g. 'Sid wished the snake would slither past.'
Onomatopoeia	Words or sounds which, when spoken, imitate the sounds they describe, e.g. 'thump', 'buzz', 'slither'.
Irony	When the meaning the audience is supposed to understand is opposite to the literal or factual meaning of the words that are said. Irony is sometimes used to portray humour, e.g. 'You look happy' said to a miserable person. Dramatic irony is often used to create tension, e.g. in a play an actor telling another 'You're safe now' when the audience knows danger is approaching.
Pace	Speed at which words or ideas are delivered.
Intonation	The way a speaker changes their pitch to express meaning, e.g. a higher pitch at the end of a sentence can indicate a question; a lower pitch can indicate a warning. Varied intonation can indicate emotional speech; limited intonation can be used to express boredom.
Rhetorical questions	Questions asked that do not require an answer. Often used to provoke thought or encourage an audience into agreement.

ACTIVITY 1

Identify the technique from the table being used in each example below:

1	'He's got a face like a stung warthog!'	7	'Listen to the throaty roar of that engine!'
2	'I'm staring down the barrel of another deadline.'	8	'Am I expected to believe that?'
3	'The sickening thud could be heard across the room.'	9	'Your enthusiasm is overwhelming,' remarked the teacher to her less than impressed class.
4	'Proper Preparation Prevents Poor Performance!'		
5	'My son is trying,' insisted his mother. 'Yes,' the teacher replied, 'very trying!' 'Take you a look and see what ye think.'	10	'If I ever see you here again it will be the high jump for you, my boy!'
6	'I'm terribly sorry,' said the stranger, 'I didn't quite understand what you just said.'		

3 | The Characteristics of Spoken Language

ACTIVITY 2

Persuasive spoken language

1 Work in groups of three. Two of you have 1 minute each to persuade each other of something – prepare a 'pitch' – e.g. to lend them £1, to help them with their homework, to buy a bicycle from them. The third member of the group should observe, note when the characteristics of spoken language (see right) are used and feed back to the others.

2 In your groups spend 3 minutes listing the language or techniques that made the pitches persuasive.

3 Now, the observer should deliver a 1-minute pitch, using as many persuasive techniques as possible.

4 Share your findings with the class and discuss:
- What kinds of things do you find persuasive? Why?
- How could you try to persuade someone?
- Is it easier to persuade somebody about something if you believe it yourself? Explain why.

The characteristics of spoken language are:

 The complexity and speed of most informal spoken language (such as conversation or group discussion) makes it difficult to plan exactly what to say in advance. The pressure to think whilst speaking encourages a looser structure than written language, with more repetition, hesitations and rephrasing. Even in planned spoken language, such as a presentation, there is a looser structure than in writing.

 The boundaries between sentences can be unclear and sentences can flow into each other or be joined with connectives such as 'and' and 'then'. This means that sentences can be fairly lengthy, although intonation and pauses often separate speech into more manageable chunks for the listener.

 In conversation or group discussion, the speaker can rely on instant feedback from others to ensure that they are understood or that their points are agreed or disagreed with. Even when giving a speech or presentation, the speaker can still get feedback from the audience by reading the facial expressions or body language of the audience to see if they are bored, confused or interested.

 Shortened expressions such as 'that one', 'in here' or 'over there' can be used, as body gestures can be used to clarify meaning.

 Informal vocabulary can be used, such as 'whatchamacallit', as there is more opportunity to clarify meaning if something is not understood by the listener. However, if you are giving a formal speech or presentation, it is better to use to formal vocabulary.

 Interruptions and overlapping often occur in conversation or discussion.

 Spoken language frequently displays ellipsis – omission of words. For example: 'I'm going cinema, you coming?'

 Many expressions are used in informal spoken language that do not really have any meaning or need to be included, e.g. 'You know what I mean' or '*Basically* I was *like* really angry'.

The difference between spoken and written language

ACTIVITY 3

Read Texts A and B and identify which is spoken language and which written. List the differences between Texts A and B that indicate to you that one is a written text and one is a spoken text. Share your findings as a class to develop a clear grasp of these differences.

Text A

An amazing thing happened me the other day . . . I'd been out shopping and I went back to this multi-storey car park that I'd parked in and it was kind of deserted . . . erm . . . and as I was walking towards my car I saw this figure sitting in the passenger seat . . . and I thought what's that I've been burgled and as I walked towards the car feeling a bit scared this person got out of the car and it was a little old lady. . . so I thought oh well probably it's not a burglar and . . . er . . . anyway I asked her and the woman said . . . er . . . apparently she'd been sitting there waiting for her daughter to arrive and the daughter hadn't turned up and she was feeling a bit faint and so she went and sat in the car . . . it seems a very strange thing to do . . . I mean . . . apparently she'd been trying all the door handles one was open so she sat in it . . . so anywa. . . erm . . . you know . . . what was I going to do now

Text B

Young people seem to love mobile phones, spending hours chatting to friends or texting messages to each other. Many adults also find them invaluable, using them for business and social purposes. Many people, however, find them intrusive and irritating and would like to see them banned from public places. As with so many issues, there are two sides to the debate about mobile phones.

One reason why mobile phones are so popular is that they give us immediate access to other people. How often have you seen shoppers in supermarkets on their mobiles, checking what they should buy for dinner that night, or people on trains phoning home to arrange a lift from the station? Mobile phones are a great means of communication; we can keep in touch with whoever we want, whenever we want, wherever we are – as long as the other person has their mobile switched on!

Another reason for their rapid rise in popularity is that, like so much modern technology, mobile phones are constantly improving. It is now possible to buy phones which allow you to send and receive photos and e-mails. You can even download games and videos from the internet. Mobile phones have become more than a means of easy communication; they are fun and fashionable and that's why they're so popular with young people.

What affects spoken language?

Spoken language is affected by:

- **Those involved (the participants):** their roles, status, expectations
- **The setting:** board room or coffee bar – though the topic may be the same
- **Its purpose:** informative, persuasive, communicative event, e.g. church service or meeting
- **The audience:** the group of people you are speaking to
- **The form the message takes:** presentation, discussion, sermon, chat
- **Long-term historic change:** words and language have changed and will continue to change over time – language and meaning are constantly evolving
- **Short-term change or language fashions:** growing out of innovation – e.g. new words such as 'megabytes' or 'docudrama'.

4 Standard English

The term **Standard English** refers to a dialect that has come to represent the English language. Standard English is used both in speech and in writing (e.g. in formal documents), but here we are concerned only with its spoken form.

This is an example of Standard English being used in a telephone conversation:

> 'Hello. I'm ringing on behalf of my wife, Mary. Unfortunately, she won't be in today because she's feeling unwell.'

Standard English in spoken form is used in formal situations such as business negotiations, public announcements, and news broadcasts. It is fairly common for a speaker to use Standard English but to deliver it with a regional accent.

We dress differently when we go out with friends to how we dress for an important interview. Similarly we change our language to suit the context. Standard English is formally and grammatically correct English. It is the language equivalent of wearing a smart suit.

ACTIVITY 4

Here is an informal comment made from one student to another. How will this student relay the message in Standard English when they find the Principal?

> 'Hey, have you seen the Head? The dragon in the office is looking for her – there's some inspector boyo has just arrived.'

Context

As well as contributing to meaning, context can also influence the actual words and sentences that we use. For example:

- Do you sometimes say 'Hi' and at other times 'Good morning'?
- Do you have a 'telephone voice'?

This variation in language may be done deliberately, but often it is not. There are two main reasons why we adjust the way we speak:

1 to fit in with our audience or what we feel they expect of us, e.g. use formal language
2 to be clearly understood by our audience, e.g. how you speak to very young children.

Rhetoric is the art of speaking or writing effectively or persuasively. It uses principles and rules of composition drawn from classical traditions.

On the next two pages is a list of rhetorical devices along with a brief explanation of what they are. You may not know these by their formal titles but you will instantly recognise many of them when you read the description.

The list is quite long but it is essential that you are familiar with these techniques so that you can analyse spoken language effectively. It is important to identify when speakers use these techniques, and also to understand their effect and why the speaker has used them.

ACTIVITY 5

One of the most famous pieces of spoken language from the second half of the twentieth century was delivered by Dr Martin Luther King on the steps of the Lincoln Memorial in Washington in 1963.

Go to the website www.americanrhetoric.com/speeches/mlkihaveadream. htm and watch and listen to his speech. You will also find a transcript of his words.

Using the list on the next two pages, identify the rhetorical devices and techniques used in the speech. Note down the effect that each of these has – the audience's reaction is a good indicator.

Accent	Features of pronunciation (speech sounds) that show regional or social identity. An individual may have a personal and distinctive accent.
Allusion	Figure of speech which makes brief, even casual reference to a historical or literary figure, event or object. For example, in John Steinbeck's *Of Mice and Men*, the surname of the character George Milton is an allusion to John Milton, author of *Paradise Lost*, as by the end of the novel, George has lost his dream of a ranch of his own with his friend Lennie.
Ambiguity	Use of language with more than one possible meaning, e.g. 'We saw her duck.'
Analogy	Comparison of two things that are alike in some respects. Metaphors and similes are both types of analogy. For example: A street light is like a star. Both provide light at night, both are in predictable locations, both are overhead, and both serve no function in the daytime. Homer Simpson: 'Son, a woman is a lot like a . . . a refrigerator! They're about six feet tall, 300 pounds. They make ice, and . . . um . . . Oh, wait a minute. Actually, a woman is more like a beer. Son, a woman is like a beer. They smell good, they look good, you'd step over your own mother just to get one!' Her eyes were glistening jewels.
Anaphora	Repetition of the same word or phrase at the beginning of successive phrases or clauses, e.g. 'We shall fight in the trenches. We shall fight on the oceans. We shall fight in the sky.'
Anecdote	Brief story about a real event or person.
Aphorism	Concise statement designed to make a point or illustrate a commonly held belief, e.g. 'Early to bed and early to rise makes a man healthy, wealthy and wise.'
Colloquial	Using ordinary, everyday language, e.g. in the US, depending on where you live, a sandwich may be called a 'sub', a 'grinder' or a 'hero'.
Contradiction	When things compared are direct opposites, e.g. 'That top looks nice, but I don't like it.'
Delayed sentence	Sentence that withholds its main idea until the end, e.g. 'Just as he bent to tie his shoe, a car hit him.'
Dialect	Speech pattern typical of a certain regional location, race or social group that is evident through unique word choice, pronunciation and/or grammatical usage.
Diction	Speaker's (or writer's) choice of words to convey a tone or effect.
Didactic	Teaching or intending to teach a moral lesson.
Eulogy	Speech (or writing) in praise of a person or thing; an oration (formal speech) in honour of someone who has died.
Euphemism	Substitution of a milder or less direct expression for one that is harsh or blunt, e.g. 'passed away' for 'dead'.
Formal language	Language that is lofty, dignified or impersonal.
Humour	Provokes laughter and provides amusement.
Hyperbole	Overstatement characterised by exaggerated language, e.g. 'I had a ton of homework to do.'

Imagery	Use of figurative language to evoke a feeling, call to mind an idea, or describe an object. Imagery may involve any or all of the five senses; sensory details.
Inflection/ Intonation	Rise and fall of voice; pitch used for expression.
Invective	Use of angry and insulting language.
Juxtaposition	Placing two items side by side to create a certain effect or reveal an attitude.
Nostalgia	Desire to return in thought or fact to a former time.
Oxymoron	Figure of speech that combines two apparently contradictory elements, e.g. 'a deafening silence'.
Paradox	A statement that seems to be contradictory, e.g. 'I know that I know nothing'. Homer Simpson often displays skilful use of the paradox (and oxymoron), e.g. 'Oh Bart, don't worry, people die all the time. In fact, you could wake up dead tomorrow.'
Personification	Treating something abstract or non-human as if it were a person by giving it human qualities, e.g. 'Opportunity knocked on the door.' Here, Homer Simpson uses personification to explain human behaviour: 'The only monster here is the gambling monster that has enslaved your mother . . . and it's time to snatch your mother from his neon claws!'
Register	The tone or way a text speaks to and addresses its readers or listeners. It is the text's 'voice'.
Repetition	Deliberate duplication of a word or words for effect.
Rhetorical question	Question asked for effect – no answer is required. For example: MOTHER SIMPSON: *(singing)* How many roads must a man walk down before you can call him a man? HOMER: Seven. LISA: No, Dad, it's a **rhetorical question**. HOMER: OK, eight. LISA: Dad, do you even know what 'rhetorical' means? HOMER: Do **I** know what 'rhetorical' means?
Sarcasm	Sharp, caustic remark; a form of verbal irony in which apparent praise is actually bitterly or harshly critical, e.g. saying 'Nice catch' when a goalkeeper misses the ball.
Satire	Humour used to make fun of or ridicule an idea or human vice.
Slang	Informal non-standard use of words. Perhaps the best known regional slang is Cockney rhyming slang, e.g. 'up the apples and pears' = stairs.

6 Types of Spoken Language

The language of interviews

When analysing the language of interviews, it is important to look at the type of question being asked. To find out specific information **closed questions** should be used, e.g. 'What is the capital of France?' This is a closed question because the answer is 'Paris', the name of the capital – there is nothing else to add. Closed questions are useful for obtaining simple answers.

To find out about something that has happened, what a person knows, or how they do something, **open questions** should be used. A chat-show host will use open questions when they want someone to talk for a while: for example, 'Can you tell us a bit about your latest film?'

ACTIVITY 6

The transcript below is from a backstage interview with Robert Pattinson by MTV at the MTV Movie Awards in 2009. Read the transcript and assess how effectively the interviewer uses questions to elicit (draw out) information from Robert Pattinson. Where does the interviewer use open or closed questions?

INTERVIEWER:	Rob, you won *Best Fight* tonight. How did it feel up there on stage?
PATTINSON:	It made me feel really tough; really hard. I don't think I've ever won a fight in my life, so it was cool.
INTERVIEWER:	And it must have been nice to be up there with Cam Gigandet again.
PATTINSON:	Yeah, Cam won. That's crazy that he's won two years in a row.
INTERVIEWER:	A year ago, people barely knew you guys when you attended the MTV Movie Awards. What's the biggest difference you see as far as the chaos, the fans, the reception?
PATTINSON:	I mean, it's completely polar-opposite. I didn't even think anyone knew who I was last year.
INTERVIEWER:	We're about to debut the *New Moon* trailer. Give us your reaction to it.
PATTINSON:	I haven't seen it yet.

INTERVIEWER:	You haven't?
PATTINSON:	This will be my first time seeing it.
INTERVIEWER:	Well, I'm sure you've seen the 15-second preview online, where you're kissing Kristen, right?
PATTINSON:	I haven't seen anything! I mean, from what I've seen from playback and stuff when I've been shooting it, it looks amazing. So I think [*New Moon*] should be [good]. I'm keeping it as a surprise from myself.
INTERVIEWER:	Are you going to have time to shoot anything before *Eclipse*? What are you going to shoot next?
PATTINSON:	I am. As yet, it's still untitled, at the moment, but I'm going on Monday to start shooting it. It's a kind of drama, love-story kind of thing. It's cool; it's a really great script.

ACTIVITY 7

Imagine you have to interview a famous person because you are writing their biography.

Write a list of ten key questions you would ask. Remember to consider the types of question you use – closed or open questions.

ACTIVITY 8

Listen to a radio or television interview. Select a short extract and study it closely.

What kinds of strategies and skills does the interviewer use?
Do they:

- create an atmosphere that is formal or friendly, hostile or protective
- take an approach that is stand-offish or gushing, sneering or flattering
- use questions that are easy and undemanding or challenging and uncompromising
- use mainly closed or open questions?

Which question in the interview generated the most interesting answer? Was it asked as a result of an earlier answer or was it, in your opinion, a question the interviewer had prepared in advance?

Speeches

MARK ANTONY:
Friends, Romans, countrymen, lend me your ears;
I come to bury Caesar, not to praise him;
The evil that men do lives after them,
The good is oft interred with their bones,
So let it be with Caesar . . . The noble Brutus
Hath told you Caesar was ambitious:
If it were so, it was a grievous fault,
And grievously hath Caesar answered it . . .
Here, under leave of Brutus and the rest,
(For Brutus is an honourable man;
So are they all; all honourable men)
Come I to speak in Caesar's funeral . . .
He was my friend, faithful and just to me:
But Brutus says he was ambitious;
And Brutus is an honourable man . . . .
He hath brought many captives home to Rome,
Whose ransoms did the general coffers fill:
Did this in Caesar seem ambitious?
When that the poor have cried, Caesar hath wept:
Ambition should be made of sterner stuff:
Yet Brutus says he was ambitious;
And Brutus is an honourable man.
You all did see that on the **Lupercal**
I thrice presented him a kingly crown,
Which he did thrice refuse: was this ambition?
Yet Brutus says he was ambitious;
And, sure, he is an honourable man.
I speak not to disprove what Brutus spoke,
But here I am to speak what I do know.
You all did love him once, not without cause:
What cause withholds you then to mourn for him?
O judgement! thou art fled to brutish beasts,
And men have lost their reason . . . . Bear with me;
My heart is in the coffin there with Caesar,
And I must pause till it come back to me.

Lupercal: festival in Roman times held on 15 February

ACTIVITY 9

Watch a video clip or listen to your teacher reading Mark Antony's speech (above) to the people in Act 3 Scene 2 of *Julius Caesar* by Shakespeare. Then answer these questions:

1 What was Mark Antony's intention in this speech?
2 How would the audience have reacted after the first ten lines?

3 What particular effect would the repetition have had on the audience?
4 How does the speech conclude?
5 What would the audience have felt?

Winston Churchill was the inspirational British Prime Minister in the Second World War. In 1940, after the retreat from Dunkirk, the military situation was bleak. His response was his famous 'we shall never surrender' speech, made in the House of Commons.

ACTIVITY 10

Look at the techniques highlighted in this famous speech. Analyse the effect that these would have had in motivating the nation and building people's confidence at this critical moment in the war.

List of three – 'if'

Personal pronoun 'we' involves the audience

Short phrases

Emotive language

Repetition

Repetition

Forceful phrase rousing nation to victory

I have, myself, full confidence that if all do their duty, if nothing is neglected, and if the best arrangements are made, as they are being made, we shall prove ourselves once again able to defend our Island home, to ride out the storm of war, and to outlive the menace of tyranny, if necessary for years, if necessary alone. At any rate, that is what we are going to try to do. That is the resolve of His Majesty's Government – every man of them. That is the will of Parliament and the nation. The British Empire and the French Republic, linked together in their cause and in their need, will defend to the death their native soil, aiding each other like good comrades to the utmost of their strength. Even though large tracts of Europe and many old and famous States have fallen or may fall into the grip of the Gestapo and all the odious apparatus of Nazi rule, we shall not flag or fail. We shall go on to the end, we shall fight in France, we shall fight on the seas and oceans, we shall fight with growing confidence and growing strength in the air, we shall defend our Island, whatever the cost may be, we shall fight on the beaches, we shall fight on the landing grounds, we shall fight in the fields and in the streets, we shall fight in the hills; we shall never surrender, and even if, which I do not for a moment believe, this Island or a large part of it were subjugated and starving, then our Empire beyond the seas, armed and guarded by the British Fleet, would carry on the struggle, until, in God's good time, the New World, with all its power and might, steps forth to the rescue and the liberation of the old.

Melodramatic imagery and alliteration

Forceful phrase rousing nation to rally and to fight on

Listen to your teacher or other students read out the three rousing battle speeches A, B and C on this page and the opposite page. Pay close attention to the use of rhetoric and other techniques employed in each speech. Which of these men would you follow and why?

Speech A: Shakespeare's Henry V

This is a fictional speech written by William Shakespeare. In it, the English King, Henry, is attempting to lift the morale of his army, which is vastly outnumbered as they prepare to fight the French at the Battle of Agincourt on St Crispin's Day.

This story shall the good man teach his son;
And Crispin Crispian shall ne'er go by,
From this day to the ending of the world,
But we in it shall be remember'd;
We few, we happy few, we band of brothers;
For he to-day that sheds his blood with me
Shall be my brother; be he ne'er so vile,
This day shall gentle his condition:
And gentlemen in England now a-bed
Shall think themselves accursed they were not here,
And hold their manhoods cheap whiles any speaks
That fought with us upon Saint Crispin's day.

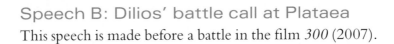

Speech B: Dilios' battle call at Plataea

This speech is made before a battle in the film *300* (2007).

DILIOS:	Long I pondered my King's cryptic talk of victory. Time has proven him wise. For from free Greek to free Greek, the word was spread that bold Leonia's and his 300, so far from home, laid down their lives; not just for Sparta, but for all Greece and the promise this country holds. Now, here on this ragged patch of earth called Plataea, let his hordes face obliteration!
SPARTAN ARMY:	HA-OOH!!
DILIOS:	Just there the barbarians huddle, sheer terror gripping tight their hearts with icy fingers – knowing full well what merciless horrors they suffered at the swords and spears of 300. Yet they stare now across the plain at 10,000 Spartans commanding 30,000 free Greeks: HA-OOH!
SPARTAN ARMY:	HA-OOH! HA-OOH! HA-OOH!
DILIOS:	The enemy outnumber us a paltry 3 to 1, good odds for any Greek. This day we rescue a world from mysticism and tyranny and usher in a future brighter than anything we can imagine.
	Give thanks, men, to Leonidas and the brave 300. TO VICTORY!!!

Speech C: General Maximus Decimus Meridius in *Gladiator*

This speech is made before a battle in the film *Gladiator* (2000) by a Roman general to his cavalry. 'Fratres' means 'Brothers'.

> Fratres!
> Three weeks from now I will be harvesting my crops.
> Imagine where you will be, and it will be so.
> Hold the line! Stay with me!
> If you find yourself alone, riding in green fields with the sun on your face, do not be troubled, for you are in Elysium, and you're already dead!!!
>
> Brothers:
> What we do in Life echoes in Eternity . . .

ACTIVITY 12

Look at the techniques highlighted in the eulogy below by Russell Crowe to Steve Irwin, an Australian wildlife expert killed by a stingray in 2006. Analyse the effect that these would have had on his audience.

Eulogies

A eulogy is a formal expression of praise for someone who has died, often delivered at a funeral.

Good morning everybody. Firstly, to Terri and all of Steve's family, from my family to yours, our deepest sympathies and condolences. I think this memorial should be a joyful one, and not mournful one. We, after all, have to keep in mind who we are here to celebrate, and what he would have preferred. I hope somebody will speak today of the specifics of what Steve achieved as a conservationist, but all I can do today is talk directly to my friend, my mate, Steven.

Your passing has suspended reality for all of us. It was way too soon, and completely unfair on all accounts. I know as humble as you always were, that you would still be pleased to know that the world sends its love and that people all over this planet have been grieving. We've all lost a friend, we've lost a champion, and we're gonna take some time to adjust to that.

I'm in New York, mate – the big city – and you have been headline news on CNN for a week. There are not many zookeepers who would command that attention, mate. And all that means is that you got your message across. You got the word out there. And you were heard. And you will be remembered.

Positive language sets tone of speech.

Personal pronoun 'my' repeated, emphasising their close relationship.

Informal style – uses 'mate' to address deceased.

Direct address 'you' used throughout gives positive message that he is still present in all their lives.

Informal style

Anaphora – repetition emphasises that they have all suffered a great loss.

Humour – playful teasing of deceased maintains upbeat tone of speech.

Repetition of 'you' in last lines confirms Steve Irwin's legacy and achievements.

ACTIVITY 13

Analyse this eulogy to Princess Diana by her brother, Charles Earl Spencer. Pay close attention to:

- the language used to discuss Diana
- language choices
- how the language matches the context.

Diana was the very essence of compassion, of duty, of style, of beauty. All over the world she was a symbol of selfless humanity. All over the world, a standard bearer for the rights of the truly downtrodden, a very British girl who transcended nationality. Someone with a natural nobility who was classless and who proved in the last year that she needed no royal title to continue to generate her particular brand of magic.

Today is our chance to say thank you for the way you brightened our lives, even though God granted you but half a life. We will all feel cheated always that you were taken from us so young and yet we must learn to be grateful that you came along at all. Only now that you are gone do we truly appreciate what we are now without and we want you to know that life without you is very, very difficult.

We have all despaired at our loss over the past week and only the strength of the message you gave us through your years of giving has afforded us the strength to move forward.

I would like to end by thanking God for the small mercies he has shown us at this dreadful time. For taking Diana at her most beautiful and radiant and when she had joy in her private life. Above all we give thanks for the life of a woman I am so proud to be able to call my sister, the unique, the complex, the extraordinary and irreplaceable Diana whose beauty, both internal and external, will never be extinguished from our minds.

ACTIVITY 14

Using the rhetorical devices you have studied, write a eulogy for yourself. This is an opportunity to write in a tongue-in-cheek manner; you could consider giving yourself many of the qualities in 'death' that you didn't have in life!

Other kinds of spoken language

The Apollo moon landing

Read this extract in which where Neil Armstrong describes stepping onto the moon. Identify the metaphor he uses and describe its impact.

. . . although the surface appears to be . . . very, very fine-grained as you get close to it. It's almost like a powder . . . Okay, I'm going to step off the LEM now. That's one small step for man; one giant leap for mankind.

This extract below is from Halle Berry's acceptance address when she won Best Leading Actress at the 2002 Oscars. Do you think it is a planned or unplanned speech? Use evidence from the passage to support your view. How does the use of language make it clear that this is a modern acceptance speech?

Oh, my god. Oh, my god. I'm sorry. This moment is so much bigger than me. This moment is for Dorothy Dandridge, Lena Horne, Diahann Carroll. It's for the women that stand beside me, Jada Pinkett, Angela Bassett, Vivica Fox. And it's for every nameless, faceless woman of colour that now has a chance because this door tonight has been opened. Thank you. I'm so honored. I'm so honored. And I thank the Academy for choosing me to be the vessel from which His blessing might flow. Thank you.

I want to thank my manager, Vincent Cirrincione. He's been with me for twelve long years and you fought every fight and you've loved me when I've been up, but more importantly you've loved me when I've been down. You have been a manager, a friend, and the only father I've ever known. Really. And I love you very much.

I want to thank my mom . . .

I want to thank Lions Gate. Thank you. Mike . . . Thank you for giving me this chance . . . Thank you.

I want to thank my agents . . . thank you. Thank you for never kicking me out and sending me somewhere else. Thank you. I, I, I, who else? I have so many people that I know I need to thank. My lawyers – Neil Meyer, thank you. Okay, wait a minute. I got to take . . . seventy-four years here!! OK. I got to take this time! I got to thank my lawyer, Neil Meyer, for making this deal. Doug Stone. I need to thank lastly and not leastly, I have to thank Spike Lee for putting me in my very first film and believing in me. Oprah Winfrey for being the best role model any girl can have. Joel Silver, thank you. And thank you to Warren Beatty. Thank you so much for being my mentors and believing in me.

Thank you! Thank you! Thank you!

Matching grades to spoken language performances

In this Controlled Assessment Task the essential qualities the examiners will be looking for are highlighted at the important grade boundaries. Read these descriptions *carefully*; they tell you what your responses should be like.

Grade C spoken language analysis displays the ability to understand and explain:

 different influences on language choices

 the effects of some regional variations in spoken language

 why spoken language shows variety and change over time

 how spoken language is adapted for a range of purposes.

Grade A/A* spoken language analysis displays the ability to understand and explain:

 subtle influences on language choices

 the significance of regional/non-standard variations in spoken language

 why various features of spoken language show variety and change over time, and in different places and contexts

 how spoken language is selected and adapted for a range of purposes in different contexts.

Spoken language: Key to success

The writing-up period for this Controlled Assessment Task is 90 minutes so make sure you have pre-planned what you are going to do and that you are ready to use the time purposefully.

Efficient essay writing

This assessment is a written one and so it is essential that you learn the rules of effective essay writing:

 The best writing results from the following process: **Think, Plan, Write.** You will have spent some weeks before the Controlled Assessment on the first of these two elements; even so, resist the temptation to start writing your answer immediately when you get in the room to start your write up.

✓ Take the time to put your plan down on paper (this will be 15 minutes well spent) – it is essential if you are to produce your best work. Using your plan will ensure that your writing leads the reader through a clearly constructed analysis of your pieces of spoken language.

✓ You now have 65 minutes for the main writing of your task.

✓ A really strong introduction can give your answer its direction and set the tone for the remainder of your answer.

✓ A thoughtful and strong conclusion leaves the marker with a favourable impression.

✓ You will have 5–10 minutes to review your finished work. You *must* review your work because when working quickly and under pressure *everyone* makes mistakes. Remember too that there are no marks for extreme neatness – it is much better that your work is accurate even if it contains a few corrections. Check for the following common mistakes and correct any that you find:

   i)   Have you paragraphed the essay?

   ii) Did you vary the sentence openings and lengths?

   iii) Have you used a varied vocabulary?

   iv) Have you left out any words or are there any sentences where the meaning is less than clear?

The content of your essay

✓ Remember to keep the focus of your writing on what you have **heard** – the focus *must* be spoken language!

✓ Don't be tempted to over-prepare – trying to memorise whole essays is folly and will probably backfire on you so don't contemplate it! Be content that you have prepared, you know what you intend to write – so go in and do it!

✓ You may well have a transcript of the pieces you have studied as you do your Controlled Assessment write-up but use them purely for reference purposes.

✓ Any quotations you use should be quite brief – you will not get credit for copying out swathes of a text you have in front of you!

Checklist for success: working towards Grade C	✔
Have you shown understanding of what you have *heard* by **offering explanations** and **drawing conclusions** about the two pieces of spoken language?	
Have you **presented supporting evidence** from both texts to sustain your conclusions?	
Have you discussed all of the **features** set out in the question?	
Have you presented your opinions on the two texts in an **organised** and **fluent** essay?	
Have you used words and phrases that help to **clarify** the subject matter?	

Checklist for success: working towards Grade A/A★	✔
Have you sustained an **analysis** and **evaluation** of what has been *heard* in both pieces of spoken language?	
Have you presented a range of **appropriate** and **insightful supporting material** from both texts to sustain your analysis?	
Have you offered a **sustained and perceptive insight** into the distinctive qualities of both pieces of spoken language as required by the question?	
Have you constructed an answer that is **fluent** and **assured in style** and is **competently structured**, using **accurate expression** confidently?	
Have you **employed vocabulary precisely** to sustain focus on the subject matter?	

Unit 4
English Language and English

Task 2 (English Language) and Tasks 1–3 (English)

Introduction to The Study of Written Language/Literature

This element of Unit 4 is a shared area of study for both English Language and English. In both cases it is tested through Controlled Assessment. The target skills and the Assessment Objectives are exactly the same for both Specifications.

Target outcome: To present an informed and insightful consideration of how a writer or writers of literature have created/presented a perspective on a subject or theme.

Target skills

The target skills you will learn about in these task(s) will enable you to:

 read and understand texts

 select material appropriate to purpose

 collate from different sources

 develop and sustain interpretation of writers' ideas

 explain and evaluate how writers use linguistic, grammatical, structural and presentational features to achieve effect and engage and influence the reader

 understand texts in their social, cultural and historical contexts.

Assessment Objective

Your Assessment Objective in these tasks is:

Responses to Literature/Literary texts

i)   Read and understand texts, selecting material appropriate to purpose, collating from different sources and making comparisons and cross-references as appropriate.

ii) Develop and sustain interpretations of writers' ideas and perspectives.

iii) Explain and evaluate how writers use linguistic, grammatical, structural and presentational features to achieve effects and engage and influence the reader.

iv) Understand texts in their social, cultural and historical contexts.

Controlled Assessment Task

In **English Language** the single Controlled Assessment piece is Task 2 in your Specification and it assesses **The Study of Written Language – Literary Texts**. It is worth 15% of your final GCSE grade.

You will have 1 hour 30 minutes under Controlled Assessment conditions in which to write an essay on one of three preset themes.

135

Controlled Assessment Task (continued)

For example:

> Analyse how the theme of war has been presented in a text you have studied.

In **English** you will be expected to complete three Controlled Assessment pieces. They are Tasks 1–3 in your Specification and assess **The Study of Literature**. They are worth 20% of your final GCSE grade.

You will be assessed on the study of three texts consisting of:

- a text from English, Welsh or Irish literary heritage
- a play by Shakespeare
- a text from a different culture or tradition.

You will have 1 hour under Controlled Assessment conditions to write each of your responses on the three texts.

These three responses will be on preset themes – these change annually and are set out in the Specification. For example, your question might be:

> How are relationships presented in *Romeo and Juliet*?

or

> How does Dickens create a sense of mystery in his writing?

1 Controlled Assessment in Unit 4

The Controlled Assessment task(s) will be based on texts chosen by the English department and your teacher. The theme(s) on which they focus are specified annually by CCEA.

You will have time (a period of weeks) in which to carry out planning and preparation. This will take the form of working in class and at home. Your teacher will help you with your preparation in class, but you should use your initiative in your own time to make sure that you plan and organise yourself thoroughly.

In addition, your whole class will receive feedback during this planning and preparation process from your teacher; and you will learn how work will be marked according to the assessment criteria.

Having completed this preparatory process, you will have a specified period of time in which to write your response(s). This will be done under formal supervision. Once this write-up has begun it must be completed without the aid of any support materials other than plain copies of the text(s). If this Controlled Assessment is done over more than one session, your work will be held in school by your teacher. Once you have had the allotted writing-up time, that's the piece finished.

Writing your response within this time frame may seem quite daunting, but if you make the most of the preparation time available to you, it will not present you with a major problem.

The rest of this Unit looks in turn at drama, prose and poetry and assesses the significant factors within each genre.

- If you are taking **English Language** then you will need to work through only one of the next three sections – depending on the focus of your study.
- If you are taking **English** then you will eventually work through all three sections.

Drama 2

Drama is designed to be watched – it is in its natural environment on a stage. Take every opportunity to see the play you are studying (or for that matter any play) on stage. It is only then that you can really appreciate the combination of factors that will lift dry, two-dimensional words off a page and give them life – the skills of the actors, the set, sound effects, lighting, make-up and costumes.

The ingredients of drama

A gripping play will use a mix of these elements in order to hold an audience's attention:

- a fascinating story or plot
- a story that builds before reaching a denouement
- characters that the audience can believe in
- situations that have to be faced up to and dealt with
- some sort of resolution – happy or tragic or somewhere in between.

Plot and structure

These are closely linked and you will have come across them before. Here's a reminder of their differences:

- **Plot:** how the storyline develops with its twists, turns and unexpected incidents
- **Structure:** how a playwright develops and divides up the storyline into different segments.

Shakespeare's plays are structured in **acts** (frequently five) with each act made up of a number of **scenes** which move the story forward.

Structure is linked to changes in **mood** or **atmosphere**. This varies in order to keep the audience interested and to help direct the audience as to how to react to the characters and action.

For example, *Macbeth* (sometimes known the 'Scottish Play'), opens with a short scene featuring witches. This sets the atmosphere for what will follow.

Often the mood will change as the story builds up to its dramatic **climax** – the play's most critical and dramatic moment (not always at the very end of the drama, as those of you studying *Macbeth* will know).

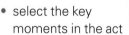

ACTIVITY 1

This exercise will help you to establish the key moments in one act of the Shakespeare play you are studying. Working in pairs with the act you are given, take 15 minutes to:

- select the key moments in the act
- pick out a quotation or exchanges between characters to represent each of these key moments
- list these in the order in which they occur.

Be prepared to share your findings with the rest of the class and to justify your choices.

The **pace** or speed at which the action unfolds varies. The rate at which events occur will be controlled in order to create particular effects like an increase in tension or a sense of excitement. Often events happen in quick succession or there is a series of crises as the action builds towards the climax of the play.

Characters

We learn about the characters in a play mainly through the **dialogue** and **action**. Some playwrights also give detailed descriptions and background information about particular characters. Shakespeare does not – he relies on the actions of his characters and his dialogue to construct three-dimensional, credible characters.

You need to focus carefully on individual characters within the play. What do they do? What types of relationships exist between them? Get to know the characters in your text and try to understand what motivates them to act as they do.

How Shakespeare sets about presenting or revealing his characters to the audience is called **characterisation**. This is also how the writer influences or controls our response to the characters and the situations they are in. As a result, we may share the anguish of one character while hoping another will get their comeuppance!

Shakespeare's control of our reactions to his characters can be extremely subtle. In *Macbeth*, by the time Macbeth resolves to fight Macduff at the climax of the play we have run through the entire range of emotional responses to this man and his behaviour. At different times he has been national saviour and hero; morally weak willed and naive; superstitious; hen-pecked and manipulated; as well as treacherous, murderous and pitiless. Despite this journey, there is still something heroic about his refusal to give in. When he dies the whole energy and dynamism of the play immediately disappears.

ACTIVITY 2

Hot seating is an effective way to gain an insight into a character.

In groups, decide which character is to be the focus and take the 'hot seat'. Take 10 minutes to agree on four constructive questions to ask this character. Then take turns to role play the character (take the hot seat) and answer these questions.

ACTIVITY 3

The extract below is from the end of Act 2 of *All My Sons* by Arthur Miller. A relationship is reaching a crisis point after a dramatic revelation.

In pairs, discuss the stance taken by each of the two characters and then use your analysis of their motives to present a reading of this excerpt based on your interpretation.

Arthur Miller

Chris, recently back from the war, realises that his father, Keller, a figure who until now he has looked up to and admired, has knowingly allowed defective cylinder heads for engines in war planes to be shipped out of his factory, resulting in the loss of 21 planes and their crew. This is the exchange between the pair when Chris finds out that his father was responsible.

CHRIS:	Then why didn't you tell them?
KELLER:	It was too late. The paper, it was all over the front page, twenty-one went down, it was too late. They came with handcuffs into the [work] shop, what could I do? *(He sits on bench.)* Chris . . . Chris, I did it for you, it was a chance and I took it for you. I'm sixty-one years old, when would I have another chance to make something for you? Sixty-one years old you don't get another chance, do ya?
CHRIS:	You even knew they wouldn't hold up in the air.
KELLER:	I didn't say that.
CHRIS:	But you were going to warn them not to use them –
KELLER:	But that don't mean –
CHRIS:	It means you knew they'd crash.
KELLER:	It don't mean that.
CHRIS:	Then you thought they'd crash.
KELLER:	I was afraid maybe –
CHRIS:	You were afraid maybe! God in heaven, what kind of a man are you? Kids were hanging in the air by those heads [the faulty cylinder heads]. You knew that!
KELLER:	For you, a business for you!
CHRIS *(with burning fury)*:	For me! Where do you live, where have you come from? For me! – I was dying every day and you were killing my boys and you did it for me!

Analysing a character

Here are some aspects you need to consider when you are analysing a character:

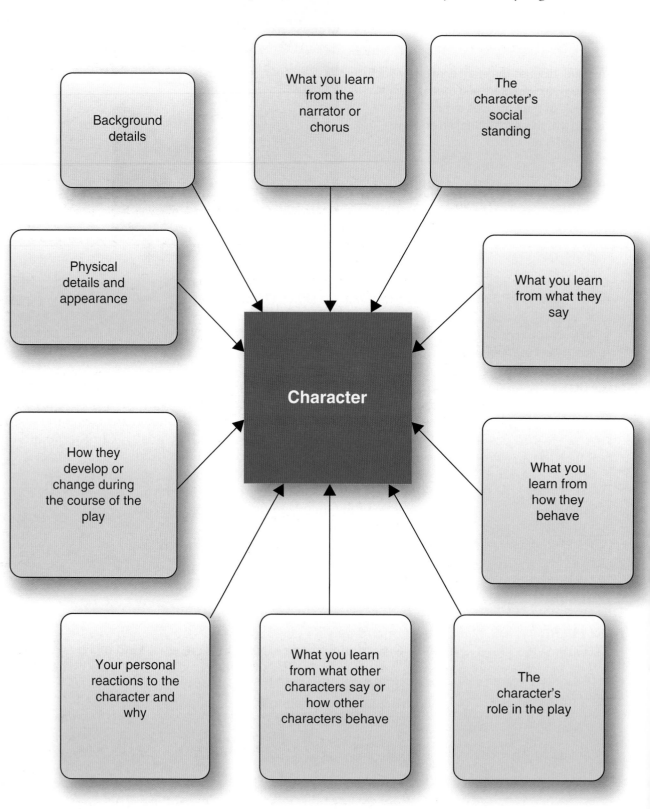

Background details

What you learn from the narrator or chorus

The character's social standing

Physical details and appearance

What you learn from what they say

Character

How they develop or change during the course of the play

What you learn from how they behave

Your personal reactions to the character and why

What you learn from what other characters say or how other characters behave

The character's role in the play

Use this checklist to help you gain a sound and detailed grasp of individual characters:

First impressions:

- how the character is introduced to the audience, if this is their first appearance on stage
- background information supplied by other characters
- details regarding physical appearance or personal facts

Dialogue:

- what the character says to others
- how others reply to them
- voice tones, e.g. anger, concern, sarcasm
- what the character says in asides or soliloquies – a strategy Shakespeare used extensively
- what a narrator or chorus says about them

Actions:

- what the character does to others
- how others behave or react in response
- any unexpected actions or responses
- how the character enters and exits the stage
- the pace of the action

Language or particular words and phrases:

- how this reflects the character's mood and that of others
- the power of particular speeches
- how the character's choice of language reveals their personality
- use of humour
- use of colloquial or formal speech

Setting:

- the importance of location to the character
- the relevance of descriptions of place in the stage directions
- how the historical setting helps the audience understand the character
- significance of social setting to the character
- use of flashbacks (or flash forwards) to another time or place
- how the general mood or atmosphere affects how the audience feels towards the character

When you are presented with your text(s) remember:

 READ! READ! READ!

 Make sure you understand the plot and structure.

 Look closely at the characters and the themes.

3 Prose

The best way to begin studying a prose text is to enjoy the story. However, the study of a prose text for Controlled Assessment is not just a matter of knowing the story, although that is fundamentally important.

You will need to be aware of the **themes** or **issues** which the writer wanted to explore. You will also need to be able to analyse the **writer's craft**: the techniques employed to make the story really interesting, such as use of language, structure and plot, narrative stance, character development. You will be expected to show a thorough understanding of the **writer's purpose**.

The key features of prose texts

A thorough, detailed knowledge and understanding of the text is your first objective. You will develop this as a result of work in the classroom, as well as your own personal study, which could include internet research. If you are going to discuss and evaluate a novel thoroughly, the most important aspects to consider are:

- **Setting:** the backdrop to the story
- **Plot:** the sequence of events that shapes the storyline
- **Characters:** including their relationships with each other
- **Language and style:** use of description, dialogue, imagery (e.g. similes and metaphors), dialect, etc.
- **Themes:** the significant, frequently underlying issues that the author is drawing to the attention of the reader.

Setting

Stories always have a specific location or are set against a certain background. For example, in John Steinbeck's novel *Of Mice and Men*, the backdrop is the Great Depression in America in the 1930s and the story is set amidst the tough life on a ranch outside the town of Soledad. This allows Steinbeck to portray the harsh existence that itinerant labourers endured at this time.

ACTIVITY 4

In pairs, identify the **main features** of the setting in a prose text you have read. Note your findings in a bullet-point list.

Outline the main **reasons why** you think the writer chose this setting.

The life and work of labourers in America during the 1930s was often very difficult.

Plot

In a prose text the linked sequence of events provides the basic storyline or plot. The plot is the skeleton of the text, around which the writer develops the flesh of their creation.

A plot can take a fairly straightforward form and be based on a time sequence. For example, *Lord of the Flies* is a chronological account; it is a frightening description of how life on the island deteriorates over a period of time. A plot may not be so straightforward and may involve flashbacks, or similar techniques like those Jennifer Johnston uses in *How Many Miles to Babylon?*

Writers often increase the suspense or add to the mystery of the story by developing unusual twists and turns in the plot, in order to sustain the reader's interest. You need to be aware of the reason for and the outcome of these devices.

The critical stage of the plot is the finale, the climax of the account, when the writer makes their point, revealing the final piece in the jigsaw. For example, in *Animal Farm*, the climax happens in the extract below where Benjamin and Clover are looking through the window at the special feast in the farmhouse. As they look from pig to man and from man to pig, they realise that they can no longer tell the difference: pigs and men are impossible to differentiate. Both are equally corrupt.

There was the same hearty cheering as before, and the mugs were emptied to the dregs. But as the animals outside gazed at the scene, it seemed to them that some strange thing was happening. What was it that had altered in the faces of the pigs? Clover's old dim eyes flitted from one face to another. Some of them had five chins, some had four, some had three. But what was it that seemed to be melting and changing? Then, the applause having come to an end, the company took up their cards and continued the game that had been interrupted, and the animals crept silently away.

But they had not gone twenty yards when they stopped short. An uproar of voices was coming from the farmhouse. They rushed back and looked through the window again. Yes, a violent quarrel was in progress. There were shoutings, bangings on the table, sharp suspicious glances, furious denials. The source of the trouble appeared to be that Napoleon and Mr Pilkington had each played an ace of spades simultaneously.

Twelve voices were shouting in anger, and they were all alike. No question, now, what had happened to the faces of the pigs. The creatures outside looked from pig to man, and from man to pig, and from pig to man again; but already it was impossible to say which was which.

Characters

When you are studying a novel or short story it is important to pay close attention to the characters. When you first read the text you will gain a general understanding of who the characters are and what they do, but you will need to reflect on the characters in more depth.

First of all let's consider the main characters. They will be three-dimensional believable individuals who change as a result of what happens to them. This makes them dynamic as they learn (sometimes not quickly enough!) from what happens to them. By the end of the text they may have gained a deeper understanding of themselves.

Changes within a character

You can identify changes within a character by focusing on:

- **Thoughts and feelings:** Consider the thoughts and feelings of the character. Look for thoughts that are repeated throughout the story. What are the goals, ambitions and values of the character and how do they change? If the thoughts and feelings of the character change it will generally be because they have learnt something about themselves and life, which will help to inform you of the theme of the text.
- **Conversations and interactions:** What do the characters say and do? Writers put words in their characters' mouths for good reasons.
- **Learning outcomes:** What does the character learn and therefore what do you learn?

Conflict

Writers frequently put their characters in a conflict situation, so you may want to focus on the conflicts that are evident within the text:

- Is there a conflict between two or more people?
- Is the main character in conflict with the world?
- Is the character in conflict with society?
- Is the character in conflict with himself or herself?

The outcome of such conflicts will usually determine what the writer wants the reader to learn, so emphasising the theme.

ACTIVITY 5

Read the extract on the opposite page from *Roll of Thunder, Hear My Cry* and answer these questions:

1 Who is the conflict between?
2 What themes or issues are hinted at through this short extract?

Mr Simms glared down at me. 'When my gal Lillian Jean says for you to get yo'self off the sidewalk, you get, you hear?'

Behind him were his sons R.W. and Melvin. People from the store began to ring the Simmses. 'Ain't that the same little nigger was cuttin' up back there at Jim Lee's' someone asked . . .

Then Mr Simms jumped into the street. I moved away from him, trying to get up. He was a mean looking man, red in the face and bearded. I was afraid he was going to hit me before I could get to my feet, but he didn't. I scrambled up and ran blindly for the wagon. Someone grabbed me and I fought wildly, attempting to pull loose. 'Stop, Cassie!' Big Ma said. 'Stop, it's me. We're going home now.'

Insight into characters

Characters do not invent themselves; they are deliberately created, shaped and perfected by the writer, who allows us to see characters only as they intend us to see them.

You need to understand how writers create and develop characters and how they control our feelings about those characters.

You can develop an insight into characters by assessing:

- what they look like
- what they do
- what they say – and how they say it!
- what they think and feel
- what other people say about them
- how other people treat them or react to them.

All of these aspects give the writer opportunities to influence our attitude towards the characters: for example, through the language or images used to present them.

ACTIVITY 6

The extract below from *Of Mice and Men* introduces George and Lennie. Steinbeck helps readers to understand the character of Lennie by linking him with animals. Explain how he does this and what the effect is.

Lennie

ACTIVITY 7

In pairs or groups, focus on one major character in your text(s) and discuss how the writer tries to **manipulate** your thoughts about the character. Identify the **ways** in which the writer does this and note your findings in a bullet-point list.

The first man was small and quick, dark of face, with restless eyes and sharp, strong features. Every part of him was defined: small, strong hands, slender arms, a thin and bony nose. Behind him walked his opposite, a huge man, shapeless of face, with large, pale eyes, and wide, sloping shoulders; and he walked heavily, dragging his feet a little, the way a bear drags his paws. His arms did not swing at his sides, but hung loosely.

The first man stopped short in the clearing, and the follower nearly ran over him. He took off his hat and wiped the sweat-band with his forefinger and snapped the moisture off. His huge companion dropped his blankets and flung himself down and drank from the surface of the green pool; drank with long gulps, snorting into the water like a horse. The small man stepped nervously beside him.

'Lennie!' he said sharply. 'Lennie, for God' sakes don't drink so much.' Lennie continued to snort into the pool. The small man leaned over and shook him by the shoulder. 'Lennie. You gonna be sick like you was last night.'

Lennie dipped his whole head under, hat and all, and then he sat up on the bank and his hat dripped down on his blue coat and ran down his back. 'That's good,' he said. 'You drink some, George. You take a good big drink.' He smiled happily.

George unslung his bindle and dropped it gently on the bank. 'I ain't sure it's good water,' he said. 'Looks kinda scummy.'

Lennie dabbled his big paw in the water and wiggled his fingers so the water arose in little splashes; rings widened across the pool to the other side and came back again. Lennie watched them go. 'Look, George. Look what I done.'

Language and style

Every writer selects a distinctive **style** of writing to suit:

- the setting they have chosen
- the characters they are creating
- the sort of story they are presenting
- what is happening in the story at a particular point.

One of the first features to note is the narrative style – the point of view from which the story is told. *To Kill a Mockingbird*, for example, is presented in the **first person**, through the eyes of one of the characters in the novel. The writer has **adopted the persona** of a character and the effect of this is to draw the reader more intimately into the events of the story, to make it somehow more personal and immediate.

By contrast, *Lord of the Flies* is presented in the **third person**, through the eyes of an outside observer. The writer therefore seems more detached and objective in their presentation of the story.

The language and style of a prose text can include a wide range of features, for example:

- **vivid adjectives** or **descriptive phrases** – e.g. in the description of the tropical island in *Lord of the Flies*: 'Here and there, **little breezes** crept over the **polished waters** beneath the **haze of heat**. When these breezes reached the platform the **palm-fronds would whisper**, so that **spots of blurred sunlight** slid over their bodies or **moved like bright, winged things** in the shade.'
- **metaphors** and **similes** – e.g. in *Of Mice and Men*, Slim's '**hatchet face** was ageless'; in *The Woodlanders*, '**the bleared white visage** of a sunless winter day emerged **like a dead-born child**.'
- **dialogue** – e.g. the tense dialogue between the signalman and the narrator in Dickens' *The Signal-man*
- **symbols** – e.g. the **conch** or the **pig's head** in *Lord of the Flies*
- **verbs of action or violence** – e.g. in *To Kill a Mockingbird*, the description of the shooting of the mad dog: 'Atticus's hand **yanked** a ball-tipped lever as he brought the gun to his shoulder. The rifle **cracked**. Tim Johnson **leaped**, **flopped over** and **crumpled** on the sidewalk in a brown and white heap.'
- **dialect** or **colloquial expressions** – e.g. in *Of Mice and Men*, Candy 'said excitedly, "We **oughtta let 'im** get away. Curly **go'n'ta wanta get 'im** lynched."'
- **building of tension** – especially towards the end of a chapter or an important event, e.g. in *Lord of the Flies* (end of Chapter 11), the writer hints at the violence that Sam and Eric are about to endure: 'Roger edged past the Chief, only just avoiding pushing him with his shoulder. The **yelling ceased**, and Samneric lay looking up in **quiet terror**. Roger advanced upon them as one wielding a **nameless authority**.'

ACTIVITY 8

In pairs, consider a prose text you have read and identify the **main features** of the use of:

- language
- style.

Note your findings in a bullet-point list.

Themes

In many cases the theme(s) will be the writer's starting point. Writers have very clear purposes in creating a novel – purposes other than simply giving the public 'a good read', or making a lot of money for themselves!

A scene from the 1962 film version of *To Kill A Mockingbird*

There is often a serious purpose behind the story; the writer may want to illustrate their views on a particular issue, or even manipulate readers' attitudes towards that issue. For example, in *To Kill a Mockingbird*, Harper Lee is exposing the problems arising from racial prejudice in the American 'Deep South' and trying to make her readers feel sympathy for victims of such prejudice.

Writers may explore more than one theme in their story and often present a range of views on the way people live their lives or on society and its values.

You can judge the writer's success in illustrating their theme(s) by the impact that you feel when you have studied and reflected upon the work. You may be savouring your pleasure as Elizabeth Bennet in *Pride and Prejudice* finally is rewarded for sticking to her principles. You may be sharing George's misery in the ultimately inevitable tragedy of Lennie in *Of Mice and Men*. Whatever you feel, the strength of your reaction is a testimony to or evidence of the writer's power.

The character Matthew reads 'Funeral Blues' in *Four Weddings and a Funeral*

Poetry can be enthralling and stunning. If you don't believe this, do an internet search and watch 'Funeral Blues' from the film *Four Weddings and a Funeral* – you will almost certainly sense its raw power and emotional depth.

Poets frequently write and redraft their work over months and years – poetry is language constructed in its most concentrated form. So it is unlikely that a hasty 5-minute skim will reveal the depth of quality that a poem may possess. Do not always expect an instant return – you may have to do a little 'Digging' (try Seamus Heaney's poem with this title).

Poetry has always been written to be heard: to be read aloud. So if you are given some poems to read, keep this in mind. It is also worth remembering that not only have the form and language been selected extremely carefully, so too has the punctuation. If you are trying to get to the heart of a poem, be careful to read it according to the punctuation rather than simply line by line.

The aim for your study of poetry is that you can:

- demonstrate a clear and confident understanding of the nature of the poetry and its implications
- illustrate this through a perceptive analysis of the use of poetic and linguistic devices
- show that you are aware of how poets deliberately exploit language to impact upon the reader.

This sounds tough – and it will be if you don't make sure that you have a thorough understanding of the poems that you are going to explore in your Controlled Assessment. Your teacher will take you through these but don't rely on a couple of readings in class. It is essential that you put in time at home so that you build up a confident and complete understanding of the poems. If your private study throws up issues or questions, your teacher will be happy to try to help you – but not if you wait till the morning of your Controlled Assessment!

Language and structure

Poets use many structural and linguistic techniques in their work – sometimes you might think that a poet is trying to use as many of these devices as possible!

Remember that simply recognising linguistic or structural features within a poem – such as simile, metaphor, oxymoron, quatrain, sonnet – is not your primary objective as you study poetry. You need to analyse the effect the poet is trying to achieve by using particular devices. Normally these devices are not used in isolation and do not have individual purposes; they are very carefully combined in an attempt to create both an aural effect on the reader (what you hear) and an emotional impact.

Analysing a poem

Your analysis of a poem can be broken down into smaller tasks, looking at the major elements of a writer's craft:

1 Begin by looking at the **subject matter** of the poem: what event, situation or experience does the poem feature?
2 Does the poet have a **purpose** or a **theme** or a **message**? What was the poet's purpose in writing this? What is being conveyed?
3 What is the **mood** or **feeling** of the poem? Is there a key emotion or mood? Does that mood change during the course of the poem? What response does the poet conjure up in the reader?
4 What are the poem's **key features**? What **techniques** has the poet used, what specific skills have been employed in creating this poem? This should be a major element within your analysis.
5 Finish off with a **summary**. You have analysed the poem, now pull together the significant information. What impact has the poem had upon you? How successful is it? Do you think that it succeeds in its purpose, or if not, why has it failed?

Key features – poetic technique

Identifying the key features of a poem and explaining **how** the poet achieves particular effects is an important part of your analysis. Use this checklist to help you tackle this:

 Structure: How is the poem structured? Does it have a conventional structure such as a sonnet, or an ode? Does it have stanzas with a regular number of lines, or any other features in its structure? What is the effect of this structure?

 Language: How would you describe the poet's use of words – are they vivid, striking, effective, drab, predictable or unusual? Is the language in keeping with the subject and/or theme? What part does the language play in the poem's impact?

 Imagery: Are there any striking examples of similes, metaphors, personification or symbols? What is their effect and what do they achieve?

 Rhythm: Does the poem have a regular (slow or fast) or fragmented rhythm? What is the effect of its rhythm?

 Sounds: Does the poem have any significant sound features, e.g. onomatopoeia, alliteration or assonance? Does the poem rhyme? How do these features influence the impact the poem has on the reader?

Responding to poems

Your Controlled Assessment will be based on a theme and you will be expected to have studied a series of poems. You are not required to make comparisons between these poems but comparison is nevertheless one way of constructing or preparing your response.

There are different ways in which you can construct your answer but remember that the **quality** of your work, rather than the structure you choose, will be most important in determining your mark. Here are the 'pros and cons' of two styles of approach.

The poem-by-poem approach

It is probably more straightforward to work through one poem and then move on to the next one. This means that you have to concentrate on only one poem at a time. The danger is that your response may appear pedestrian or rather plodding in style and you may miss the opportunity to make perceptive cross-references.

To analyse one poem at a time, for each poem use the approach below or follow the 'Analysing a poem' guidelines on page 150.

The **general subject or approach to the theme** taken in the poem. The **context** of the poem – when and where is the poem set and how does this appear to impact on the poem?

Assess the poem in the light of **your own personal preferences**. (Don't feel you have to be too lavish with your praise!) What are the highlights for you? And what didn't really work or wasn't as effective in your view?

The *theme* at the heart of the question

The **poet's purpose** in creating the poem – are they giving us an insight into a personal struggle or observing a situation and presenting their observations as a result?

Use of mood and tone – how does the poet create mood and tone and what effect does this have?

The poet's **use of:**
- **structure** – quatrains/stanzas/sonnets, etc.– what effect does the structure have as the poet explores the theme?
- **vocabulary** – imagery/sounds of words or phrases – striking or unusual use of language? Is there archaic usage? In what way does this affect the mood of the poem?
- **rhythm and rhyme** – has the poet achieved effects using rhyme and rhythm and to what purpose?

Comparing and contrasting poems

Working across poems and poets is a more complicated process but offers you a more dynamic approach. This will require you to be confident enough to spend quite a bit of time on analysis and planning after you have developed a sound understanding of all the poems.

This approach gives you the opportunity to appear insightful and in control of a more complex style of response. As this is a Controlled Assessment you do have the chance to plan thoroughly in advance and organise the shape your response will take.

Compare and contrast:
- The **general subject/approach to the theme** taken in the poems.
- The **context** of each poem – when and where are the different poems set? How does this appear to impact on the poems?

Compare and contrast:
- Assess the poems in the light of **your own personal preferences**. (Don't feel you have to be too lavish with your praise!)
- What are the highlights for you in each poem? What didn't really work or wasn't as effective in your view?

The *theme* at the heart of the question

Compare and contrast:
- The **poets' purposes** in creating the poems – are they giving us an insight into a personal struggle or observing a situation and presenting their observations as a result?
- **Use of mood and tone** – how and why do they differ or in what ways are they similar?

Compare and contrast:
The poets' use of:
- **structure** – quatrains/stanzas/sonnets, etc. – what effect do the structures have as the poets explore the theme?
- **vocabulary** – imagery/sounds of words or phrases – striking or unusual use of language? Is there archaic usage? In what way does this affect the mood of the poems?
- **rhythm and rhyme** – have the poets achieved different effects using rhyme and rhythm and to what purpose?

Preparation will be key to completing this piece successfully. Poetry is the form of literature that often causes most difficulty to GCSE candidates, so be prepared to spend more time on it – not less!

It is important that you write a strong structured essay which constantly refers back to the question asked.

The introduction

Try to begin in an interesting way. Your opening should grab the reader's attention straight away.

You could begin with a 'hook or grabber' to catch their attention. Aim for something which will immediately engage the reader: something thought provoking such as a proverb, a quotation or a question, but make sure that you can relate it to the theme specified in the task or to the text.

The attention grabbers below are all supported by examples that relate to the theme 'Old Age'. Notice how the second sentence leads back to the focus of the study.

Quotation

This could be a quotation about the theme in general, from the writer, about the text or from someone else who has commented on the text or writer. It could even be a line from a song. Here's an example:

Abraham Lincoln said, 'In the end, it's not your years in life that count. It's the life in your years.' Lincoln's words reflecting on how a life has been spent remind us directly of the theme of old age, which is the focus of . . .

Statistic or fact

This could be a statistic or fact about the theme such as:

There are over 296,000 people of pensionable age living in Northern Ireland – that's 16 % of the population. This startling statistic is a reminder that old age is certainly a universal issue. It is no surprise that writers often focus on this issue as a theme. The novel . . .

Proverb

This could be a proverb about the theme. For example:

Life can only be understood backwards, but it must be lived forwards. This proverb relates directly to the theme of old age, which is explored in the short story . . .

ACTIVITY 9

Choose **one** of these themes to insert in the task below.
- Love
- Death
- Conflict
- War
- Racial Tension
- Childhood
- Friendship
- Betrayal

Analyse how the theme of [your choice] has been presented in a text you have studied.

Produce three different engaging openings to the response to this task that make use of:
- a quotation – could be from a song, poem or novel
- a statistic or fact
- a proverb.

The main body of the essay

Here you should aim to explore a range of significant areas. These areas will depend on which text(s) you are studying, but you can adjust the outline below to meet your individual needs. You may need to re-order, prioritise or omit sections so that your essay best meets the requirements of the text(s) you have studied and the question you are asked.

Suggested outline

- **Section 1:** How the writer(s) develop a plot, situation, predicament or scenario in order to focus the reader's attention on the theme
- **Section 2:** How the writer(s) convey the thoughts and feelings of the characters in order to reflect the theme (remember: narrative stance may be important here)
- **Section 3:** How the writer(s) use conversations and interactions between the characters to develop the theme
- **Section 4:** How the writer(s) use symbolism to reflect the theme
- **Section 5:** How the writer(s) use language to reflect the theme

Support what you have to say with brief quotations or references to relevant incidents from the text.

Remember **PEE – Point, Evidence, Explain** – but vary the way in which you construct your points, evidence and explanation so that there is not an increasingly mechanical or formulaic feel to your writing. Use the lists of words and phrases below to help you.

Connectives and discourse markers

- also
- as well as
- moreover
- too
- next
- then
- first
- second
- third
- finally
- meanwhile
- above all
- in particular
- significantly
- equally
- similarly
- likewise
- as with
- whereas
- instead of
- alternatively
- otherwise
- unlike
- on the other hand
- for example
- as revealed by
- however
- indeed
- notably
- so
- thus
- therefore
- except
- if
- yet
- apart from
- because
- although
- unless
- especially

Point	Evidence	Explain
• firstly	• for example	• we can conclude that
• initially	• as revealed by	• it appears that
• furthermore	• this is shown when	• it is possible that
• also	• demonstrated by	• this suggests
• to begin with	• for instance	• this makes it seem
• in addition	• an instance	• which makes us think
• to start with	• to show that	• perhaps the reader can infer
• additionally	• such as	
• moreover		
• then		
• to conclude		
• finally		

It is important to bear in mind that there are two basics to be balanced here:

- what you say
- how you say it.

As you complete each paragraph, look back at its content and ask yourself if have you answered the question. Doing this will ensure that you are not straying off the point and failing to address the question properly!

Use **connectives** and **discourse markers**, such as those on the left, to link your paragraphs.

Concluding the essay

Round off your piece with a conclusion in which you summarise and reinforce the points which you have already made.

You want the final impression to be a positive one. Never finish on a completely new point. It is a good idea to summarise your previous key ideas and then round off with a concluding thought. Try to end your essay in an interesting way, just as you began it in an attention-grabbing manner. This will allow your concluding statement or thought to stay in the mind of the reader long after they have finished reading your piece.

When writing a thematic essay you might end with how the text has made you feel or how it has challenged any ideas that you had about the theme. Here is an example of a conclusion to a piece on the theme of love:

The media bombards teenagers with a romanticised view of love. I should know – I'm one of them! I dream of my Prince Charming sweeping me off my feet, however what I have realised through the study of this text is that the old adage 'The course of love ne'er did run smooth' is true of real life. I will try to wait a bit longer before I fall in love!

 Student response

'They who are of the opinion that money will do everything, may very well be suspected to do everything for money.' George Savile

Money is the focus of many of Maupassant's stories including the story I will be studying, 'A Day in the Country'. This story makes us question whether or not money is the root of all evil. In 'A Day in the Country' we meet two very poor families and one very rich couple. When one poor family sells a child to the rich couple it sparks off jealousy in the other family who then become unbearable.

In this story, whether money is the root of all evil or not depends on the social and historical circumstances the characters are in. In his life, Maupassant had been through the circumstances of being well-off and very poor which clearly influenced his writing.

In 'A Day in the Country' money can be seen as both good and evil. An obvious circumstance in which it seems to be evil is whenever a child is actually sold for money, 'I would very much like to take your little boy away.' However, the Vallins have, by selling their child, not only ensured a better life for young Jean, but also for themselves and the rest of their family, 'the Vallins pottered along quite comfortably on their pension.' Money does not change the Vallins family or even Jean, who receives a much better education than would have been possible if he had not been sold. Money does not spoil Jean and he does not feel any anger against, or that he is above, his mother or father. 'He walked straight into the Vallins hovel as though it was his own.'

ACTIVITY 10

Below and on the next page is an example of a student's response to the short story *A Day in the Country* by the French writer Guy de Maupassant. The question asked was:

> Analyse how the theme of money has been presented in the story studied.

Read the response and identify the strengths of the essay as a response to a literary text. (Don't be too concerned if you have not read the story, it's the response that is the focus!) Note your findings in a bullet-point list.

Guy de Manpassant

In Madame d'Hubiere's case however, money does spoil her, as well as thinking the money can make everyone happy, 'think about his happiness', money has made Madame d'Hubieres think that she can always have her own way, 'In the tear choked voice of a little girl who always got her own way.' The Tuvache family are another example of where money can be seen to be the root of all evil. Having refused to sell their child on the basis of what they believe is morally right, 'You want us to sell our son? No! Never!' the Tuvaches, especially Madame Tuvache, become increasingly embittered and seemingly jealous of their neighbours, 'each day coarse jeers were bellowed on one doorstep'.

Young Charlot Tuvache grows up believing that he is something special because he was not sold, when he sees Jean Vallin return in all his finery his pride and arrogance is stung and he lashes out at his parents, 'I'll never forgive you. Never.' After years of believing they were right not to sell their son, the Tuvaches are repaid by the arrogant young man they have raised leaving them with no one to support them, 'and he vanished into the night'. The Vallins on the other hand have not lost Jean as he returned to them. Maupassant's description of the two peasant families reflects the peasants he saw living in Normandy. The Vallins seem to represent the boisterous, energetic side Maupassant saw in them. However the Tuvache family show his belief that their 'dreary lives' could give them 'narrow souls'.

The story presents the dilemma of whether it is right to sell your child; most people would initially say that it is definitely wrong to do so but Maupassant's writing makes us question our own beliefs. It seems clear that the child and family which were the happiest were the Vallins who do sell their child. The Tuvache family, who seemed at first to represent what was morally right become so embittered, and cause Charlot to become so arrogant, that we would find it very hard to take their side on the issue. Perhaps if the Vallins had not been so very poor we would not be able to find selling a child morally right but in this instance it would seem to be so.

I do not believe that it is money that is the root of all evil, but, as it tells us in the Bible it is the love of money. The Tuvaches jealousy of the Vallins and, basically money, makes them stubborn and bitter and Charlot arrogant and ungrateful. Money can bring happiness and opportunities, as shown through Jean Vallin's grateful character but whenever people become too obsessed with money itself it changes their character for the worse.

Study of Written Language/ Literature: Controlled Assessment Success

Matching grades to studies of written language/literature

In these Controlled Assessment Tasks the essential qualities the examiners will be looking for are highlighted at the important grade boundaries. Read these descriptions *carefully*; they tell you what your responses should be like.

Grade C writing:

 shows an engaged, personal response to literary texts

 refers to relevant aspects: language, main ideas, themes and characters (and context)

 shows some understanding of the intended impact upon the reader

 makes references from text to support straightforward, valid ideas and interpretations.

Grade A/A* writing:

 demonstrates a discriminating analysis that offers critical and perceptive interpretations of literary texts

 explores key aspects of use of language, structure and presentation (and social, historical and cultural context)

 explores how these key aspects engage and affect the reader

 makes aptly selected textual references that indicate a confident awareness of the text.

Literary responses: Key to success

Efficient essay writing

 Keep your essay focused. Always link what you have to say back to the question – but vary how you do this so think of synonyms for words that occur frequently in your essay, such as:

- facts: factors, areas or aspects
- discuss: consider or evaluate.

 Try to use an extensive range of words which will enable you to say exactly what you want to say. Reading helps expand your vocabulary.

 Generally try to avoid abbreviations: etc., e.g., i.e., TV

 Write out numbers unless they are awkwardly long: write 1 as one but 123,476

Check your spelling and grammar.

 Use signpost words and phrases:

- for development: in addition . . . furthermore . . . also . . . similarly . . .
- for emphasis: in particular . . . especially . . .

 A range of punctuation will demonstrate that you can handle language confidently and will clarify what you are saying by controlling the pace. Semi-colons and colons are particularly useful and you can also use exclamations when appropriate.

 Use a new paragraph for each area being explored. Avoid too many short paragraphs as they give a disjointed feel to your work. Equally, avoid very long paragraphs as the reader's concentration will be tested.

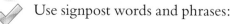 You will be credited for using brief quotations to back up points that you are making. If you are quoting more than one line of a play or poem, then use the line spacing and layout as it appears in the text. Individual words and phrases can simply be put in inverted commas and presented in the body of your answer without any formatting.

 When you are referring to the title of a text it should be put in inverted commas – this will clarify whether you are writing about 'Macbeth' (the play itself) or writing about Macbeth as a character in the play of the same name.

The content of your essay

Maintain focus on the purpose of the task – the question!

Show a sustained awareness of the intended audience – the examiner – and use language that is appropriate to that audience.

Content coverage needs to deal with all aspects of the question and be well judged and detailed.

Interpretations/arguments need to be convincingly developed and supported by relevant detail from the text(s).

Ideas should be carefully selected and prioritised to construct a coherent discussion – so make sure that you plan and prioritise.

Paragraphs should have a topic sentence – this will help you stay on task.

Use this **writing template/planner** to help you develop your ability to write a response to literary text(s). Remember to adapt it to suit you and your purpose!

Paragraph section		Jot down notes, key words or key ideas you might use:
Introduction ● 'Attention grabber' ● Link 'attention grabber' to theme and text ● Outline the areas you aim to explore in this essay		
Section 1 How the writer(s) develop a plot/ situation in order to focus the reader's attention upon the theme.	Throughout the body of the essay remember to use: ✓ quotes to support your writing ✓ a wide range of vocabulary ✓ accurate spelling, punctuation and grammar ✓ connectives and discourse markers.	
Section 2 How the writer(s) convey the thoughts and feelings of the characters in order to reflect the theme (remember narrative stance may figure largely here).		
Section 3 How the writer(s) use the conversations and interactions of the characters to develop the theme.		
Section 4 How the writer(s) use symbolism throughout to reflect the theme.		
Section 5 How the writer(s) use language to reflect the theme.		
Last paragraph ● Conclusion ● Write an engaging/thoughtful conclusion ● Relate the theme presented in the text to your own personal experience		

It is quite likely that in the course of your preparations for the Controlled Assessment Tasks you will be given the opportunity to write an essay (not on the actual Controlled Assessment question that you will be answering) to get used to the write-up process.

Below are checklists for success which may prove useful both before and after you have attempted any such 'practice writing'.

Checklist for success: working towards Grade C	✔
Have you shown a straightforward understanding of the **writer's intentions**?	
Have you shown recognition of the **central theme(s)**?	
Have you demonstrated an understanding of some of the use that has been made of **literary devices**?	
Have you discussed all of the **features** set out in the question?	
Have you presented your interpretations in an **organised and fluent** essay?	
Have you used words and phrases that help to **clarify meaning**?	

Checklist for success: working towards Grade A/A★	✔
Have you demonstrated a clear and confident understanding of the **text and its implications**?	
Have you presented a perceptive analysis of the **literary techniques and devices**?	
Have you shown a clear awareness of how writers **exploit literary techniques and language** to impact upon the reader/audience?	
Have you constructed a **fluent and assured answer** that is **confidently structured and** competently **sustains a perceptive discussion**?	
Have you employed an **appropriate, extended vocabulary** precisely to **sustain focus** on the issues under discussion?	

Unit 4
English Language and English

Task 3 (English Language) and Tasks 4–5 (English)

Introduction to Writing Creatively for Purpose

This element of Unit 4 is for both English Language and English. In both cases it is tested through Controlled Assessment and assesses **Writing**.

Target outcome: To deliberately mould language to create a specific written outcome that has a definite audience and purpose.

Target skills

The target skills are exactly the same for both Specifications. The target skills you will learn about in the task(s) will enable you to:

 write to communicate clearly, effectively and imaginatively

 select a form appropriate to purpose

 demonstrate knowledge of the conventions of the form selected

 organise information and ideas

 select vocabulary appropriate to task

 use a range of sentence structures for effect

 use accurate grammar, spelling and punctuation.

Assessment Objective

Your Assessment Objective in the task(s) is:

Writing

i) Write clearly, effectively and imaginatively to engage the reader.

ii) Use a form and select vocabulary that matches purpose and audience.

iii) Organise ideas/information logically into sentences and paragraphs.

iv) Make use of language and structural features for effect.

v) Use a range of sentence structures as well as punctuate and spell accurately.

Controlled Assessment Task(s)

In **English Language** you will be expected to complete **one** Controlled Assessment piece. This is Task 3 and is worth 15% of your final GCSE grade.

You will have 2 hours under Controlled Assessment conditions to respond.

You will choose an audience and appropriate form and then write imaginatively to engage.

In **English** you will be expected to complete **two** Controlled Assessment pieces to inform, persuade, entertain or engage. In one of these you will be required to use transactional writing skills (a newspaper article, leaflet or blog etc.). These are Tasks 4 and 5 and are worth 20% of your GCSE grade.

You will have 3 hours under Controlled Assessment conditions to write. For both **English Language** and **English** you will write on any three themes.

1 Writing Creatively/Writing for Purpose

The task will allow you to:

 choose a **theme** from the selection supplied by CCEA

 decide on a clear **purpose** for your writing – to inform, persuade or entertain your audience

 choose an **audience** for your writing

 select an appropriate **form** for your writing (one of the pieces must be transactional).

You will have the opportunity to show an awareness of different formats, such as:

• newspaper article	• report	• podcast
• letter	• brochure	• story
• leaflet	• editorial	• script
• account	• polemic	• biography
• diary entry	• review	• speech
• blog	• commentary	• poem.

To give you an idea of the range of possible tasks, here are some examples:

- Write a newspaper article reporting on the competitive nature of a local sporting derby.
- Write a blog on the conflict between the increased use of CCTV and the individual's right to privacy.
- Write a polemic (a passionate, strongly worded, and often controversial argument) against female celebrity role models.
- Write Katherine's (Kate's) diary entry revealing her thoughts about Petruchio in *The Taming of the Shrew*.
- Write a short story creating an atmosphere of suspense.
- Write a review of a film explaining how it created an atmosphere of suspense and how successful this was.

Remember: It is important to select an appropriate form for your writing – to engage your audience on your topic.

This gives you the opportunity to create an original piece of writing using your own imagination, invention and ideas.

You will need to:

Whatever form your creative piece takes, you should set out to influence the reader to reflect upon the theme being considered. To achieve this you need to engage the interest and, perhaps, challenge the views of your audience, so put into practice all you have learnt about writing effectively.

The planning period for this Controlled Assessment is much longer than the planning time available in an exam, so make the most of it and make sure you are properly prepared when you go into the formally supervised writing session.

One of the most obvious ways you can sustain the reader's attention is by writing effective openings and conclusions.

Openings

Depending on which form you have chosen, there are many different techniques you could use to begin your creative writing. Here are some ideas:

- humour to entertain
- a dramatic moment
- dialogue between characters
- an intriguing situation
- descriptive writing, e.g. a character or place
- an emotive opening, e.g. to provoke shock or fear
- a first-person narrator for direct appeal
- a provocative or emphatic statement
- persuasive devices, e.g. questions, repetition or a list
- a personal anecdote or real-life scenario
- an apt quotation
- effective use of factual material.

ACTIVITY 1

In small groups, discuss the effectiveness of the techniques used to capture the reader's attention in the openings of texts A–D. As well as the list on this page, also consider the use of:

- narrative stance
- verb tense
- figures of speech
- word choice
- sentence lengths and structures
- informal structures.

Text A

This is the opening of a newspaper feature article.

The television chef Jamie Oliver launched a one-man crusade against Turkey Twizzlers, but what about that other favourite of our nation's school canteens: the chicken nugget? Reading the ingredient lists on boxes of nuggets from various major supermarkets makes for a nauseating experience. Look closely at the packets and you will see just how little chicken each actually contains.

Felicity Lawrence, who investigated the state of the chicken nugget industry for her book, *Not on the Label*, says that at the low end – manufacturers that produce nuggets for school menus, for example – 'mechanically recovered meat' is used. This involves placing a butchered chicken carcass through a machine to produce a 'slurry of protein, which is then bound back together with polyphosphates and gums'. Fat and skin are often added. Now, do you fancy some chicken with that nugget?

Text B

This is the opening of a teenager's blog.

Hey, what's so bad about Bebo?? My parents have been on my case AGAIN about the amount of time I spend online. Major stress! They don't seem to realise that things have moved on since the olden days when they were young! They don't even TRY to understand when I explain what's good about Bebo. They don't LISTEN! Aghhhhh!!

I think Bebo is brilliant. It was incredibly simple and soooo easy to set up a fun, colourful personal webpage. I can now stay in touch with my mates through music, pictures, jokes and games as well as words. I also really, really, really enjoy watching the funny videos, leaving comments and reading the comments people put on my page. Got to be good for my communication skills!! Plus, it's fun!! Where's the harm in that?

Text D

This is the opening of the novel *Caught in the Crossfire* by Alan Gibbons.

There is something in the shadows. Rabia Khan is worried. She has found herself in the wrong place at the wrong time. She sees the long fingers of the night clawing into the alley and gives a little shudder. She ought to know better than to be this end of the Ravensmoor Road after dark. Things have a habit of happening here. This stretch of road has a history. Rabia's father has warned her often enough – warned her until all she could do was defy him and go there anyway, just to remind him of her growing independence, her right to think for herself and take risks. Now she is regretting the way she has ignored his advice not to go on her own. It seems Dad knew best after all.

Text C

This is the opening of the short story *The Balaclava Story* by George Layton.

Tony and Barry both had one. I reckon half the kids in our class had one. But I didn't. My mum wouldn't even listen to me.

'You're not having a balaclava! What do you want a balaclava for in the middle of summer?'

I must've told her about ten times why I wanted a balaclava.

'I want one so's I can join the balaclava boys . . .'

'Go and wash your hands for tea, and don't be so silly.'

She turned away from me to lay the table, so I put the curse of the middle finger on her. This was pointing both your middle fingers at somebody when they weren't looking. Tony had started it when Miss Taylor gave him a hundred lines for flicking paper pellets at Jennifer Greenwood. He had to write out a hundred times: 'I must not fire missiles because it is dangerous and liable to damage someone's eye.'

Tony tried to tell Miss Taylor that he hadn't fired a missile, he'd just flicked a paper pellet, but she threw a piece of chalk at him and told him to shut up.

Alan Gibbons

Endings

Endings are as important as openings so you need to plan carefully how to conclude your piece effectively.

ACTIVITY 2

The spider diagram below contains some options for effective endings. In groups, complete the diagram by adding your suggestions.

Share your ideas with the rest of the class so that everyone has as many ideas as possible.

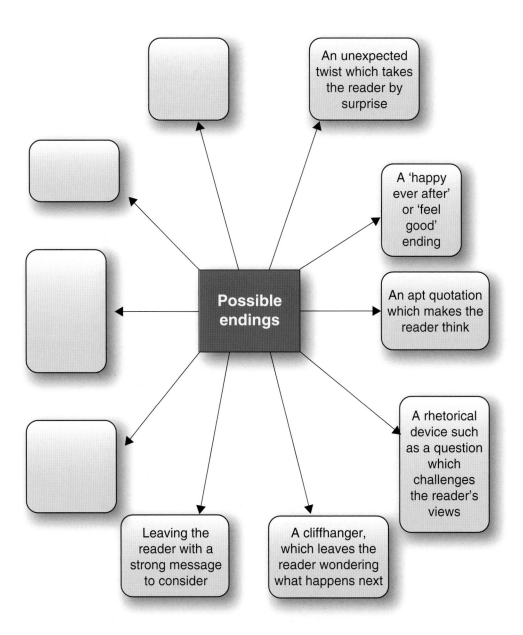

An unexpected twist which takes the reader by surprise

A 'happy ever after' or 'feel good' ending

An apt quotation which makes the reader think

A rhetorical device such as a question which challenges the reader's views

A cliffhanger, which leaves the reader wondering what happens next

Leaving the reader with a strong message to consider

Possible endings

One option is to write a story which reflects your chosen theme. A great story is something everyone enjoys but there are a number of key elements you need to consider to make your story enjoyable:

- **Plot:** This is the basic storyline. It can be relatively straightforward and uncomplicated or contain unexpected twists and turns.
- **Structure:** How your story begins; how events unfold and develop, perhaps to a dramatic climax; how your story ends; how you use different sentence structures for maximum effect.
- **Narrative stance:** The viewpoint from which the story is told – most writers use first- or third-person narrators.
- **Characters:** You will have time to develop only one main character and perhaps two or three others. The storyline should revolve around these characters and how they interact.
- **Setting:** Where the events of the story take place. This is an important factor in generating mood and atmosphere as well as pulling the reader into the narrative.
- **Language:** The words and phrases and linguistic techniques selected are at the heart of creating a story that will absorb the reader.

Plot and structure

In any narrative, whether the story is told through poetry, prose or drama, plot and structure are closely connected:

- A story is often structured as a series of **key moments** each of which move the narrative forward. Some of these key moments may surprise or shock the reader.
- The **time sequence** of how events are presented is a crucial feature of the structure. A common structural device is the use of **flashback**. Letting the reader glimpse the past in this way can add dramatic impact. It can also provide insight into what motivates characters, so helping the reader understand their behaviour. For example, a plot can unfold in a **chronological** manner or **time shifts** can be used such as starting in the present, going back to past events and concluding by coming back full circle to the present.
- Structure is also linked to changes in **mood** or **atmosphere**. This should be varied in order to keep the audience interested. For example, the opening could be light-hearted with the mood gradually darkening as the story builds up to a dramatic **climax**. **Tonal shifts** can be introduced through description, the use of setting and how characters are presented.
- **Foreshadowing** is a more complex device used to good effect in Steinbeck's *Of Mice and Men*. The shooting of Candy's dog foreshadows the tragic end to this famous novel.

- The **pace** or speed at which the action is revealed should vary in order to create effects such as an increase in tension or a sense of excitement. Events can happen in quick succession or there could be a series of crises as the action builds up to an exciting conclusion.

ACTIVITY 3

Find and read a short story. (You might choose *The Signal-man* by Charles Dickens or *The Fib* by George Layton.)

Charles Dickens

Using the bullet list on plot and structure above and opposite, identify how the writer develops the narrative for maximum impact on the reader. Note your findings in a grid like the one below.

Key or significant moments	Time sequence	Mood and atmosphere	Pace of action
Opening sequence			
First key moment			
Second key moment			
Next key moment			
Next key moment (and so on as required)			
Climax			
Ending			

You can also use a grid like the one above to help you plan your narrative writing. It will help you think through how the key moments in your story can connect to changes in time, mood and pace.

Remember: The climax of your story does not have to occur at the end.

4 Creating Characters

When you are describing your characters, you need to think about how you wish the reader to react to them – you may want the reader to feel negatively towards one character but empathise with another. You are in charge. You are the writer, so you can manipulate the reader's response by **how** you present your characters.

Look at how this has been achieved in the following example:

> Mr Cassidy is **introduced to the reader** in a way which immediately creates a negative impression. Note the references to the teachers' nicknames and the use of punctuation to emphasis the word 'disaster' (it is parenthesised – set apart – by the use of hyphens).

> The description of Mr Cassidy's **appearance** reinforces the initial negative impression through use of adjectives, e.g. 'old and grey', 'mean little eyes', 'grotty tweed jacket'. The classroom **setting** reflects his unpleasantness. The chewing gum 'stuck on the edges of the tables' neatly conveys how little his students respect him.

> Note the use of repetition and a list of three to summarise his character. The references to his **behaviour**, e.g. 'slouched at his desk' and 'never looked at us' portray him as an uncaring, inadequate teacher.

> The **reactions** of the students reveal much about this teacher. It is clear they do not enjoy his classes. The simile and reference to the wasp highlight the nasty atmosphere in his classroom.

Mr Carew was on a career break. Instead of him we had Mr Gormless Gormley for English and – disaster – Sad Case for History. His real name was Mr Cassidy but he had always been called Sad Case, though it could just as well have been Bad Case or Mad Case.

He was old and grey, had mean little eyes, always wore the same grotty tweed jacket and hadn't a clue how to teach, which was sad when you realised he'd been a teacher for about thirty years. You could tell that he hated teaching, hated kids, hated everything about school. When you went into his room, he'd be slouched at his desk pretending to read. He never looked at us coming in. There was always litter on the floor, everything was shabby, loads of graffiti, masses of chewing-gum stuck on the edges of the tables not underneath like in all the other rooms. The tables were crammed together and Sad Case never bothered to straighten them out. He was always losing his temper and threatening terrible things. The atmosphere in his classroom was brutal, like eating porridge on a picnic. You knew that nobody had enjoyed one of Sad Case's classes in years and he hadn't enjoyed one either. The only buzz you got in his room was when a wasp flew in by mistake.

He was rude too. 'Shut up, ya shower of tramps,' he'd say. 'You over there, ya good-for-nothing lout without a brain in your head, sit down and shut up.' He never knew our names. He just didn't bother to learn them.

Our first Sad Case class was awful. He snarled and growled for the first five minutes then handed out grubby, graffiti-covered pages with the smudgy heading, 'First Year Revision Test'.

> The use of **dialogue** brings this character to life. His rudeness is demonstrated this through the use of direct speech.

> The **narrator** conveys his dislike for Mr Cassidy throughout. The **intended effect on the audience** is that we 'see' through his eyes so we share his disapproval and empathise with the students, e.g. we too are outraged to learn that he hands out a revision test in his first lesson and that it is 'grubby' and 'graffiti-covered'. There is also a sense of **anticipation** of conflict to come.

ACTIVITY 4

Have a go at creating an interesting character of your own. Use the analysis of Mr Cassidy and the spider diagram below to help you. Remember – don't be boring!

Background details such as information about family or giving your character a 'past' will make them more convincing for the reader. These details can be woven into the story or you can reveal a particular detail at a key moment for dramatic impact.

Decide on a name. This helps bring a character to life. Sometimes writers decide to keep a character nameless to make a point, e.g. Curley's wife in *Of Mice and Men*.

Take **inspiration** from people you know or have met. Most characters are a mixture of 'real life' and invention.

You can reveal a lot about your character from the **use of direct speech**: what your character says and what is said about him/her.

Writers often introduce a character through a description of **physical details** and **appearance**. This can also be done as the story unfolds. It helps the reader get to know a character.

How to create a character

The way your character **behaves** – what he/she does or doesn't do – in certain situations and at key moments is a vital aspect of how he/she is presented to the reader.

A character can be shaped if they **develop** or **change** during the narrative.

Other characters' **reactions** to your character add another dimension: how other characters behave towards the person as well as what they say and think about them.

Carefully consider the **intended effect on the reader**: how you wish the reader to react to your character and to how they interact with others is important in sustaining interest.

A character's thoughts and feelings can be revealed through an **internal monologue**. A first person narrator can pull the reader into a situation by speaking directly to the audience.

The setting:

- locates your narrative in a specific time and place, making your story more believable
- creates visual images which make it possible for the reader to imagine the scenes you describe
- helps you develop a character as it allows you to reveal more about them
- can evoke the mood and atmosphere you want to create
- can foreshadow what is to come in the story, so building up a sense of anticipation in your reader.

Creating appropriate background details and surroundings for your characters and events is essential to engage your reader.

The contribution of setting in involving the reader is clearly demonstrated in the following extract. Here, the main character, Ian, is being pursued by McClean, a villain also known as wolfman. He has taken refuge in an empty flat in a tower block but McClean is closing in on him. At this point in the story Ian feels his only choice and chance of escape is to climb out onto a ledge that is eleven floors up.

Ian is clinging to the wall, his face pressed into it, the muscles in his leg starting to buzz and ache, the tendons round his ankles tugging as they take the strain of holding him on that eight-inch ledge. But that is only half of it. McClean's head is sticking out of the window no more than a yard or two away.

Have you seen me? You must have.

But McClean is squinting straight ahead. He squeezes the rain from his eyes. He's half-blinded by the whip and sting of the wind.

What the hell is this? You must have seen me.

But McClean's eyes fail to fasten on Ian. The wolfman looks down not sideways, then, incredibly, he starts to withdraw his head. A moment later, Ian hears the click of the catch. There is no way back. He has to go forward. Even as he braces himself to take his first step he can't believe he hasn't been seen.

This is just a stupid game of cat and mouse. It's got to be. How can you have missed me? You must have seen me. You must!

But as quickly as he appeared McClean has gone. It's too good to be true. Ian tries to imagine himself in McClean's place. Could I possibly be that close to somebody and not see anything?

No, you've seen me.

I know what this is. You're just going to work your way round to the other side of the building and wait for me there.

Cold as it is up there on his precarious eleventh-floor perch, Ian is sweating. His palms are slimy against the wall. Ever so slowly he moves his right hand from the wall and wipes it on his shirt. Then, returning his right hand to the wall and easing his left off, he repeats the operation. Finally, realising he has no choice but to go on, he makes his first move since McClean's head appeared at the window.

Trying not to look down the dizzying precipice of the building, Ian takes the weight on his toes and on the balls of his feet and starts to inch forward. A few more steps and those aching muscles will be shrieking with pain.

You can do this, he tells himself.

He barks insults at himself under his breath. Coward! Idiot! It doesn't matter how much noise he makes, not in this howling wind.

Come on! You can do it.

But, as he feels the tendons in his legs starting to shudder again, as he feels the wind trying to suck him off the wall, he isn't sure he can . . .

He knows that the keenness of his mind is all that is standing between him and fatal impact with the ground below. So, heels over the drop, toes cling to the ledge, he edges forward, sliding his feet. And it is left foot, right foot, palms flattened against the bricks, fingernails clawing at the narrow crevice.

Not far now.

He continues to shuffle along the ledge. His movements are slow and deliberate, all the more so because of the rain that is trickling down the brickwork, sluicing over the ledge and puddling round his feet.

A few more steps.

On he goes. Out of the corner of his eye he can see street lamps and the necklace of lights strung along the motorway. The night wind is a dark muzzle sucking at him, trying to chew him loose off that wall.

Just a few more steps.

There's the balcony! With a little stretching he could put his hand on the rail.

But I mustn't. If I rush now I could throw it all away.

Instead, Ian actually forces himself, completely against instinct, to slow down. Legs quivering, muscles crying out, he shuffles slowly along to the balcony. Then he can't move any more. He tries to take a step, but something is holding his foot to the ledge.

This can't be happening.

He tries to see what can be gluing him to the ledge like this. His whole body quivering, the rain dripping off his eyebrows and his nose, he slides his forehead down the brickwork. There's the ground below.

Oh God. Oh my God!

He tries to shift his foot, doing it by force, kicking at the obstruction. It's the wrong move. The sole of his shoe slips off the ledge. Slithers into the black void below him. Death has hold of his ankle, pulling him down.

No!

He wants to scream but bites down in terror and clamps his foot back on the ledge. He gulps down icy breaths of air.

Oh Jeez!

Now he can see. His right shoelace has come undone and he is standing on it with his left. Even after kicking his foot right off the ledge he has stood back down on it.

Stupid.

He raises his foot and shakes the wet shoelace from the sole of his shoe. He does it carefully this time. With control. He is free. Wearily, hardly able to believe that it is over, he hauls himself over the balcony rail then slides down and lies exhausted on the other side.

These questions (right) are intended to highlight the writer's strategies. Using similar techniques to craft your narrative writing will help you sustain the reader's interest.

ACTIVITY 5

Read the account on pages 170–171 and then answer the questions below.

1 What is the intended effect on the reader of using the present tense in the opening paragraph and throughout the piece?
2 How does the writer use descriptive details to create a sense of where this action is taking place?
3 Ian is in real danger. How is this impression conveyed to the reader?
4 How do Ian's physical reactions to his situation and the use of internal monologue contribute to developing an extremely tense atmosphere?
5 Find examples of figures of speech. Explain how these help reinforce Ian's predicament.
6 How does the writer appeal to the reader's senses? Pick out examples and analyse how these enhance the reader's involvement.
7 How is this piece of writing structured to sustain the reader's interest in Ian's plight? Comment on how the variety of sentence structures contributes to highlighting Ian's precarious situation.
8 In what other ways does the writer use setting to create a memorable scene?

Use this mnemonic to help you remember the key features to bring your setting to life.

L **Location:** Establish a sense of where different scenes take place.

Language: Select words and phrases that will influence your reader's reactions and emotions. Dialogue or direct speech can play an important role in creating setting.

A **Atmosphere:** This is the mood or tone you wish to convey to the reader. You can use setting to bring about tonal shifts and contrasts to add interest, e.g. start a story with a happy mood but build up a growing sense of tension. Pathetic fallacy (using the weather or landscape to reflect mood) can be used to reinforce a particular atmosphere or reflect a character's feelings.

D **Descriptive** Descriptive or visual details bring a scene to life
D **Details:** by adding convincing touches. A well-placed detail can have real impact.

E **Effect on the reader:** Aim to create interest through appealing to emotions such as fear, anger, joy or shock. Encouraging a sense of empathy with a character will also engage the reader.

R **Reactions of the characters:** The physical and emotional reactions of the characters within a setting also pull the reader into what is happening. Thoughts and feelings can be revealed through internal monologue.

S **Senses:** As well as creating imagery, appeal to other senses – smell, taste or touch – to make your writing more vivid.

Structure: Sustain the reader's participation through a variety of sentence structures.

ACTIVITY 6

Create your own setting for a narrative, putting into practice what you have learnt in this section.

A familiar situation might be the easiest to start with – a family or classroom scenario, for example.

Direct speech can be used to develop believable characters and to create atmosphere. However, writers also use dialogue to generate interest, involvement and excitement.

We do this ourselves when we are relating something that has happened to us. Without even thinking about it, we usually quote what was said to us. This is because we instinctively know that using direct speech will make the anecdote more interesting for our listener.

The opening (below) to Alan Gibbons' novel *The Edge* shows this in action. What actually happens is that a mother wakes up her son and tells him to get out of bed. It's not very exciting when expressed like that! Gibbons, however, has added dialogue and internal monologue to bring the scene to life, so creating an opening full of tension.

Note how the dialogue in this extract is set out and punctuated. (You may need to revise how to do this.) Observe also the effect of using a variety of 'saying' verbs such as 'hisses' and 'whispers'.

He awakes with a start. Somebody is shaking him. Roughly.

'What. . .?'

A hand covers his mouth, choking off the question. For a moment he gives in to a surge of panic, then he makes out a face in the darkness. His mother. She is crouching by his bed, one hand on the headboard, one clamped to the lower half of his face. He can see her properly now, her features slightly illuminated by the streetlamp a couple of doors away. It's her eyes he notices first, the frightened, pleading expression. Oh no, don't tell me it's happening again. He has learned to read his mother's face. Interpreting her looks, her mouthed warnings, has been essential to his survival. But this he can't read. It is too sudden, too unexpected. He gives a questioning frown.

'We've got to go,' Mum hisses. 'Now.'

'Go? Go where?'

Her hands are waving, palms down, reinforcing the pleading look in her eyes. 'Keep your voice down, Danny,' she whispers. 'Please!'

He does as he is told. His next words are barely audible, 'What's going on?'

'Can't explain. But we have to go. Right now.'

'Chris?'

She shakes her head. Chris. No, not Chris. Danny breathes a sigh of relief. At least this doesn't involve him. Let the Animal rot, please let him rot.

Some stories are told mainly through conversations or exchanges between characters. Much of Steinbeck's novel *Of Mice and Men* is structured in this way. In the next extract Candy, an old man, reluctantly agrees to allow his beloved but ancient dog to be shot.

The dialogue generates a real sense of **empathy** for Candy. What the characters have to say here and elsewhere in this novel, however, also relates to the themes raised in the book. This scene highlights the loneliness and vulnerability of old age. You, too, could reflect upon a given theme through the use of dialogue or by writing a play script.

Notice the use of colloquial, informal speech, which adds authenticity to Steinbeck's writing. Also, Candy's anguish is conveyed in the **way** he speaks and this is **contrasted** by the rough speech of Carlson. Interestingly, Steinbeck mostly uses the straightforward verb 'said' for speech. He does, however, use adverbs such as 'proudly', 'softly' and 'hopefully' to convey feelings.

John Steinbeck

The thick-bodied Carlson came in out of the darkening yard. He walked the other end of the bunk house and turned on the second shaded light. 'Darker'n hell in here,' he said . . . He stopped and sniffed the air, and still sniffing, looked down at the old dog. 'God awmighty, that dog stinks. Get him outta here, Candy! I don't know nothing that stinks as bad as an old dog. You gotta get him out.'

Candy rolled to the edge of his bunk. He reached over and patted the ancient dog, and he apologised, 'I been around him so much I never notice how he stinks.'

'Well, I can't stand him in here,' said Carlson. 'That stink hangs around even after he's gone.' He walked over with his heavy-legged stride and looked down at the dog. 'Got no teeth,' he said. 'He's all stiff with rheumatism. He ain't no good to you, Candy. An' he ain't no good to himself. Why'n't you shoot him, Candy?'

The old man squirmed uncomfortably. 'Well – hell! I had him so long. Had him since he was a pup. I herded sheep with him.' He said proudly, 'You wouldn't think it to look at him now, but he was the best damn sheep dog I ever seen.'

George said, 'I seen a guy in Weed that had an Airedale could herd sheep. Learned it from the other dogs.'

Carlson was not to be put off. 'Look, Candy. This ol' dog jus' suffers hisself all the time. If you was to take him out and shoot him right in the back of the head –' he leaned over and pointed, '– right there, why he'd never know what hit him.'

Candy looked about unhappily. 'No,' he said softly. 'No, I couldn't do that. I had 'im too long.'

'He don't have no fun,' Carlson insisted. 'And he stinks to beat hell. Tell you what. I'll shoot him for you. Then it won't be you that does it.'

Candy threw his legs off his bunk. He scratched the white stubble whiskers on his cheek nervously. 'I'm so used to him,' he said softly. 'I had him from a pup.'

'Well, you ain't bein' kind to him keepin' him alive,' said Carlson. 'Look, Slim's bitch got a litter right now. I bet Slim would give you one of them pups to raise up, wouldn't you, Slim?'

The skinner had been studying the old dog with his calm eyes. 'Yeah,' he said. 'You can have a pup if you want to.' He seemed to shake himself free for speech. 'Carl's right, Candy. That dog ain't no good to himself. I wisht somebody'd shoot me if I got old an' a cripple.'

Candy looked helplessly at him, for Slim's opinions were law. 'Maybe it'd hurt him,' he suggested. 'I don't mind takin' care of him.'

Carlson said, 'The way I'd shoot him, he wouldn't feel nothing. I'd put the gun right there.' He pointed with his toe. 'Right back of the head. He wouldn't even quiver'. . . He continued to look down at the old dog. Candy watched him uneasily. At last Carlson said, 'If you want me to, I'll put the old devil out of his misery right now and get it over with. Ain't nothing left for him. Can't eat, can't see, can't even walk without hurtin'.'

Candy said hopefully, 'You ain't got no gun.'

'The hell I ain't. Got a Luger. It won't hurt him none at all.'

Candy said, 'Maybe tomorra. Le's wait til tomorra.'

'I don't see no reason for it,' said Carlson. He went to his bunk, pulled his bag from underneath it and took a Luger pistol. 'Let's get it over with,' he said. 'We can't sleep with him stinkin' around in here.' He put the pistol in his hip pocket.

Candy looked a long time at Slim to try to find some reversal. And Slim gave him none. At last Candy said softly and hopelessly, 'Awright – take 'im.' He did not look down at the dog at all. He lay back on his bunk and crossed his arms behind his head and stared at the ceiling . . .

Slim said, 'Carlson.'

'Yeah?'

'You know what to do.'

'What ya mean, Slim?'

'Take a shovel,' said Slim shortly.

'Oh, sure! I get you.' He led the dog out into the darkness.

The easiest way to write from someone else's point of view is to imagine you are a particular person or character in a text and narrate your thoughts and feelings in the first person. This narration could take many different forms: for example, dairy entry, letter, stream of consciousness, speech or blog.

You can explore a theme very effectively in this way as you can really get inside another person's situation.

ACTIVITY 7

This activity gives you an opportunity to practise creating empathy. Read this extract in which Stanley, a young boy, has been brought to a tough prison camp. In this scene, he doesn't say much but you can imagine his inner turmoil at the thought of what lies ahead.

Imagine you are Stanley. Write a diary entry describing your thoughts and feelings about your first day at Camp Green Lake.

We have looked at how dialogue can connect a character to the reader and help create a sense of empathy. Writing with empathy means writing from someone else's point of view.

Stanley felt somewhat dazed as the guard unlocked his handcuffs and led him off the bus. He'd been on the bus for over eight hours.

'Be careful,' the bus driver said as Stanley walked down the steps.

Stanley wasn't sure if the bus driver meant for him to be careful going down the steps, or if he was telling him to be careful at Camp Green Lake. 'Thanks for the ride,' he said. His mouth was dry and his throat hurt. He stepped onto the hard, dry dirt. There was a band of sweat around his wrist where the handcuff had been.

The land was barren and desolate. He could see a few rundown buildings and some tents. Farther away there was a cabin beneath two tall trees. Those two trees were the only plant life he could see. There weren't even weeds.

The guard led Stanley to a small building. A sign on front said, YOU ARE ENTERING CAMP GREEN LAKE JUVENILE CORRECTIONAL FACILITY.

The guard led Stanley into the building, where he felt the welcome relief of air-conditioning.

A man was sitting with his feet up on a desk. He turned his head when Stanley and the guard entered, but otherwise didn't move. Even though he was inside, he wore sunglasses and a cowboy hat. He also held a can of soda, and the sight of it made Stanley even more aware of his own thirst.

He waited while the bus guard gave the man some papers to sign. He had a tattoo of a rattlesnake on his arm, and as he signed his name, the snake's rattle seemed to wiggle . . .Then the man in the cowboy hat walked around the desk to Stanley. 'My name is Mr Sir,' he said. Whenever you speak to me you must call me by that name, is that clear?'

Stanley hesitated. 'Uh, yes, Mr Sir,' he said, though he couldn't imagine that was really the man's name.

'You're not in the Girl Scouts anymore,' Mr Sir said.

Stanley had to remove his clothes in front of Mr Sir, who made sure he wasn't hiding anything. He was then given two sets of clothes and a towel. Each set consisted of a long-sleeve orange jumpsuit, an orange T-shirt, and yellow socks . . .

Stanley got dressed. The clothes smelled like soap.

Mr Sir told him he should wear one set to work in and one set for relaxation. Laundry was done every three days. On that day his work clothes would be washed. Then the other set would become his work clothes, and he would get clean clothes to wear while resting.

'You are to dig one hole each day, including Saturdays and Sundays. Each hole must be five feet deep, and five feet across in every direction. Your shovel is your measuring stick. Breakfast is served at 4:30.'

Stanley must have looked surprised, because Mr Sir went on to explain that they started early to avoid the hottest part of the day. 'No one is going to baby-sit you,' he added. 'The longer it takes you to dig, the longer you will be out in the sun. If you dig up anything interesting, you are to report it to me or any other counsellor. When you finish, the rest of the day is yours.'

Stanley nodded to show he understood.

'This isn't a Girl Scout camp,' said Mr Sir . . .Then he led Stanley out into the blazing heat.

'Take a good look around you,' Mr Sir said. 'What do you see?'

Stanley looked out across the vast wasteland. The air seemed thick with heat and dirt. 'Not much,' he said, then hastily added, 'Mr Sir.'

Mr Sir laughed. 'You see any guard towers?'

'No.'

'How about an electric fence?'

'No, Mr Sir.'

'There's no fence at all is there?'

'No, Mr Sir.'

'You want to run away?' Mr Sir asked him.

Stanley looked back at him, unsure what he meant.

'If you want to run away, go ahead, start running. I'm not going to stop you.'

Stanley didn't know what kind of game Mr Sir was playing.

'I see you're looking at my gun. Don't worry. I'm not going to shoot you.' He tapped his holster. 'This is for yellow-spotted lizards. I wouldn't waste a bullet on you.'

'I'm not going to run away,' Stanley said.

'Good thinking,' said Mr Sir. 'Nobody runs away from here. We don't need a fence. Know why? Because we've got the only water for a hundred miles. You want to run away? You'll be buzzard food in three days.'

Stanley could see some kids dressed in orange and carrying shovels dragging themselves toward the tents.

'You thirsty?' asked Mr Sir.

'Yes, Mr Sir,' Stanley said gratefully.

'Well, you'd better get used to it. You're going to be thirsty for the next eighteen months.'

8   Selecting an Appropriate Form

Selecting an appropriate form for your creative writing is an important decision as you need to select a form which will showcase your skills and give you the opportunity to investigate and/or highlight aspects of the theme.

All forms of writing are open to you so remember all the advice you have been given about producing different types of writing. For example, you will find useful tips in Unit 1: Section A where form is explored in more detail.

Whatever form you choose, remember to consider **the three Ws**.

What you are going to write
Who you are addressing
Why you are writing

For your creative writing task(s) you will have time to work in groups to generate ideas and time for individual research. This Controlled Assessment element will be worth 15% of your marks for English Language or 20% of your marks for English, so it is well worth planning and preparing carefully **what** you are going to write.

Who you are addressing in your writing will be strongly linked to the form you choose.

Before you write be very clear **why** you are writing.

The final activities in this section give you the opportunity to think through the process of selecting an appropriate form.

ACTIVITY 8

Imagine you are one of the characters in a text you have read recently. Decide on an appropriate form and audience for the theme you are exploring. For example:

- For the theme of Women, you could choose the form of Lady Macbeth's diary entries which detail her evil plans. The audience would be the public who would read it after her death.
- You could choose the form of Candy's internal monologue as he lies in his bunk at the end of the day his dog was shot. This piece could explore themes such as Conflict and Relationships.

ACTIVITY 9

In pairs, read and consider the images and texts below and on the next page. They are based on the theme of Society or Homelessness.
Make a list of possible forms of creative writing stimulated by this material.
Then write one of the forms you have thought of. You will need to carry out some further research on this issue.

This is the opening of Robert Swindells' novel *Stone Cold*, which tells the story of sixteen-year-old Link, who is homeless on the streets of London:

> You can call me Link. It's not my name, but it's what I say when anybody asks, which isn't often. I'm invisible, see? One of the invisible people. Right now I'm sitting in a doorway watching the passers-by. They avoid looking at me. They're afraid I want something they've got, and they're right. Also, they don't want to think about me. They don't like reminding I exist. Me, and those like me. We're living proof that everything's not all right and we make the place untidy.
>
> Hang about and I'll tell you the story of my fascinating life.

ANGELS OF THE SLUMS

In the African city of Nairobi, where the poorest of the poor are reduced to scavenging from rubbish dumps, some people are fighting to turn back the tide of human misery.

Priscilla Higham reports.

Kibera slum is home to 1.2 million people and is one of 29 slums, which house 60 percent of the population of Nairobi – Kenya's capital city. It was here I met Sarafina who runs a feeding programme from her café. She is one of the 'Angels of the Slums' – men and women who are fighting the extremes of poverty in order to help children and the elderly and diseased in their communities.

Trailed by hordes of squealing children, I arrive at Sarafina's café in the heart of the slum. It's a heartbreaking scene. The benches lining the walls of the corrugated iron shack are full of young mothers with their sickly, crying babies and skeletal old people with racking coughs. Homeless slum children flock in for their supper: 'This one with the little sister has no mother,' says Sarafina, pointing to a child of eight carrying a malnourished baby with a swollen belly. 'Many of them are orphans but we can't afford medicine for those who are sick.'

The stories make difficult listening. Helen, who helps Sarafina, tells me, 'We found another baby in a dustbin today. We took it to the hospital but I don't think it will survive.'

My next visit was to Rose Omia who visits sick people in the Matare slum. In common with Kenya's other slums, Matare is a maze of alleys and crammed with a haphazard arrangement of houses.

Between the houses run open sewers which are overflowing and clogged with garbage. Urban services are non-existent and huge piles of uncollected rubbish mingle with rotting waste. This lack of sanitation poses a major health hazard.

Rose took me through the narrow, filthy streets of Matare. Everything is enveloped in a film of dust. In this bleak landscape, we are trailed by more ragged, barefoot children. We knock on the door of one dwelling and enter a cramped, dingy room where Pauline, 28, lives with her mother and her three children. Pauline has a large septic wound on her leg which gives her a lot of pain.

Korogocho slum, where I was introduced to Stephen Oumo, was unimaginably squalid. Stephen has set up the only library to exist in the Kenyan slums. We walk along a muddy, deeply rutted track broken up with pools of stagnant water. The atmosphere is oppressive. There is a dark cloud overhead, due to the closeness of the city dump – 20 acres of burning rubbish – where hundreds of people live under plastic sheets scavenging on a mountainside of garbage. We cross a river choked with rubbish where people are bathing, despite the fact that a few hundred yards upstream all the sewers are emptying into it. Hundreds of vultures circle in the sky; the air is thick with smoke and the smell of burning refuse is overwhelming. At first the vast dump looks deserted. Then I notice that the whole mass is moving and hundreds of people are sifting through the rubbish. There is even a makeshift school here dug into the refuse and roofed in plastic.

As I made my way home to the prosperous West, I was left with nothing but admiration for worthy men and women such as Sarafina, Rose and Stephen who have decided to do something about the wretched poverty they live in. They truly are 'Angels of the Slums'.

9 Writing Creatively: Controlled Assessment Success

Matching grades to creative writing

In this Controlled Assessment the essential qualities the examiners will be looking for are highlighted at the important grade boundaries. Read these descriptions *carefully*; they tell you what your responses should be like.

> **Grade C** writing aims to produce a competent and engaging piece that demonstrates:
>
> a clear awareness of the form and style that is appropriate to purpose
>
> paragraphing that is used effectively to sequence events or develop ideas
>
> a range of sentence structures and varied vocabulary that are used to generate interest
>
> vocabulary that is selected to suit the task and audience
>
> mainly accurate punctuation that clarifies meaning
>
> correct spelling of common and most irregular words.

> **Grade A/A*** writing aims to produce a highly engaging piece that wholly engages the audience and demonstrates:
>
> sophisticated awareness of a form and style that is suitable to the task and purpose
>
> fluent linking of key points that are clearly and fully developed
>
> the confident use of complex ideas and information which are presented with flair
>
> a wide range of appropriate vocabulary spelt correctly
>
> assured control of a wide range of punctuation which is used to enhance meaning
>
> a sophisticated appreciation of the conventions of written language.

Writing creatively: Key to success

The Controlled Assessment writing-up has to be completed within a specified period of time, so you have to pre-plan what you are going to do and use this time purposefully.

Before you start your own creative writing, read these key pointers and put them into practice.

Efficient writing

 You have prepared for your Controlled Assessment creative writing sessions and you are aware that it has to be completed in a relatively short period of time but remember, the best writing results from the following process: **Think, Plan, Write.** Resist the temptation to start immediately; take the time to put your plan down on paper. This will be a well-spent 15 minutes in both English Language and English, and it is central if you are to produce your best work.

 Make your writing engaging – the last thing the examiner wants is to read something dull!

 There are no prizes for finishing first so use all of your time wisely – the only reward for finishing early could be a low grade!

 Remember you have about 90 minutes in English Language and 65 minutes in English in which to complete the actual writing.

 Review your finished work (in this proposed time scheme you have been left with 15 minutes in English Language and 10 minutes in English).You *must* review your work to get the most out of your answer because when working quickly and under pressure *everyone* makes mistakes. Remember too that there are no marks for extreme neatness, it's much better that your work is accurate even if it contains a few corrections.

As you check your work, consider the following questions and correct any mistakes that you find:

i)   Have you paragraphed the essay?

ii) Did you use a range of sentence lengths?

iii) Did you vary the sentence openings?

iv) Have you used a varied vocabulary?

v)   Have you left out any words?

vi) Are there any sentences where the meaning is less than clear?

The content of your writing

 Maintain focus on the purpose of the task.

 Careful pre-planning is essential if you are to have the opportunity to produce a well-judged and detailed piece of creative writing.

 Carefully plan the structure to construct a coherent piece of creative writing.

 Use language effectively in order to produce a convincing piece.

 Ensure paragraphs have topic sentences – this will help you stay on task.

It is possible that you will, in the course of your preparations for the Controlled Assessment tasks, be given the opportunity to write a creative piece (not on the actual Controlled Assessment that you will be answering) or snippets of creative pieces to get used to the write-up process.

Below are checklists for success which may prove useful both before and after you have attempted any such creative writing practice.

Checklist for success: working towards Grade C	✔
Have you produced **a competent, engaging** piece of writing?	
Have you shown **awareness of form and style** that are appropriate to your **purpose?**	
Have you used **paragraphs** to sequence events/develop ideas clearly for the reader?	
Have you tried to make use of a range of **sentence structures** and a **varied vocabulary** to create different effects and engage the reader's interest?	
Have you selected **vocabulary** to suit both **audience and purpose**?	
Have you used **punctuation** to clarify meaning and **spelt common words correctly**?	

Checklist for success: working towards Grade A/A★	✔
Have you produced a highly convincing piece of writing that demonstrates sophisticated awareness of **form and style** and that is suitable to the task and the **audience**?	
Have you presented key points that are **clearly linked, fully developed** and expressed in a **fluent manner** so as to wholly engage the audience?	
Have you presented **complex ideas and information with flair**?	
Have you deployed a wide range of **appropriate vocabulary**?	
Have you demonstrated an assured awareness of the **conventions** of a full range of **punctuation?**	
Have you **spelt** your wide-ranging **vocabulary** correctly?	

Exam Practice

Answering Exam Questions

This section looks at the process of answering exam questions and gives you opportunities to practise working at exam speed.

Remember that you have to be ready to write your responses in the actual time allotted for each answer. This is the final piece in the examination jigsaw.

We shall look in turn at Sections A and B of Paper 1 and Sections A and B of Paper 2.

Paper 1 – Section A: Personal Writing

Section A of Paper 1 tests **Personal Writing**. Read and discuss the sample exam question below. It has been annotated to help familiarise you with the process of producing your response.

> Key issues are highlighted in red in this example.

Section A: Personal Writing

Up to **16 marks** are available for an interesting and organised piece of writing.

Up to **8 marks** are available for the use of a range of sentence structures and correct spelling, punctuation and grammar.

Task 1
Write about an occasion when you suffered real embarrassment.

In your answer you should:

- inform the examiner of the reasons for your choice
- describe the occasion and what it was like
- explain what made it so awful. **[24]**

Planning your answer. . .
It is suggested that you organise your time like this:

- **5–10 minutes** planning your answer
- **25–30 minutes** writing your essay
- **5 minutes checking over** your writing.

> This is basic information you should be familiar with but read it – doing this will help you settle down and get into your pre-planned routine.

> A section like this will appear only in the Foundation tier exam paper but it offers valuable advice for all students. The three bulleted prompts are there to get you thinking along the right lines.

> This is the topic for your piece of personal writing.

> The timings for organising your work will help you produce your best possible piece of personal writing in 45 minutes – so **follow them!**

> For a question with only one task, you don't need to worry about the number of marks. Concentrate on writing an engaging, organised and competently structured answer.

ACTIVITY 1

Now it's your turn to have a go at answering the example exam question on page 183.

1 Take 45 minutes and produce your answer.

2 When you have finished, switch with a partner – read their essay and fill in the strengths and areas for improvement in a table like the one below. Use the Mark Schemes on pages 201–202 (Foundation tier) or pages 203–204 (Higher tier) to help you with your assessment.

Strengths of this essay	Areas that need to be improved
1.	1.
2.	2.

Here is another task. Before you begin this, think about what you did well the last time you undertook a personal writing task and what areas you need to be more conscious about or improve.

ACTIVITY 2

1 Take 45 minutes and answer the question below.

2 When you have finished, read your work again and assess its strengths and areas for improvement. Use the Mark Schemes on pages 201–202 (Foundation tier) or pages 203–204 (Higher tier) to help you with your assessment.

Section A: Personal Writing

Up to **16 marks** are available for an interesting and organised piece of writing.

Up to **8 marks** are available for the use of a range of sentence structures and correct spelling, punctuation and grammar.

Task 1

Write about an occasion when you have been really touched by the kindness of a friend.

In your answer you should:
- describe the situation to the examiner
- explain how your friend helped you
- reflect on why this was so important to you.　　**[24]**

Planning your answer. . .

It is suggested that you organise your time like this:
- **5–10 minutes** planning your answer
- **25–30 minutes** writing your essay
- **5 minutes** checking over your writing.

Note: The two bullet lists would appear only in the Foundation version of the exam paper.

Paper 1 – Section B: Reading Multi-Modal Texts

Read and discuss the annotated sample exam question below. You will find images of the two DVD covers on pages 186 and 187.

You will find images of the two DVD covers on pages 186 and 187.

> **Key issues are highlighted in red in this example.**

Unless you take 10–15 minutes to make a proper analysis of both texts you won't have anything significant to say – you **must** give yourself this preparation or thinking time before you start your answers.

Don't describe these devices; consider the effect they have on the reader: analysis not description is what's required! What effects are achieved through the images, background, design and layout? Remember: you can write about the font, size, positioning or colour of the writing but not the words in the body of the text!

This bulleted section will appear only in the Foundation tier exam paper.

This bulleted section will appear only in the Foundation tier exam paper.

Section B: Reading Multi-Modal Texts – Foundation tier

The DVD covers of *Close Encounters of the Third Kind* and *E.T.* are designed to make these classic Sci-Fi movies an attractive purchase.

Complete **both** tasks.

Task 2

Compare how **presentational devices** are used in **both** DVD covers to make each film appealing to its audience.

In your answer comment on:
- the use of images and colour
- the layout. **[9]**

Task 3

Compare how **language** has been used in **both** DVD covers to persuade you that these are exciting films. **[15]**

Comment on the use of words and phrases in:
- the titles, headings and subheadings
- the text written to promote the films.

Planning your answer. . .

It is suggested that you organise your time like this:
- **10–15 minutes** reading the DVD covers
- **10 minutes** responding to Task 2
- **20 minutes** responding to Task 3

You are told both covers share the same purpose. Your answer needs to focus on how they have delivered enough sense of drama and excitement to persuade the public to buy the product.

Time is short – you have only **10 minutes** to complete this answer. Make each point quickly and move on to the next one. Ideally, your answer will consist of about six short paragraphs each making a perceptive comparative point on the two covers.

Allow about **20 minutes** to complete your answer. More marks = more time! Focus on how the words and phrases have been chosen to capture, engage, intrigue and finally persuade the would-be purchaser to part with their money. Remember to **compare and contrast** the strategies used in each cover.

Take this advice very seriously – it informs you of the most effective way to use your 45 minute time allowance! There's no such thing as 'running out of time' – it's time mismanagement!

THE COLLECTOR'S EDITION

CLOSE ENCOUNTERS
OF THE THIRD KIND

CLOSE ENCOUNTERS
OF THE THIRD KIND

"SPECTACULAR! BRILLIANT!
'CLOSE ENCOUNTERS'
DESERVES AN HISTORIC PLACE
IN MOVIE ENTERTAINMENT."
JACK KROLL, NEWSWEEK

Columbia TriStar Home Entertainment proudly presents the definitive director's cut of Steven Spielberg's masterpiece. "Literate in plotting and dazzling in execution, CLOSE ENCOUNTERS OF THE THIRD KIND is "an absolute stunner!" (*Variety*)

And now, for the first time on DVD, Steven Spielberg's enduring achievement can be seen and enjoyed as he always intended, in this director's cut, remastered from the original film elements. "Of all the UFO films ever made this is the most edifying...a feast for the eyes! The appeal of this film was enormous and still is." (*The Motion Picture Guide*)

SPECIAL FEATURES
DIGITALLY MASTERED AUDIO & ANAMORPHIC VIDEO
AUDIO: ENGLISH 5.1 (DTS AND DOLBY DIGITAL), ENGLISH 2-CHANNEL (DOLBY SURROUND), FRENCH, SPANISH.
SUBTITLES: ENGLISH, FRENCH, SPANISH, PORTUGUESE, CHINESE, KOREAN, THAI.
ANIMATED MENUS.
PRODUCTION NOTES.

DISC ONE
WIDESCREEN PRESENTATION
SCENE SELECTIONS WITH MOTION IMAGES

DISC TWO
MAKING OF DOCUMENTARY, 1977 FEATURETTE "WATCHING THE SKIES",
11 DELETED SCENES, FILMOGRAPHIES, THEATRICAL TRAILERS.

A COLUMBIA/EMI PRESENTATION
"CLOSE ENCOUNTERS OF THE THIRD KIND: THE COLLECTOR'S EDITION"
A PHILLIPS PRODUCTION A STEVEN SPIELBERG FILM
STARRING RICHARD DREYFUSS TERI GARR MELINDA DILLON AND FRANCOIS TRUFFAUT
MUSIC BY JOHN WILLIAMS VISUAL EFFECTS BY DOUGLAS TRUMBULL DIRECTOR OF PHOTOGRAPHY VILMOS ZSIGMOND, A.S.C.
PRODUCED BY JULIA PHILLIPS AND MICHAEL PHILLIPS WRITTEN AND DIRECTED BY STEVEN SPIELBERG

www.sonypictures.com

10202 W. Washington Blvd. Culver City, California 90232-3195
©1977 Columbia Pictures Industries, Inc. All Rights Reserved.
©2001 Layout and Design Columbia TriStar Home Entertainment, Inc. All Rights Reserved.

COLUMBIA
PICTURES

Approx. 137 Minutes   Printed in U.S.A.

01138

ISBN 0-7832-4691-1

Presented in WIDESCREEN VERSION which preserves the original theatrical aspect ratio of approx. 2.35:1

ACTIVITY 3

Now take 45 minutes to answer:
- **either** the annotated exam question on page 185 (Foundation tier)
- **or** the exam question below (Higher tier).

When you have finished, read your work again and assess its strengths and areas for improvement. Use the Mark Scheme on pages 205–206 (Foundation tier) or pages 207–208 (Higher tier) to help you with your assessment.

Section B: Reading Multi-Modal Texts – Higher tier

These two DVD covers of a film called *Eternal Dusk* are designed to be appealing to the film's potential audience. (You will find images of the two DVD covers on pages 189 and 190.)

Complete the two tasks below.

Task 2

Compare and contrast how **presentational devices** have been used in both covers in order to appeal to the target audience. In your answer you should comment on the use of images and colour and the layout.   **[9]**

Task 3

Compare and contrast how **language** has been used in both texts to support and reinforce the visual appeal. **[15]**

Cover A

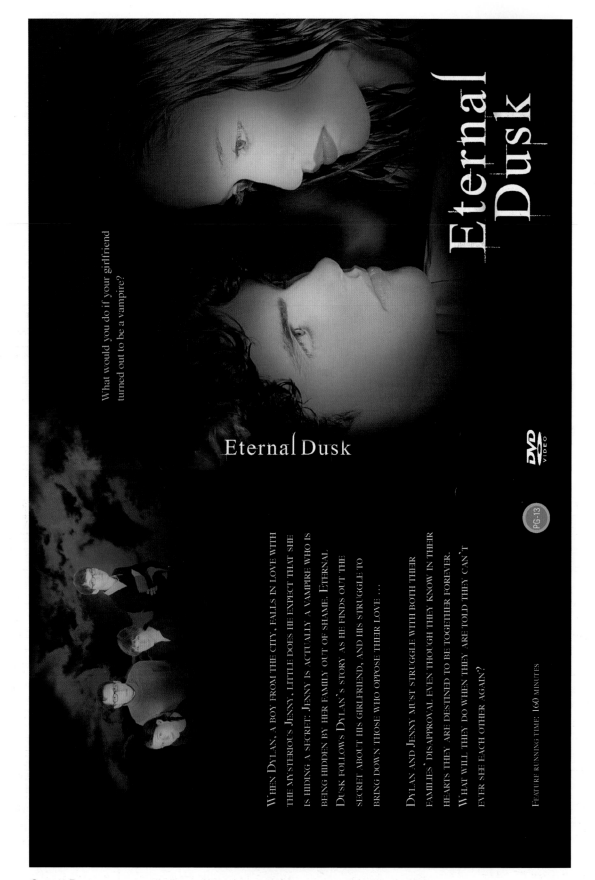

Cover B

Paper 2 – Section A: Functional Writing

Section A of Paper 2 tests **Functional Writing** so a range of writing scenarios are possible. Because the Foundation and Higher tier formats differ, an annotated sample question is given for each. Read and discuss the example that's appropriate for you. Higher tier students will also find important advice on planning in the Foundation tier question.

> Key issues are highlighted in red in these examples.

Section A: Functional Writing – Foundation tier

Up to **16 marks** are available for an organised, appropriate and interesting response.

Up to **8 marks** are available for the use of a range of sentence structures and correct spelling, punctuation and grammar.

Task 1

Write the speech/talk you would give to your classmates on the following topic:

'Charity begins at home but it shouldn't stop there!' **[24]**

Planning your answer. . .

It is suggested that you organise your time like this:

- **5–10 minutes** planning your answer
- **25–30 minutes** writing your essay
- **5 minutes checking over** your response.

> The type of writing required.

> The audience for your speech/talk.

> This advice will appear only in the Foundation tier exam paper but it is just as important that students taking the Higher tier paper adopt a similar strategy in order to produce an effective piece of writing.

> This is the form your writing should take. A discursive essay is a reasoned discussion that comes to a conclusion – it doesn't require a balanced discussion of every point of view; it can focus primarily on your own perspective.

> Remember to **plan your answer**! The timings suggested in the Foundation tier example would be a suitable model.

Section A: Functional Writing – Higher tier

Up to **16 marks** are available for an organised, appropriate and interesting response.

Up to **8 marks** are available for the use of a range of sentence structures and correct spelling, punctuation and grammar.

Task 1

Write a discursive essay on the following issue:

'Charity begins at home and it should stop there!'

Consider other viewpoints and put forward your own opinion on this subject. **[24]**

> This is basic information you should be familiar with, but read it – doing this will help you settle down and get into your pre-planned routine.

> This is deliberately quite a controversial statement. Even if you feel strongly about the subject, don't allow your personal feelings to get in the way of making sure that you write a strong, well organised and engaging discussion!

> Remember to refer to the views of others.

191

ACTIVITY 4

1 Now take 45 minutes and answer **one** of the exam-type questions below. You will find ideas and opinions that might be useful in developing your writing opposite.

2 When you have finished, read your work again and assess its strengths and areas for improvement. Use the Mark Schemes on pages 209–210 (Foundation tier) or pages 211–212 (Higher tier) to help you with your assessment.

Section A: Functional Writing – Foundation tier

Up to **16 marks** are available for an organised, appropriate and interesting response.

Up to **8 marks** are available for the use of a range of sentence structures and correct spelling, punctuation and grammar.

Task 1

Write the talk you would give to your classmates on the following issue:

'Watching television is only second-hand living. Get out and make a life of your own!'

[24]

You may wish to make use of some of the ideas and opinions (see opposite) if you think they would be useful in developing your piece of writing.

Planning your answer. . .

It is suggested that you organise your time like this:

- **5–10 minutes** planning your answer
- **25–30 minutes** writing your essay
- **5 minutes checking over** your response.

Section A: Functional Writing – Higher tier

Up to **16 marks** are available for an organised, appropriate and interesting response.

Up to **8 marks** are available for the use of a range of sentence structures and correct spelling, punctuation and grammar.

Task 1

Write a discursive essay on the following issue:

'Watching television is only second-hand living. Get out and make a life of your own!'

[24]

Consider other viewpoints and put forward your own thoughts and views on this subject.

You may wish to make use of some of the ideas and opinions (see opposite) if you think they would be useful in developing your piece of writing.

These general prompts provided for the exam questions in Activity 4 should help to get you thinking along the right lines. **Build your piece around your own ideas**, making use of some of these prompts if you wish but not necessarily all of them! Put them **in your own words**. **Do not copy them out** and then comment on them!

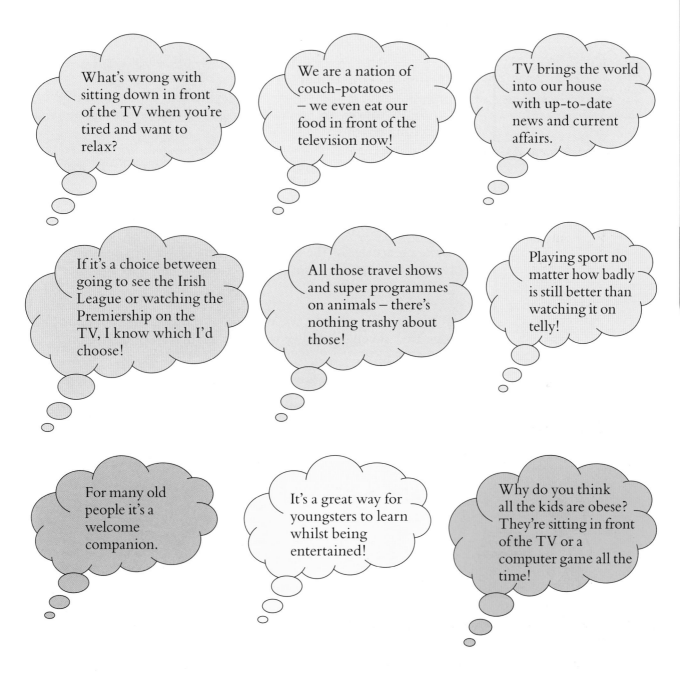

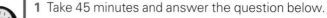

ACTIVITY 5

Here is another opportunity to practise your functional writing for Paper 2 Section A. You will find facts and opinions that might be useful in your discussion on page 195.

1 Take 45 minutes and answer the question below.
2 When you have finished, read your work again and assess its strengths and areas for improvement. Use the Mark Schemes on pages 209–210 (Foundation tier) or 211–212 (Higher tier) to help you with your assessment.

Section A: Functional Writing

Up to **16 marks** are available for an organised, appropriate and interesting response.

Up to **8 marks** are available for the use of a range of sentence structures and correct spelling, punctuation and grammar.

Task 1

Write an article for the school magazine in which you urge all its readers to become a lot more serious about looking after the environment. **[24]**

You may wish to make use of some of the facts and opinions (see page 195) if you think they would be useful in your discussion.

The future of the planet is at stake!

Take greener holidays, switch off lights, recycle, think about Fair Trade – there are so many things we could do!

If we are to do this as responsible adults then surely school should be leading the way by setting a practical example that we can follow!

We still throw too much away – and that's just the litter you see blowing around the place!

A school in Nottinghamshire replaced their old, inefficient oil boilers which were producing high CO_2 emissions. Through a boiler replacement programme the school was given the opportunity to have a wood-fuelled boiler installed to replace the old system. That's what should be happening in our school.

What about all that packaging and those plastic bags?

Could we not be recycling paper in school – we certainly write enough!!

Being green needs to be seen as more than the latest fad – it has to become a way of life.

Facts

- UK households produced 30.5 million tonnes of waste in 2003/04, of which 17% was collected for recycling (source: defra.gov.uk). This figure is still quite low compared to some of our neighbouring EU countries, some of which recycle over 50% of their waste.
- 1 recycled tin can would save enough energy to power a television for 3 hours.
- 1 recycled glass bottle would save enough energy to power a computer for 25 minutes.
- 1 recycled plastic bottle would save enough energy to power a 60 watt light bulb for 3 hours.
- Up to 60% of the rubbish that ends up in the dustbin could be recycled.
- The unreleased energy contained in the average dustbin each year could power a television for 5000 hours.
- The largest lake in Britain could be filled with rubbish from the UK in 8 months.
- On average, 16% of the money you spend on a product pays for the packaging, which ultimately ends up as rubbish.
- As much as 50% of waste in the average dustbin could be composted.
- Up to 80% of a vehicle can be recycled.
- 9 out of 10 people would recycle more if it were made easier.
- 70% less energy is required to recycle paper compared with making it from raw materials.
- If all cans in the UK were recycled, we would need 14 million fewer dustbins. £36,000,000 worth of aluminium is thrown away each year.
- Glass is 100% recyclable and can be used again and again. Glass that is thrown away and ends up in landfills will never decompose.
- 275,000 tonnes of plastic are used each year in the UK, that's about 15 million bottles per day. Most families throw away about 40 kg of plastic per year, which could otherwise be recycled. Plastic can take up to 500 years to decompose.

Paper 2 – Section B: Reading Non-Fiction

Section B of Paper 2 tests **Reading Non-Fiction** and will consist of a single question on the reading and interpretation of a previously unseen non-fiction text. This text can take a range of different formats.

Read and discuss the annotated example exam question below. You will find the text on page 197. (The same comments will apply to similar questions for Higher tier.)

> Key issues are highlighted in red in this example.

Section B: Reading Non-Fiction – Foundation tier

Read the following extract from a travel book. The writer has expressed his very personal views on visiting Blackpool for the first time. He does this in a manner which sustains the reader's interest.

Complete the task below.

Task 2

Explain how the writer holds the reader's interest.

In your answer show how the writer has:
- used a style of writing that is lively and personal
- included facts and his own opinions
- selected words and phrases for effect
- made use of sentence structuring and paragraphing. **[24]**

These are the key words – you are looking at **how** the writer has held our interest.

These will act as useful paragraph headings – work your way through them.
You don't have the time to waste on a lengthy introduction and conclusion that restate points you have already made.

You are given the writer's intention in the text and this will be at the heart of your answer.

Don't report or summarise each of these. Consider how they build up the writer's intended effect – analysis not description is your aim!

You can support your analysis by simply referring to an incident or detail; or with very short quotations or collections of single words.
Don't copy out chunks of text – you'll only be wasting time!

Blackpool – and I don't care how many times you hear this, it never stops being amazing – attracts more people every year than Greece and has more holiday beds than the whole of Portugal. More chips are consumed there than anywhere else on the planet. (It goes through 40 acres of potatoes a day!) It has the largest concentration of roller-coasters in Europe. It has Europe's second most popular tourist attraction – the 42-acre Pleasure Beach and it has the most famous illuminations. In fact, Blackpool has increased its visitor numbers by 7 per cent! This is quite an achievement when you consider the British climate, the fact that Blackpool is ugly and dirty, a long way from anywhere interesting, has a sea that is an open toilet and has attractions that are nearly all cheap and nasty.

It was the illuminations that brought me there. I had been hearing and reading about them for so long, that I was genuinely keen to see them. I rushed to the sea-front in a sense of expectation. Well, I could not see what all the fuss was about – Blackpool's illuminations were dreary and dismal. There is, of course, always the danger of disappointment when you finally experience something you have wanted to see for a long time, but in terms of letdown, it would be hard to exceed Blackpool's light show. I thought there would be lasers sweeping the sky, strobe lights tattooing the clouds and other gasp-making dazzlements. Instead there was just a rumbling procession of old trams decorated as rocket ships or Christmas crackers and several miles of pathetic decorations on lamp posts. I suppose if had never seen electricity in action, it would be pretty breathtaking but I'm not sure of that. It all just seemed tacky on a rather grand scale, like Blackpool itself.

What was no less amazing were the crowds of people who had come to witness this miserable show. Traffic along the front was bumper to bumper, with childish faces pressed to the windows of every creeping car, and there were masses of people walking happily along the spacious promenade. I once read that half of all visitors to Blackpool have been there at least ten times. Goodness knows what they find in the place. I walked for a mile or so along the promenade and couldn't understand the appeal of it. Perhaps I was just weary but I couldn't wake up any enthusiasm for it at all. I wandered through brightly lit arcades and peered in bingo halls but the festive atmosphere that seemed to seize everyone failed to rub off on me. I decided to have an early night.

In the morning I got up early to give Blackpool another chance. It wasn't much better by daylight. One of the sights that I knew would stick firmly in my mind was the long promenade and the three piers at Blackpool. I will long remember the people sitting in deck chairs underneath a dark sky, some with their shirts off, some with their mouths open and clutching copies of the daily papers. Tomorrow they would be using them for wrapping fish and chips. They were waiting for the sun to shine, but the forecast was rain for the next five months! I escaped from Blackpool as soon as I could.

ACTIVITY 6

Now take 45 minutes to answer:
- **either** the annotated exam question on page 196 (Foundation tier)
- **or** the exam question below (Higher tier).

When you have finished, read your work again and assess its strengths and areas for improvement. Use the Mark Scheme on page 213 (Foundation tier) or 214 (Higher tier) to help you with your assessment.

Section B: Reading Non-Fiction – Higher tier

Read the following extract from a travel book. The American writer has expressed his very personal views on coming to Europe for the first time in a manner which sustains the reader's interest.

Complete the task below.

Task 2

Explain how the writer holds the reader's interest.

In your answer show how the writer has:
- used a style that is engaging and personal
- made use of his own opinion
- selected words and phrases for effect
- made use of sentence structuring and paragraphing. **[24]**

You will find the text for this question below.

In this extract from a travel book, the writer is recalling his first visit to Europe almost 20 years earlier.

The first time I came to Europe was in 1972, skinny, shy, alone. In those days the only cheap flights were from New York to Luxembourg, with a re-fuelling stop en route at Keflavik Airport, Reykjavik. The aeroplanes were old and engagingly past their prime – oxygen masks would sometimes drop unbidden from their overhead storage compartments and dangle there until a stewardess with a hammer and a mouthful of nails came along to put things right, and the door of the lavatory tended to swing open on you if you didn't hold it shut with a foot, which brought a certain dimension of challenge to anything else you planned to do in there – and they were achingly slow. It took a week and a half to reach Keflavik, a small grey airport in the middle of a flat grey nowhere, and another week and a half to bounce on through the skies to Luxembourg.

. . . .

I was secretly watching out of the window for Europe. I still remember my first sight. The plane dropped out of the clouds and there below me was this sudden magical tableau of small green fields and steepled villages spread across an undulating landscape, like a shaken-out quilt just settling back onto a bed. I had flown a lot in America and had never seen much of anything from an aeroplane window but endless golden fields on farms the size of Belgium, meandering rivers and pencil lines of black highway as straight as taut wire. It always looked vast and mostly empty. You felt that if you squinted hard enough you could see all the way to Los Angeles, even when you were over Kansas. But here the landscape had the ordered perfection of a model-railway layout. It was so green and minutely cultivated, so compact, so tidy, so fetching, so . . . European. I was smitten. I still am.

I brought with me a yellow backpack so enormous that when I went through customs I half expected to be asked, 'Anything to declare? Cigarettes? Alcohol? Dead horse?', and spent the day teetering beneath it through the ancient streets of Luxembourg City in a vivid daze – an unfamiliar mixture of excitement and exhaustion and intense optical stimulation. Everything seemed so vivid and acutely focused and new. I felt like someone stepping out of doors for the first time. It was all so different: the language, the money, the cars, the number plates on the cars, the bread, the food, the newspapers, the parks, the people. I had never seen a zebra-crossing before, never seen a tram, never seen an unsliced loaf of bread (never even considered it an option), never seen anyone wear a beret who expected to be taken seriously, never seen feathered pheasants and unskinned rabbits hanging in the butcher's window or a pig's head smiling on a platter, never seen a packet of Gitanes or the Michelin man. And the people – why, they were Luxembourgers. I don't know why this amazed me but it did. I kept thinking, That man over there, he's a Luxembourger. And so is that girl. They don't know anything about the New York Yankees, they don't know the theme tune to *The Mickey Mouse Club*, they are from another world. It was just wonderful.

Mark Schemes

This section contains the mark schemes for the examinations for GCSE English Language and English. These mark schemes have two purposes:

 to allow you to assess the overall standard of your own work

 to enable you to work out what you have done well and what areas you can improve upon.

In terms of content and level descriptors, the mark schemes are exactly the same as what would be used to assess your answers in the actual examinations (although they have been slightly cut down here to make them more useable). You can use these mark schemes to assess the work you have been doing throughout this book, particularly in the exam sections at the end of Units 1A (pages 19–22), 1B (pages 44–47), 2A (pages 74–78) and 2B (pages 93–98) and in the Exam practice section (pages 183–199).

There are mark schemes provided for Paper 1, Sections A and B, and Paper 2, Sections A and B, for both Foundation and Higher level so you can assess your work against the right level for you. The mark schemes provided are:

- Paper 1 – Section A: Personal Writing, Foundation level, AO 4(i) and (ii) on page 201
- Paper 1 – Section A: Personal Writing, Foundation level, AO 4(iii) on page 202
- Paper 1 – Section A: Personal Writing, Higher level, AO 4(i) and (ii) on page 203
- Paper 1 – Section A: Personal Writing, Higher level, AO 4(iii) on page 204
- Paper 1 – Section B: Reading Multi-Modal Texts, Foundation level, AO 3(i) and (ii) on page 205
- Paper 1 – Section B: Reading Multi-Modal Texts, Foundation level, AO 3 (i), (ii) and (iii) on page 206
- Paper 1 – Section B: Reading Multi-Modal Texts, Higher level, AO 3(i) and (ii) on page 207
- Paper 1 – Section B: Reading Multi-Modal Texts, Higher level, AO 3 (i), (ii) and (iii) on page 208
- Paper 2 – Section A: Functional Writing, Foundation level, AO 4(i) and (ii) on page 209
- Paper 2 – Section A: Functional Writing, Foundation level, AO 4(iii) on page 210
- Paper 2 – Section A: Functional Writing, Higher level, AO 4(i) and (ii) on page 211
- Paper 2 – Section A: Functional Writing, Higher level, AO 4(iii) on page 212
- Paper 2 – Section B: Reading Non-Fiction, Foundation level, AO 3(i), (ii) and (ii) on page 213
- Paper 2 – Section B: Reading Non-Fiction, Higher level, AO 3(i), (ii) and (ii) on page 214

The Assessment Objectives that are referred to in these mark schemes can be seen in full on page 3.

Foundation tier
Paper 1 – Section A: Personal Writing
Response time: 45 minutes

Sample tasks

- **Task 1:** Write about an occasion when you suffered real embarrassment. (Activity 1, page 183)
- **Task 1:** Write about an occasion when you have been really touched by the kindness of a friend. (Activity 2, page 184)

This checklist outlines the writing skills for AO 4(i) and (ii) that all candidates would be expected to try to use in their responses to these or similar tasks. The examiner would also credit other valid strategies that are not mentioned below.

Communicate clearly and effectively and imaginatively, demonstrating:

- a handling of the topic in such a way as to attempt to positively develop the reader's interest
- use of a style that endeavours to build a positive relationship with the target audience
- possible use of anecdotes/humour to engage the audience

Adapting form and vocabulary to task and purpose in ways that engage the reader, demonstrating:

- an awareness of the examiner as audience
- a use of tone that is meant to engage and sustain the audience's attention
- use of a straightforward vocabulary that is in keeping with the task and audience and that, occasionally, may enliven the writing

Organise information and ideas into structured, sequenced sentences, paragraphs and whole texts, demonstrating:

- a sense of progression – the reader being taken through the writer's experience
- an awareness of opening and closing paragraphs
- some use of topic sentences for different paragraphs
- development that uses organisation in an attempt to hold the audience's interest

Use a variety of linguistic and structural features for cohesion and coherence, demonstrating:

- some variety of sentence length for effect
- occasional use of connectives to give coherence to paragraphing
- the use of rhetorical devices – the rule of three, questions, hyperbole, etc.

Assessment Objectives: AO 4(i) and (ii)
Marks available: up to 16 marks

Competence level 1 [1–4]

Characterised by:

- some general, rather sketchy development
- an unconvincing grasp of purpose and audience
- some attempt at simple structuring using a rudimentary style

Competence level 2 [5–8]

Characterised by:

- a simple development, relating events in a elementary manner
- a broad sense of purpose and/or audience that may be sustained
- a basic structuring and an elementary style

Competence level 3 [9–12]

Characterised by:

- an uncomplicated development, relating the incident in a deliberate fashion
- a general sense of purpose and audience
- a logical structuring and a straightforward style

Competence level 4 [13–16]

Characterised by:

- a generally effective development that maintains the reader's interest
- a recognition of purpose and audience
- a clear structuring and an increasingly fluent style

Foundation tier
Paper 1 – Section A: Personal Writing
Response time: 45 minutes

Sample tasks

- **Task 1:** Write about an occasion when you suffered real embarrassment. (Activity 1, page 183)
- **Task 1:** Write about an occasion when you have been really touched by the kindness of a friend. (Activity 2, page 184)

This checklist outlines the writing skills for AO 4(iii) that all candidates would be expected to try to use in their responses to these or similar tasks. The examiner would also credit other valid strategies that are not mentioned below.

Range and effectiveness of sentence structures:

- The wider the control that a candidate exhibits with regard to sentence structuring, the greater is their ability to sustain interest and establish a rapport with the examiner. The more competent and varied that manipulation of sentence structure is, the higher will be the mark awarded.

Use of accurate punctuation and spelling:

- Inextricably woven into the fabric of sentence structure is the control that comes from the accurate use of appropriate punctuation. Here too there is scope for variety that can help to engage the examiner. The greater the range of punctuation appropriately used, the higher will be the reward.

- Accuracy in spelling is, in isolation, potentially misleading; it needs to be viewed in conjunction with the range and precision of the vocabulary that a candidate draws upon. A limited and mundane vocabulary spelt with unerring accuracy is unlikely to capture the examiner's attention. Credit attempts to use vocabulary ambitiously where the word may not always be accurately spelt but has been chosen with care.

Assessment Objectives: AO 4(iii)
Marks available: up to 8 marks

Competence level 1 [1–2]

Characterised by:

- little control of sentence structuring – instead, simple connectives used to link ideas; verbs often repeated
- occasional use of full stops and commas tends to be the limit of punctuation
- some accuracy in the spelling of simple words
- the range of vocabulary is narrow

Competence level 2 [3–4]

Characterised by:

- a use of basic sentence structuring that offers little variation in construction or length
- generally correct use of full stops and the use of some other forms of punctuation
- basic vocabulary is usually spelt accurately
- a limited vocabulary

Competence level 3 [5–6]

Characterised by:

- a controlled use of straightforward sentence structuring – there will be evidence of some variety in sentence construction and length
- a generally secure use of basic punctuation to support structure
- generally accurate spelling of straightforward, regular vocabulary
- an uncomplicated vocabulary will be evident

Competence level 4 [7–8]

Characterised by:

- increasingly sustained competence in the handling of a variety sentence structures – occasionally these may be used for effect
- the basics of punctuation – full stops, commas, exclamation and question marks – used accurately, adding clarity to the work
- generally accurate spelling including some words with irregular patterns
- a greater precision in the use of a widening vocabulary

		Assessment Objectives: AO 4(i) and (ii) **Marks available:** up to 16 marks

Higher tier
Paper 1 – Section A: Personal Writing
Response time: 45 minutes

Sample tasks

- **Task 1:** Write about an occasion when you suffered real embarrassment. (Activity 1, page 183)
- **Task 1:** Write about an occasion when you have been really touched by the kindness of a friend. (Activity 2, page 184)

This checklist outlines the writing skills for AO 4(i) and (ii) that all candidates would be expected to try to use in their responses to these or similar tasks. The examiner would also credit other valid strategies that are not mentioned below.

Communicate clearly and effectively and imaginatively, demonstrating:

- a handling of the topic in such a way as to positively develop the reader's interest
- use of a style that builds a positive relationship with the target audience
- possible use of anecdotes/humour to enliven the writing and so engage the audience

Adapting form and vocabulary to task and purpose in ways that engage the reader, demonstrating:

- a conscious awareness of the examiner as audience
- a use of tone that is designed to engage and sustain the audience's attention
- use of vocabulary that is in keeping with the task and audience to enhance, enrich and enliven the writing

Organise information and ideas into structured, sequenced sentences, paragraphs and whole texts, demonstrating:

- a sense of logical progression – the reader being led through the writer's experience
- the use of opening and closing paragraphs
- the deployment of topic sentences for different paragraphs
- development that uses conscious organisation to sustain the audience's interest

Use a variety of linguistic and structural features for cohesion and coherence, demonstrating:

- a conscious varying of sentence length for effect
- the use of connectives to give coherence to paragraphing
- the use of rhetorical devices such as the rule of three, questions, hyperbole, etc., to develop interest and a rapport with the audience

Competence level 1 [1–4]

Characterised by:

- an uncomplicated development, relating the incident in a deliberate fashion
- a general sense of purpose and audience
- a logical structuring and a straightforward style

Competence level 2 [5–8]

Characterised by:

- a generally effective development that maintains the reader's interest
- a recognition of purpose and audience
- a clear structuring and an increasingly fluent style

Competence level 3 [9–12]

Characterised by:

- a competent development that clearly interests the reader
- a confident awareness of purpose and audience
- proficient structuring with evidence of a developing, lively style

Competence level 4 [13–16]

Characterised by:

- a poised and sophisticated development that commands the reader's attention throughout
- a positive rapport with the audience
- assured competence in terms of structure underpinned by a confident style

Higher tier
Paper 1 – Section A: Personal Writing
Response time: 45 minutes

Assessment Objectives: AO 4(iii)
Marks available: up to 8 marks

Sample tasks

- **Task 1:** Write about an occasion when you suffered real embarrassment. (Activity 1, page 183)
- **Task 1:** Write about an occasion when you have been really touched by the kindness of a friend. (Activity 2, page 184)

This checklist outlines the writing skills for AO 4(iii) that all candidates would be expected to try to use in their responses to these or similar tasks. The examiner would also credit other valid strategies that are not mentioned below.

Range and effectiveness of sentence structuring:

- The wider the range and greater the degree of originality and control used in sentence structuring, the more opportunity candidates give themselves to establish a positive rapport with the reader.
- More assured and varied manipulation of sentence structuring demonstrates higher levels of competence and is to be rewarded accordingly.

Use of accurate punctuation and spelling:

- Linked to the control of sentence structure is the control of a variety of appropriate punctuation. Here too there is scope for creativity that can help to engage the examiner's interest.
- The greater the control and innovation in the use of punctuation the higher will be the reward. Accuracy in spelling, in isolation, can be misleading; it needs to be viewed beside the range and precision of the vocabulary used.
- A limited and mundane vocabulary spelt with unerring accuracy is unlikely to capture the examiner's attention. Examiners should credit ambitious use of vocabulary – where the word may not always be accurately spelt but has been chosen with care to capture the essence of a situation.

Competence level 1 [1–2]

Characterised by:

- a controlled use of straightforward sentence structuring – there will be evidence of some variety in sentence construction and length
- a generally secure use of basic punctuation to support structure
- generally accurate spelling of straightforward, regular vocabulary
- an uncomplicated vocabulary will be evident

Competence level 2 [3–4]

Characterised by:

- increasingly sustained competence in the handling of a variety sentence structures – occasionally these may be used for effect
- the basics of punctuation – full stops, commas, exclamation and question marks – used accurately, adding clarity to the work
- generally accurate spelling including some words with irregular patterns
- a greater precision in the use of a widening vocabulary

Competence level 3 [5–6]

Characterised by:

- a deliberate manipulation of a range sentence structures – conscious control of sentence variety for effect
- a proficiently handled range of punctuation that enhances the writing
- accurate spelling of most words
- an extended vocabulary which is employed with increasing precision

Competence level 4 [7–8]

Characterised by:

- an assured use of a wide range of sentence structures that enhances the overall effect of the writing in terms of clarity, purpose and audience
- confident deployment of a full range of punctuation that facilitates fluency and complements meaning
- an extended, apposite vocabulary used with precision – errors will be one-off mistakes or, occasionally, the outcome of ambitious attempts to use complex language

Foundation tier
Paper 1 – Section B: Reading Multi-Modal Texts
Task 2: Presentational devices
Response time: 10 minutes

| | **Assessment Objectives:** AO 3(i) and (ii) **Marks available:** up to 9 marks |

Sample task

The DVD covers of *Close Encounters of the Third Kind* and *E.T.* are designed to make these classic sci-fi movies an attractive purchase.

Task 2: Compare how **presentational devices** are used in **both** DVD covers to make this film appealing to its audience.

Comment on the use of image, colour and the layout. (Activity 3, page 185)

This checklist outlines material and evidence that candidates at all competence levels may be expected to include in their response to this task. The examiner would also credit other valid suggestions or comments.

Use made of images and colour

- Given the highly visual nature of DVDs, both covers naturally rely heavily on image and colour to create impact.
- Both front covers are built around a very strong central image: the sense of something out of this world happening over the horizon on the cover of *Close Encounters* and the spark engendered by the touch of the index finger of a child and the alien suggests the magic of their encounter.
- Both covers feature night scenes with starred backdrops. The *E.T.* cover features the moon, which highlights the silhouette of a boy cycling through the sky. The *Close Encounters* cover gives less away and relies much more on building suspense and our natural fascination with the unknown. There is a very small image on the back of the cover that gives a taste of what the film has in store. The similarity of setting isn't surprising given their shared sci-fi genre.
- Both feature the dark-blue background of night and this adds excitement and atmosphere and therefore help to set the mood/tone for the DVDs and heighten our expectations.
- Some of the 'action' from each DVD is featured, giving a glimpse of what the buyer can expect – this is more evident on the *E.T.* cover whereas the *Close Encounters* cover is more reliant on mood and lighting with vaguely distinguishable shapes looming out of the darkness.
- The layouts of the spines of the DVDs are very similar; they are fairly functional, like a book spine, featuring the title in its own particular font so that it almost takes on the role of a logo for the movie.

The layout

- The layouts of the covers are very similar – major images and titles dominate the front covers and the back covers follow very similar formats: barcodes; the use of phrases in bold from favourable reviews; a collage of images; a very prominent segment given over to 'special features' using heavy, striking colour, subheadings and boxes to showcase these.
- *E.T.* prominently displays its PG status on the front, back and spine – no such prominence is afforded on the *Close Encounters* DVD, where the PG status is buried among the logos at the bottom of the back cover.
- Both front covers imply that these DVDs are special: one is a '2– Disc Special Edition' whilst the other claims to be 'The Collector's Edition'. These are not just ordinary DVDs – the appeal is to the acquisitive side of our nature.
- The layouts of the back covers are very similar: some interwoven smaller images add snippets from the movies to enhance their appeal, while the section on special features is designed to tempt the potential purchaser.
- There is dense technical text at the bottom of both covers. It is not very user-friendly – there is a profusion of logos all adding to the authenticity of the products but not really of significance in promoting the movies.

Competence level 1 [1–3]

Characterised by:

- a basic recognition that use has been made of presentational devices
- some reference to a few very obvious examples
- a very general linking of the examples of these devices to their purpose

Competence level 2 [4–6]

Characterised by:

- an understanding of how some of these presentational devices generate excitement
- reference to a series of examples, some supported by straightforward comment
- some appropriate use of comparison and contrast at a straightforward level

Competence level 3 [7–9]

Characterised by:

- a sound overall consideration of how some of the presentational devices generate excitement
- a straightforward explanation and comparison of how these devices have been used to engage and influence the reader
- the development of an appropriate interpretation of the stimulus through an uncomplicated drawing together of mainly appropriate evidence from both sources

Foundation tier
Paper 1 – Section B: Reading Multi-Modal Texts
Task 3: Language
Response time: 20 minutes

Assessment Objectives: AO 3(i), (ii) and (iii)
Marks available: up to 15 marks

Sample task

The DVD covers of *Close Encounters of the Third Kind* and *E.T.* are designed to make these classic sci-fi movies an attractive purchase.

Task 3: Compare how **language** has been used in **both** DVD covers to persuade you that these are exciting films.

Comment on the use of words and phrases in the titles, headings and subheadings; and in the text written to promote the films. (Activity 3, page 185)

This checklist outlines material and evidence that candidates at all competence levels may be expected to include in their response to this task. The examiner would also credit other valid suggestions or comments.

Language employed to promote these films

- Because neither of these films is a new release, there is emphasis on suggesting that these DVDs are 'new': *Close Encounters* 'proudly presents the definitive director's cut' (alliteration) 'for the first time on DVD'. *E.T.* has 'special edition', 'never-before-seen' and 'unseen footage'.
- In an attempt to make what is not a new release seem attractive, the following terms are used: 'classic', 'enduring'.
- *E.T.* presents the prospective buyer with a synopsis of the story and uses suitably emotive language to engage the reader in this 'family' film about 'a lost little alien . . . a lonely ten-year old boy' – 'a timeless adventure . . . no earthly bounds'.
- Both lay much emphasis on their reviews: in bold *E.T.* is described as 'A captivating classic . . . embrace everyone . . . magic touch', 'a warm, touching and funny family classic'. For *Close Encounters* there is no synopsis of the storyline but three hugely positive comments from critics. The following words give the key message that the advertisers wish to get across: 'Spectacular! Brilliant!' and 'dazzling in execution . . . an absolute stunner!' and 'a feast for the eyes!'
- Despite the greater emphasis of *Close Encounters* on its reviews, it cannot match the success of *E.T.* in the Oscars and Golden Globes, which is rather understated.

The way the language is used in headings, etc.

- Naturally both DVDs use the front cover to focus the reader's attention on the film's title, whilst both use the back to present reviews and, for *E.T.*, a synopsis of the movie.
- The paragraphing is designed to be extremely reader friendly: the paragraphs are very brief, a couple of sentences at most.
- The technical and legal information has to be there but plays no part in promoting the DVDs – the minuscule size of the font and the less than generous spacing are ample evidence that the designers of the covers are not using these sections as a means of selling the DVDs.

Competence level 1 [1–5]

Characterised by:

- some basic sense of how language and/or structure have been used positively
- reference to a few obvious examples
- a very general linking of the examples of these devices to their purpose of reinforcing a sense of excitement

Competence level 2 [6–10]

Characterised by:

- an understanding of how some of these linguistic and structural effects can be employed to generate excitement
- reference to a series of examples, some of which will be supported by straightforward comment
- some appropriate use of comparison and contrast at a straightforward level

Competence level 3 [11–15]

Characterised by:

- a sound overall consideration of how some of the linguistic and structural devices achieve their effects
- a straightforward explanation and comparison of how these effects have been used to support a sense of excitement
- the development of an appropriate interpretation of the stimulus materials through an uncomplicated drawing together of mainly appropriate supporting evidence from both sources

Higher tier
Paper 1 – Section B: Reading Multi-Modal Texts
Task 2: Presentational devices
Response time: 10 minutes

Assessment Objectives: AO 3 (i) and (ii)
Marks available: up to 9 marks

Sample task

The two covers of the DVD *Eternal Dusk* are designed to be appealing to the film's potential audience.

Task 2: Compare and contrast how **presentational devices** have been used in both covers in order to appeal to the target audience. In your answer you should comment on the use of images and colour and the layout. (Activity 3, page 188)

This checklist outlines material and evidence that candidates at all competence levels may be expected to include in their response to this task. The examiner would also credit other valid suggestions or comments.

Use of images and colour

- Given the highly visual nature of DVDs, both covers naturally rely heavily on images to create impact: Cover B is simpler in approach than Cover A. The central characters are the sole focus of an extremely tight close-up on Cover B whereas Cover A, whilst still concentrating on the two central characters, uses a wider shot backed by atmospheric clouds, an eclipse and a spectacular bolt of lightning – very melodramatic! Clearly these covers are aimed at the target teenage audience.

- Both front covers create a strong, central image: both are similar in their composition – Cover B gives equal prominence to the unsmiling central characters looking directly at each other whilst Cover A centres its attention on the stern, determined and resolute looking young hero with the girl, again, unsmiling, in the background. In both cases we are given the impression that they have a relationship – if an uneasy one. This adds to the quality of brooding intrigue and suspense.

- Both front covers feature eerie, backlit images. The background throughout is dark and helps to set the sombre/ threatening mood for the DVDs. This is particularly true of Cover B which generates a sense of intimacy by showing only the faces of the unsmiling couple to develop the tense, moody atmosphere. Cover B is less cluttered or busy than Cover A and as a result has possibly more visual impact than its competitor. The back of Cover B continues its simpler approach with the predominantly black background to highlight the white text. There is a single image of other supporting characters – shot from above against a night sky background. Again this reinforces the threatening mood. By contrast, some of the 'action' from Cover A is featured on the back cover offering glimpses of what the buyer can expect – these take the form of exciting, over-lapping images: the skeleton, wide-eyed, screaming characters the primitive wooden church. etc. (The image of the grotesque mask is mirrored in the appearance of one of the characters featured there.)

The layout

- The spine of both DVDs are similar, functional like book ends, featuring the distinctive font so that acts as a logo

- the highlighted claim 'Recommended for mature audiences' is a subtle piece of flattery by Cover A for the target audience.

- Both DVDs make use of white print on the very dark background which adds to the dramatic feel. Cover B uses uppercase text – the effect/ readability is perhaps questionable.

- Cover A carries the silver background at the top of the cover (which mirrors the background of the main picture) through from the front cover, to the spine and on to the back, creating a series of natural breaks that are used to highlight different sections on the cover – including a bullet pointed list for 'Special Features'. Cover A has the usual plethora of technical logos that are such a feature of DVD covers. This is in marked contrast to the much 'cleaner' presentation on the back of Cover B.

Competence level 1 [1–3]

Characterised by:

- a sound overall evaluation of how some of the presentational devices achieve their effects
- a straightforward explanation and comparison of how these devices have been used to engage and influence the reader positively
- the development of an appropriate interpretation of the stimulus material through an uncomplicated drawing together of mainly appropriate evidence

Competence level 2 [4–6]

Characterised by:

- a clear evaluation of how the presentational devices have been deployed to achieve their effects
- a competent explanation of how these devices have been manipulated to engage and influence the reader positively
- the development of an accurate interpretation of the stimulus materials through a drawing together of a range of appropriate evidence from both sources

Competence level 3 [7–6]

Characterised by:

- an assured evaluation of how the presentational devices have been deployed to achieve their particular effects
- a confident explanation and comparison of how these devices interact to positively influence and generate engagement within the target audience
- the development of an perceptive interpretation of the stimulus material through a purposeful comparison of a range of precisely selected, supporting evidence

Higher tier
Paper 1 – Section B: Reading Multi-Modal Texts
Task 3: Language
Response time: 20 minutes

Assessment Objectives: AO 3(i), (ii) and (iii)
Marks available: up to 15 marks

Sample task

The two covers of the DVD *Eternal Dusk* are designed to be appealing to the film's potential audience.

Task 3: Compare and contrast how **language** has been used in both texts to support and reinforce the visual appeal. In your answer comment on the use of language in headings and subheadings; and the way language is used to describe the film. (Activity 3, page 188)

This checklist outlines material and evidence that candidates at all competence levels may be expected to include in their response to this task. The examiner would also credit other valid suggestions or comments.

Language employed to promote these films

- Cover A uses language to market the product vigorously: 'never-before-seen' is used on two separate occasions as well as 'special edition'/'special features'/'TWO-DISC SPECIAL EDITION' whereas Cover B doesn't employ this promotional style – it goes for dramatic simplicity with the striking front cover question: 'What would you do if your girlfriend turned out to be a vampire?'
- Both covers feature a synopsis of the story: Cover A presents a two sentence resume whilst Cover B presents a more extensive two paragraph summary.
- The synopses are quite similar – in each case they present the starting point of the movie from the perspective of Dylan as he leaves 'the city' and meets Jenny. These are a series of phrases that are common to both.
- In a further paragraph/sentence, the Cover B synopsis goes on from where Cover B finishes with Dylan's 'struggle'.
- Given the target audience – teenage girls – both describe the ensuing relationship in suitably clichéd terms: 'the mysterious Jenny'/'hiding a secret'/'hidden by her family out of shame'/'struggle to bring down those who oppose their love'.
- There are plenty of extravagant claims for the film: Cover A is described in the following terms: 'they know in their hearts they are destined to be together forever' while Cover B saves its melodrama for its description of their relationship: 'Dylan and Jenny must struggle with both their families' disapproval'.
- Cover A concludes its resume by using an ellipsis to generate engagement with the readers, whereas Cover B uses a cliff-hanging question to finish with: 'What will they do ... each other again?'

The way the writing is structured on these two DVD covers

- Naturally both use the front cover to focus the reader's attention on the film's title although Cover B supplements this with the cryptic and intriguing question: 'What would you do if your girlfriend turned out to be a vampire' to further intrigue and directly engage the reader.
- Both use the back of the DVD to present synopses – although this is not the only material here in Cover A which chooses to promote its 'Special Features'.
- There is no paragraphing used in Cover A – this is not unsurprising because it consists of only two sentences. The relatively more extensive Cover B synopsis is presented in two paragraphs; however the use of uppercase is visually rather off-putting – possibly the designers were hoping that the strong visual appeal would be sufficient to sell their product.
- The designers of Cover A included some of the usual technical data on their DVD cover while Cover B has completely omitted the technical blurb, staying with the 'uncluttered' style, giving only the running time and the viewing classification.

Competence level 1 [1–4]

Characterised by:

- a sound overall evaluation of how some of the linguistic, grammatical and structural devices achieve their effects
- a straightforward explanation of how these devices have been used to engage the audience
- the development of an appropriate interpretation of the stimulus material through an uncomplicated drawing together of mainly appropriate supporting evidence from both sources

Competence level 2 [5–8]

Characterised by:

- a clear evaluation of how the linguistic, grammatical and structural devices have been deployed to achieve their effects
- a competent explanation of how these devices have been used in an attempt to engage and manipulate the audience
- the development of an accurate interpretation of the stimulus through a drawing together of a range of a range of appropriate supporting evidence from both sources

Competence level 3 [9–12]

Characterised by:

- an assured evaluation of how the linguistic, grammatical and structural devices have been deployed to achieve their particular effects
- a confident explanation of how these devices interact to positively influence and generate engagement within the target audience
- the development of an perceptive interpretation of the stimulus material through a purposeful comparison of a range of precisely selected supporting evidence.

Foundation tier
Paper 2 – Section A: Functional Writing
Response time: 45 minutes

Sample tasks

- **Task 1:** Write the talk you would give to your classmates, urging them to watch less television and be more active, on the following issue: 'Watching television is only second-hand living. Get out and make a life of your own!' (Activity 4, page 192)
- **Task 1:** Write an article for the school magazine in which you urge all its readers to become a lot more serious about looking after the environment. (Activity 5, page 194)

This checklist outlines the writing skills for AO 4(i) and (ii) that all candidates would be expected to try to use in their responses to these or similar tasks. The examiner would also credit other valid strategies that are not mentioned below.

Communicate clearly and effectively and imaginatively, demonstrating:

- a handling of the topic in such a way as to attempt to positively develop the reader's interest
- use of a style that endeavours to build a positive relationship with the target audience
- possible use of anecdotes/humour to engage the audience

Adapting form and vocabulary to task and purpose in ways that engage the reader, demonstrating:

- an awareness of the examiner as audience
- a use of tone that is meant to engage and sustain the audience's attention
- use of a straightforward vocabulary that is in keeping with the task and audience and that, occasionally, may enliven the writing

Organise information and ideas into structured, sequenced sentences, paragraphs and whole texts, demonstrating:

- a sense of progression – the reader being taken through the writer's experience
- an awareness of opening and closing paragraphs
- some use of topic sentences for different paragraphs
- development that uses organisation in an attempt to hold the audience's interest

Use a variety of linguistic and structural features for cohesion and coherence, demonstrating:

- some variety of sentence length for effect
- occasional use of connectives to give coherence to paragraphing
- the use of rhetorical devices – the rule of three, questions, hyperbole, etc.

Assessment Objectives: AO 4(i) and (ii)
Marks available: up to 16 marks

Competence level 1 [1–4]

Characterised by:

- some general, rather sketchy development of their views on the issue
- an unconvincing grasp of purpose and audience
- some attempt at simple structuring using a rudimentary style

Competence level 2 [5–8]

Characterised by:

- a simple development, relating their views about the issue in an elementary manner
- a broad sense of purpose and/or audience that may not be sustained
- a basic structuring and an elementary style

Competence level 3 [9–12]

Characterised by:

- an uncomplicated development, relating their point of view in a deliberate fashion
- a unsophisticated understanding of purpose and audience
- a logical structuring and a straightforward style

Competence level 4 [13–16]

Characterised by:

- a generally effective development that maintains the reader's interest in the subject
- a recognition of purpose and audience
- a clear structuring and an increasingly fluent style

Foundation tier Paper 2 – Section A: Functional Writing Response time: 45 minutes	Assessment Objectives: AO 4(iii) Marks available: up to 8 marks

Sample tasks

- **Task 1:** Write the talk you would give to your classmates, urging them to watch less television and be more active, on the following issue: 'Watching television is only second-hand living. Get out and make a life of your own!' (Activity 4, page 192)
- **Task 1:** Write an article for the school magazine in which you urge all its readers to become a lot more serious about looking after the environment. (Activity 5, page 194)

This checklist outlines the writing skills for AO 4(iii) that all candidates would be expected to try to use in their responses to these or similar tasks. The examiner would also credit other valid strategies that are not mentioned below.

Range and effectiveness of sentence structures

- The wider the control that a candidate exhibits with regard to sentence structuring, the greater is their ability to sustain interest and establish a rapport with the examiner.
- The more competent and varied that manipulation of sentence structure is, the higher will be the mark awarded.

Use of accurate punctuation and spelling

- Inextricably woven into the fabric of sentence structure is the control that comes from the accurate use of appropriate punctuation. Here too there is scope for variety that can help to engage the examiner. The greater the range of punctuation appropriately used, the higher will be the reward.
- Accuracy in spelling is, in isolation, potentially misleading; it needs to be viewed in conjunction with the range and precision of the vocabulary that a candidate draws upon. A limited and mundane vocabulary spelt with unerring accuracy is unlikely to capture the examiner's attention. Credit attempts to use vocabulary ambitiously where the word may not always be accurately spelt but has been chosen with care.

Competence level 1 [1–2]

Characterised by:

- little control of sentence structuring – instead, simple connectives used to link ideas; verbs often repeated
- occasional use of full stops and commas tends to be the limit of punctuation
- some accuracy in the spelling of simple words
- narrow range of vocabulary

Competence level 2 [3–4]

Characterised by:

- a use of basic sentence structuring that offers little variation in construction or length
- generally correct use of full stops and the use of some other forms of punctuation
- basic vocabulary that is usually spelt accurately
- a limited vocabulary

Competence level 3 [5–6]

Characterised by:

- a controlled use of straightforward sentence structuring – there will be evidence of some variety in sentence construction and length
- a generally secure use of basic punctuation to support structure
- generally accurate spelling of straightforward, regular vocabulary
- an uncomplicated vocabulary

Competence level 4 [7–8]

Characterised by:

- increasingly sustained competence in the handling of a variety of sentence structures – occasionally these may be used for effect
- the basics of punctuation – full stops, commas, exclamation and question marks – used accurately, adding clarity to the work
- generally accurate spelling including some words with irregular patterns
- a greater precision in the use of a widening vocabulary

Higher tier
Paper 2 – Section A: Functional Writing
Response time: 45 minutes

Sample tasks

- **Task 1:** Write a discursive essay on the following issue: 'Watching television is only second-hand living. Get out and make a life of your own!' (Activity 4, page 192)
- **Task 1:** Write an article for the school magazine in which you urge all its readers to become a lot more serious about looking after the environment. (Activity 5, page 194)

This checklist outlines the writing skills for AO 4(i) and (ii) that all candidates would be expected to try to use in their responses to these or similar tasks. The examiner would also credit other valid strategies that are not mentioned below.

Communicate clearly and effectively and imaginatively, demonstrating:

- a handling of the topic in such a way as to positively develop the reader's interest
- use of a style that builds a positive relationship with the target audience
- possible use of anecdotal evidence to enliven the writing and so engage the audience

Adapting form and vocabulary to task and purpose in ways that engage the reader, demonstrating:

- a conscious awareness of the examiner as audience
- a use of tone that is designed to engage and sustain the audience's attention
- use of vocabulary that is in keeping with the task and audience to enhance, enrich and enliven the writing

Organise information and ideas into structured, sequenced sentences, paragraphs and whole texts, demonstrating:

- a sense of logical progression – the reader being led through the writer's point of view/ thoughts
- the use of opening and closing paragraphs
- the deployment of topic sentences for different paragraphs
- development that uses conscious organisation to sustain the audience's interest

Use a variety of linguistic and structural features for cohesion and coherence, demonstrating:

- a conscious varying of sentence length for effect
- the use of connectives to give coherence to paragraphing
- the use of rhetorical devices such as the rule of three, questions, hyperbole, etc., to develop interest and a rapport with the audience

---

Assessment Objectives: AO 4(i) and (ii)
Marks available: up to 16 marks

Competence level 1 [1–4]

Characterised by:

- an uncomplicated development, that presents their point of view
- a general sense of purpose and audience
- a logical structuring and a straightforward style

Competence level 2 [5–8]

Characterised by:

- a generally effective development that maintains the reader's interest
- a recognition of purpose and audience
- a clear structuring and an increasingly fluent style

Competence level 3 [9–12]

Characterised by:

- a competent development that clearly engages with the reader
- a confident awareness of purpose and audience
- proficient structuring with evidence of a developing, lively style

Competence level 4 [13–16]

Characterised by:

- a poised and sophisticated development that commands the reader's attention throughout
- a positive rapport with the audience
- assured competence in terms of structure underpinned by a confident style

Higher tier
Paper 2 – Section A: Functional Writing
Response time: 45 minutes

Assessment Objectives: AO 4(iii)
Marks available: up to 8 marks

Sample tasks

- **Task 1:** Write a discursive essay on the following issue:: 'Watching television is only second-hand living. Get out and make a life of your own!' (Activity 4, page 192)
- **Task 1:** Write an article for the school magazine in which you urge all its readers to become a lot more serious about looking after the environment. (Activity 5, page 194)

This checklist outlines the writing skills for AO 4(iii) that all candidates would be expected to try to use in their responses to these or similar tasks. The examiner would also credit other valid strategies that are not mentioned below.

Range and effectiveness of sentence structures

- The wider the repertoire and greater the degree of originality and control that a candidate exhibits with regard to sentence structuring, the greater is their ability to sustain interest and establish a rapport with the examiner. The fresher, the more assured and varied that manipulation of sentence structure is, the higher will be the mark awarded.

Use of accurate punctuation and spelling:

- Inextricably woven into the fabric of sentence structure is the control that comes from the accurate use of appropriate punctuation. Here too there is scope for variety and creativity that can help to engage the examiner. The greater the range and innovation in relation to the use of punctuation, the higher will be the reward.
- Accuracy in spelling is, in isolation, potentially misleading; it needs to be viewed in conjunction with the range and precision of the vocabulary that a candidate draws upon. A limited and mundane vocabulary spelt with unerring accuracy is unlikely to capture the examiner's attention. Credit ambitious use of vocabulary where the word may not always be accurately spelt but has been chosen with care to capture the essence of a situation.

Competence level 1 [1–2]

Characterised by:

- a controlled use of straightforward sentence structuring – there will be evidence of some variety in sentence construction and length
- a generally secure use of basic punctuation to support structure
- generally accurate spelling of straightforward, regular vocabulary
- an uncomplicated vocabulary

Competence level 2 [3–4]

Characterised by:

- increasingly sustained competence in the handling of a variety of sentence structures – occasionally these may be used for effect
- the basics of punctuation – full stops, commas, exclamation and question marks – used accurately, adding clarity to the work
- generally accurate spelling including some words with irregular patterns
- a greater precision in the use of a widening vocabulary

Competence level 3 [5–6]

Characterised by:

- a deliberate manipulation of a range sentence structures – conscious control of sentence variety for effect
- a proficiently handled range of punctuation that enhances the writing
- accurate spelling of most words
- an extended vocabulary which is employed with increasing precision

Competence level 4 [7–8]

Characterised by:

- an assured use of a wide range of sentence structures that enhances the overall effect of the writing in terms of clarity, purpose and audience
- confident deployment of a full range of punctuation that aids fluency and complements meaning
- an extended, apposite vocabulary used with precision – errors will be one-off mistakes or, occasionally, the outcome of ambitious attempts to use complex language

Foundation tier
Paper 2 – Section B: Reading Non-Fiction
Response time: 45 minutes

Assessment Objectives: AO 3 (i), (ii) and (iii)
Marks available: up to 24 marks

Sample tasks

Task 2: Explain how the writer of the extract from a travel book holds the reader's interest. In your answer show how he has used a style of writing that is engaging and personal; included facts and his own opinions; selected words and phrases for effect; made use of sentence structuring and paragraphing. (Activity 6, page 198)

This checklist outlines material and evidence that candidates at all competence levels may be expected to include in their response to this task. The examiner would also credit other valid suggestions or comments.

Lively and personal style and tone

- First-person narrator adds immediacy and a degree of curiosity about writer's reaction to the resort: 'I had been hearing . . . I was genuinely keen. . . I rushed to the sea-front', 'Perhaps I was just weary', 'I escaped . . . as I could'.
- Contrast between his expectations and his experience involves reader in familiar situation of anticipation followed by disappointment: he had expected 'lasers sweeping the sky . . . strobe lights . . . dazzlements' but he found 'just just a rumbling procession of old trams'.
- Unrestrained style of writer's criticism amuses and engages our interest: 'in terms of letdown . . . hard to exceed Blackpool's light show', 'Blackpool is ugly and dirty', 'tacky on a rather grand scale, like Blackpool itself'.
- Initial tone matches writer's optimism and positive anticipation before he arrives – 'the largest concentration of roller-coasters in Europe. . . Europe's second most popular tourist attraction. . . the most famous illuminations' – but by the end of the first paragraph the tone has changed completely and the resort is roundly condemned in the final sentence.
- Amusing use of exaggeration engages reader: 'a sea that is an open toilet', 'the forecast was rain for the next five months!'
- Use of internal monologue amuses and sustains reader's attention: 'Perhaps I was just weary'.
- Throughout, the writer continues to engage the reader by creating the impression that he really wanted to like the place – 'I was genuinely keen . . . I rushed to the sea-front . . . expectation' – but his attempts to be positive fail and he 'escaped . . . as soon as I could.'

Use of fact and opinion

- In quite a striking opening the writer presents a series of quirky and interesting facts that provide a backdrop to his own opinions that follow: 'attracts more people every year than Greece . . . more holiday beds than the whole of Portugal. More chips are consumed there than anywhere else on the planet . . . 40 acres of potatoes a day! . . . largest concentration of roller-coasters . . . Europe's second most popular tourist attraction'.
- His brutally honest opinion engages the reader and forms an interesting contrast with the facts: 'several miles of pathetic decorations on lamp posts', 'attractions that are nearly all cheap and nasty'.

Selection of words and phrases for effect

- Use of a lively vocabulary: unusual and effective metaphor 'lights **tattooing** the clouds'; creation of his own word (noun), 'dazzlements'; preceded by unusual combination 'gasp-making'.
- Use of alliteration in the description sustains interest: 'dreary and dismal', 'creeping car'.
- Writer's views are captured in hard-hitting words: 'pathetic', 'cheap and nasty', 'tacky', 'open toilet'.
- The description of the holiday-makers in deck chairs is a depressing, bleak and yet amusing image.

Use of sentence structuring and paragraphing

- The paragraphing supports the progression of the visit – e.g. the chronological connective between the third and fourth paragraphs: 'I decided to have an early night.// In the morning . . .'
- Lists feature quite frequently – in the first two paragraphs. The final sentence of the first paragraph contrasts with the factual list that precedes it and consists of a list of opinions stated forcefully in the style of facts.
- The final two paragraphs end with short sentences. 'I . . . early night' leads on to the action in the final paragraph and 'I escaped . . .' used to summarise humorously his reaction to Blackpool.

Competence level 1 [1–6]

Characterised by:

- basic comments in relation to some of the features in the bullet points
- reporting that may offer some simple points that may be supported from the text
- a partial and simple interpretation of some features

Competence level 2 [7–12]

Characterised by:

- a very straightforward consideration of most of the features highlighted in the bullet points
- some basic analysis that may be supported by appropriate evidence
- some development of valid, if simple interpretations occasionally supported by straightforward evidence

Competence level 3 [13–18]

Characterised by:

- a consideration of the features highlighted in the bullet points in relation to the desired outcome – sustaining the reader's interest
- straightforward analysis supported by uncomplicated explanations
- appropriately developed interpretations backed up by mainly straightforward supporting evidence

Competence level 4 [19–24]

Characterised by:

- an analysis of features highlighted in the bullet points
- an examination supported by appropriate explanations
- the development of a competent interpretation of the stimulus material through the presentation of appropriate supporting evidence

Higher tier
Paper 2 – Section B: Reading Non-Fiction
Response time: 45 minutes

Assessment Objectives: AO 3(i), (ii) and (iii)
Marks available: up to 24 marks

Sample tasks

Task 2: Explain how the writer of the extract from a travel book holds the reader's interest. In your answer show how he has used a style that is engaging and personal; made use of his own opinion; selected words and phrases for effect; made use of sentence structuring and paragraphing. (Activity 6, page 198)

This checklist outlines material and evidence that candidates at all competence levels may be expected to include in their response to this task. The examiner would also credit other valid suggestions or comments.

Engaging and personal style and tone

- Use of first-person narrative helps to sustain the reader's interest: 'I felt like someone stepping out of doors for the first time. It was all so different', 'I was secretly watching', 'I had flown a lot'.
- Wry observations are dropped in to engage the reader's interest: 'oxygen masks would sometimes drop unbidden from their overhead storage compartments', 'the door of the lavatory tended to swing open on you if you didn't hold it shut. . .'.
- The piece is built around personal reactions that capture and sustain our interest in the writer's experiences: 'below me was this sudden magical tableau of small green fields and steepled villages spread across an undulating landscape'.
- Amusing use of exaggeration throughout: 'It took a week and a half to reach Keflavik', 'endless golden fields on farms the size of Belgium'.
- Use of lists adds detail, colour and humour: 'It was all so different: the language, the money, the cars, the number plates on the cars, the bread, the food, the newspapers, the parks, the people', '"Anything to declare? Cigarettes? Alcohol? Dead horse?"'
- The light-hearted tone conveys the writer's personality: 'a stewardess with a hammer and a mouthful of nails . . . to put things right'

Use of writer's opinion

- The writer strongly conveys his thoughts and opinions: 'if you squinted hard enough you could see all the way to Los Angeles, even when you were over Kansas', 'never seen anyone wear a beret who expected to be taken seriously', 'Everything seemed so vivid and acutely focused and new'.
- Use of detail sustains reader's interest: 'feathered pheasants and unskinned rabbits hanging in the butcher's window'.

Competence level 1 [1–6]

Characterised by:

- basic comments in relation to some of the features in the bullet points reporting that may offer some simple points that may be supported from the text
- a partial and simple interpretation of some features

Competence level 2 [7–12]

Characterised by:

- a very straightforward consideration of most of the features highlighted in the bullet points
- some basic analysis that may be supported by appropriate evidence
- some development of valid, if simple, interpretations occasionally supported by straightforward evidence

Competence level 3 [13–18]

Characterised by:

- a consideration of the features highlighted in the bullet points in

relation to the desired outcome – sustaining the reader's interest
- straightforward analysis supported by uncomplicated explanations
- appropriately developed interpretations backed up by mainly straightforward supporting evidence

Competence level 4 [19–24]

Characterised by:

- an analysis of features highlighted in the bullet points
- an examination supported by appropriate explanations
- the development of a competent interpretation of the stimulus material through the presentation of appropriate supporting evidence

Selection of words and phrases for effect

- Use of imagery to enhance the reader's enjoyment: the simile 'like a shaken-out quilt just settling back onto a bed' is effective in conveying his sense of the 'miniature' nature of Europe; the metaphor 'pencil lines of black highway' concisely captures the aerial view of these roads and is rounded off with the apt simile 'as straight as taut wire'.
- Careful and precise use of language: 'the ordered perfection of a model-railway layout', 'a pig's head smiling on a platter'.
- Use of repetition emphasises the newness of his perspective: 'I had never seen a zebra-crossing . . . never seen a tram, never seen . . .'.

Use of sentence structuring and paragraphing

- The striking, brief, opening sentence is bluntly honest, juxtaposing information with a concise description of what the writer was like physically and emotionally at the time of his first visit.
- Short sentences act as a contrast at the end of the second paragraph, powerfully emphasising his continuing affection for Europe: 'I was smitten. I still am.' The verb 'smitten' reinforces this relationship.
- Short sentences are used to mirror the thought processes in the writer's head and that further engages the reader: 'That man over there, he's a Luxembourger. And so is that girl.'
- Use of lists and repetition for emphasis: 'I had never seen a zebra-crossing before, never seen a tram'.
- Brackets and dashes add liveliness and develop the conversational nature of the writing: '(never even considered it an option)', 'And the people – why, they were Luxembourgers'.